HISTORY'S
TURNING
POINTS

History's
Turning Points

Revel Guest and Andrew St George

Foreword by Asa Briggs

BOXTREE

ACKNOWLEDGEMENTS

History's Turning Points grew out of an international television series. It therefore relies heavily on the contributions of a team which not only produced an incisive and dramatic television series, but whose work has formed the backbone of research for the book: Neil Cameron, Patrick Fleming, Emma De'Ath, Greg Lanning, Fiona Caldwell, Sarah Booth, Christine Garabedian, Elaine Sharp, Fiona Garlick, Jesus G. Montero, Naranhuar, Leigh Jackson, Jos Krah, Haruko Fukuda, John Murray, James Norton, Corisande Albert, Sue Howells, Liz Ihre and Sohrab Sorooshian. From the Learning Channel we would like to thank the Executive Producer Bill Cosmas, Michael Dingley, Georgeanne Kane and Harry Hanbury.

Throughout the series, we have been steered by expert consultants. We would like to thank them for variously correcting our mistakes, inspiring our stories, guiding our thoughts and generally making the whole process of writing this book a thoroughly enjoyable adventure through history.

In addition, we are grateful to John Ford (Senior Vice President of The Learning Channel) and Justin Albert who, with John Man, helped to shape the original idea; and to Katy Carrington and Peter James at Boxtree for tirelessly casting a sharp editorial eye on the content of this book.

First published in Great Britain in 1995 by Boxtree Limited

Concept © Transatlantic Films 1992
Text © Revel Guest and Andrew St George 1995

The right of Revel Guest and Andrew St George to be identified as Authors of this Work has been asserted by them in accordance with the Copyright, Designs and Patents Act 1988.

1 3 5 7 9 10 8 6 4 2

Designed by Robert Updegraff
Printed and bound in Portugal by Printer Portuguesa for

Boxtree Limited
Broadwall House
21 Broadwall
London SE1 9PL

A CIP catalogue entry for this book is available from the British Library.

ISBN 1 85283 958 9

HALF TITLE PAGE: Detail from relief of Persian noblemen in the Palace of Persepolis, one of the capitals of the fifth-century BC Persian Empire.

TITLE PAGE: The British assault on Quebec in 1759: *A View of the Landing Place Above the Town of Quebec, Describing the Assault of the Enemy*, by Francis Swaine, 1759.

Contents

FOREWORD

OPPOSITE: *Machu Picchu, the Lost City of the Incas, in Peru.*

Measured in terms of the age of the earth, human history covers only a short span, thousands of years against a backdrop of millions. The history of living creatures also stretches far back in time, as nineteenth-century science first revealed. Evolutionary processes were protracted, but there were prehuman disasters. Every dinosaur was destroyed millions of years before man entered the scene.

It is only in the twentieth century that the unprecedented advance of scientific knowledge has revealed some of the secrets of life and also provided the means to expunge it from the globe. During this century, too, human beings for the first time have been able to contemplate this planet from space. This fascinating book, accompanied by a television series, deals with turning points in human history, ending with the man-made mushroom cloud which turned a city into a desert. Nuclear power can fuel ultimate disaster, and the men controlling it have the power of gods.

The first chapter in *History's Turning Points* is called 'Clash of the Titans', who in Greek mythology were the giant children of the sky-god Uranus, the first ruler of the universe. Led by Cronus, they deposed their father before they were themselves destroyed by the Olympians. Two of their descendants were Prometheus and Atlas. How myth is related to history at every stage in the human story focuses imaginatively on the perception of human character, its strengths and its limits, and if only for this reason literature and history are intimately interconnected. Clio, the Muse of History, was a daughter of Zeus.

Echoes of ancient myth sound across the centuries. One of the most publicized human disasters of the twentieth century was the sinking of the White Star liner, named the Titanic, in 1912. When the American historian David Landes, fascinated by time (and clocks), wrote a careful account of the industrial revolutions of the eighteenth and nineteenth centuries that changed the material conditions of life, he chose as his title *Prometheus Unbound*. Modern psychology draws deep on myth. So too does literature.

The interpretation of the past, however, has been the special concern of historians, who for centuries were chroniclers – and often propagandists – before they became professionals. They now argue with each other, as well as or sometimes instead of reaching a wider public. History, like politics, is debate, and the media now pick it up.

The first chapter in this book introduces 'the father of history', Herodotus, a historian with the unlimited curiosity that all good historians need. The last chapter, 'The Atomic Bomb', has more to say of physicists than of historians. In both chapters, however, politicians figure in the scenario, controversial politicians who raise profound ethical questions. The story of Themistocles in the fifth century BC has a lasting interest of its own, personal as well as political. The decision of Harry S. Truman in 1945 to attack Japan with a terrifying, hitherto unused, weapon was and has remained controversial. The Los Alamos physicist, Robert Oppenheimer, who pondered long afterwards on its consequences, regarded the making of the bomb as a scientific necessity. 'If you are a scientist you believe . . . that it is good to find out what the realities are: that it is good to turn over to mankind at large the greatest possible power to control the world and to deal with it according to its lights and values.'

Each of the chapters in this book is concerned inevitably not only with power and glory but with 'lights and values'. And these have never been constant, whether or not 'human nature' has changed. Chapter 5 on 'The Black Death', a term used at the time (the mid-fourteenth century), describes the ravages of a momentous epidemic in a world without scientists capable of understanding it or being able to control it. Human decisions did not initiate it. The epidemic was carried initially by two hosts – the common black rat and the oriental rat flea. Twenty million Europeans died from it. Reactions to it reflected existing 'lights and values', but these were changed, along with much else in society, as the 'great plague' spread along the trade routes and across the globe.

Epidemics, often brilliantly and movingly described by contemporaries, have their own history. Nor was the Black Death the last of them. In the nineteenth century, cholera crossed many frontiers. In the twentieth century, AIDS has not yet found a cure. The effects of epidemics on individual lives have been immense: no less so, however, were the effects of endemic diseases like smallpox, typhus and tuberculosis, which were eventually brought under control. It was the epidemics that forced commentators to deal in aggregates; and they did this long before statistics became a science.

Changes in world population, now regularly if not always reliably tabulated, always lie in the background of history, related to subsistence and to what in the eighteenth century came to be called 'political economy'. The huge increase of world population in the present century has encouraged forecasting of the next millennium, and how it is distributed and will be distributed is bound to affect the social and political relationship between north and south. The examination of trends is a different pursuit from that of looking for and identifying 'turning points'. Yet the latter stand out only when the trends are charted.

In recent years, historians have become increasingly aware of how family history, much of it private, sets the terms of public history and of how family relationships between men, women, children and dependents, important in themselves as themes to explore, often shape events of the kind that assume global importance. Cleopatra is the main character in the drama of Roman life in the first century BC described in Chapter 3. Had her nose been sorter, the philosopher Pascal speculated, 'the whole face of the world would have been changed'. Once again myth and literature come into a story which attracted both William Shakespeare and George Bernard Shaw, while at the time, the historian Cassius Dio saw Antony as playing the role of Dyonsius or Osiris, and Cleopatra that of Silene or Isis.

In this century, the United States' 1961 decision to make oral contraceptives available on general prescription may well stand out as a turning point in global history. The society that devised them exercises an exceptional worldwide influence, and it is sharply separated from the societies of the past. Despite its global reach, it is separated too from many of the societies of the present, like those of China and of the Arab states, whose early histories are dealt with in Chapters 2 and 4. Before the European discovery of America there had been a Muslim discovery of Europe, and the great fourteenth-century Muslim traveller Ibn Batuta had as strong a sense of place, time and distance as his near-contemporary, the great Christian traveller, Marco Polo.

The three chapters on Europe and the Americans which form the core of this book introduce a 'new world', the first of them tracing the consequences of a Spanish 'voyage into the unknown', the second casting the spotlight on an American Indian princess, who provides the first legend of the New World, and the third centring on bitterly contested colonial conflicts on American soil. With the declaration of American independence in 1776 the great society of the future was ready to begin its own voyage into the unknown – with far more legends being woven around George Washington than around the princess, Pocahontas.

Much happened in the world between the 1759 battle for Quebec, described in Chapter 9, and the 1879 battle for Isandlwana in Africa, described in Chapter 10. The French Revolution of 1789 was undoubtedly a turning point. So, too, was the advent of steam-driven industry, which has usually been described as an 'industrial revolution'. It was through the force of steam and the opening up through invention and technology of a world that thought of itself as 'shrinking' that we move – in the case of this book, through Africa – into the twentieth century. It is a very different world from that of 1759 or 1789 or even 1851 when Britain, then 'the workshop of the world', held a great exhibition to survey and present 'human progress'. Of the building in which it was housed, the Crystal Palace, the historian Thomas Babington Macaulay wrote, 'I cannot think that the Caesars ever exhibited a more splendid spectacle.'

There was a Classical flavour too to the remark made by the tough and uncompromising Admiral Togo, Japanese victor at the Battle of Tsushima, the central figure in Chapter 11. Japan had been transformed since the Meiji restoration of 1868, and it now had its own industrial base. The battle against the Russian fleet in 1905 started with a pre-emptive strike. Togo knew the waters as well as Themistocles had known the waters at Salamis. It seemed apposite, therefore, that at the Japanese victory celebrations in 1905 Togo could declare that 'the gods award the crown to those who, by their training in peacetime, are victorious, even before they go into battle. But the gods soon take the crown away from those who relax in the pleasures of peace. After a victory tighten your helmet.'

The Japanese enemy in 1905, Tsarist Russia, underwent its own transformation after humiliating defeat. An attempt at revolution failed in 1905, but in the midst of world war it succeeded in 1917. After more than 300 years of Tsarist rule the Romanov family was deposed. The ultimate victor in an unplanned revolution that went through many phases was Lenin, who was in exile when both revolutions began. Inspired by Marxist ideology, he took control of events. His personality – and his ideas – were very different from those of other characters who shape history in this book, and it was because of this that history turned in 1917. The American John Reed's *Ten Days That Shook the World*, published in 1919, caught the mood. Its author died of typhoid fever in Moscow in 1920 and is buried under the Kremlin wall.

In 1989, the bicentenary year of the French Revolution, the Soviet regime was to collapse in days that again shook the world, and history turned again – in some ways backwards. There were some historians, indeed, who claimed that history had come to an end. It was one sign of difference between 1917 and 1989 that the debates of the Congress of People's Deputies in the latter year were televised, and so much attention was paid to them that the proceedings had to be recorded and shown in the evening.

The perception of recent history owes much to the 'media', a term not used until this century. So, too, does the reconstruction of past history, technically possible only in this century. Reinforcement has come also from powers of recording, visual and oral. Drawing on a wide range of evidence – everything is now grist to the historian's mill – it is possible to recapture a sense of immediacy while acquiring a sense of perspective. Any choice of events, however, is bound to be highly selective. Those chosen in this book – and for the television series – are revealing not only in their drama but in their setting. They belong to the mainstream history of the world.

ASA BRIGGS
July 1995, Sussex

INTRODUCTION

Our ignorance of history makes us libel our own times.
People have always been like this. (Gustave Flaubert)

We like to believe the world is ours for the shaping. In an age when we have so much information at our fingertips, it is tempting to believe that our own vision of the future is easily realizable. In this collection of thirteen accounts of remarkable moments in history, we decided to test this illusion.

There have been countless turning points in history. Every selection would suggest a different picture of history and a fresh view of the past. This first selection of thirteen turning points range over almost 2,500 years of man's recorded development. Each moment produced extraordinary leaders; each turned on circumstances that no one could have predicted; and each had an impact on the course of subsequent events.

This is where the lowliest players count, a new factor emerges, a leader is assassinated, a new virus kills indiscriminately or a new land is discovered. Each of history's turning points not only effected dramatic changes at the time but continues to have consequences for us today. Looking back at the past to understand why events happened as they did may help us to deal more wisely with the problems of our own time. Equally important for us, each turning point we chose caught our imagination as a great story.

It was the film-maker Justin Guest Albert who first suggested to us the idea of filmed and written history through the perspective of isolated moments. We have worked in close collaboration with the film and multimedia directors and together have found the essence of history's excitement and appeal: the story.

In telling the stories behind history's turning points, we have tried to be impartial and to investigate the inevitability of conflict given the attitudes and backgrounds of the principal characters. Where possible, we have used diaries, memoirs and letters so that the agonizing decisions and often violent actions are explained in the original words of the people involved. In this way, we have attempted to raise issues, to find new clues, that ever so slightly change our perception of events. Of course, this detective work is never ending, but it is work more akin to a guessing game than to a history lesson. We hope our readers will share our fascination with the task.

The thirteen turning points which we recount here, from the Battle of Salamis in 480 BC to the dawn of the nuclear age in 1945, show that speculation plays a crucial role in the process of reconstructing history. Are the hidden links between people and events stronger than the more obvious links? From Salamis to Hiroshima, do the principals in each turning point possess a vision of history and of their place in it? While stories come from detailed knowledge of the facts, do broader patterns emerge from a longer view of history?

OPPOSITE:
De Bry's dramatic representation of the Jamestown Massacre of 300 English colonists by the Powhatans, in Virginia, 1622.

These turning points begin with a war, 'the father of all' according to Herodotus, who was himself for so many 'the father of history'. The Persian King, Xerxes, dreamt of a great empire, and he helped form a greater one, the golden age of fifth-century Athens, by losing to the Greeks at Salamis Bay. That naval battle found a nation defending itself against an aggressive empire, its resources depleted and military guile its only weapon.

In 221 BC an empire was born in the East. Emperor Ch'in completed the Great Wall that defined the map of China, meanwhile using force to impose his personality on a nation. His rule showed the speed with which despotism could bring about sweeping and lasting change. From that moment, China had created a model for the achievement of power through aggression and cruelty. Ch'in's remarkable example has influenced many other politicians down the centuries determined to achieve ultimate power. His dynasty eventually gave way to another form of tyranny, the twentieth-century dictatorship of Mao Tse-tung. China could not escape the consequences of that moment in 221 BC.

Two hundred years later, Augustan Rome emerged from the civil war which had seen Antony and Cleopatra defeated at the Battle of Actium in 31 BC and their young rival Augustus Caesar emerge as the Emperor who would heal his country's wounds. Augustus initiated the greatest epoch of the Roman empire, by launching one of the most effective public relations campaigns in history and essentially recreating himself in his own image. He understood the importance of strong leadership reinforced by clever political campaigning and a shrewd assessment of the opposition, techniques valued just as highly by successful politicians today. He also knew that in government (as Napoleon Bonaparte was to say nearly 2,000 years later) justice means force as well as virtue. It was Augustus who invented and imposed the famous *pax Romana*.

Another powerful civilization, Islam, spread itself throughout North Africa and Spain in 711. It was a moment in history where the political weakness of one power gave opportunity to an outside power. The Muslim influence stretched north from Arabia into Spain and beyond, bringing local tax, toothpaste, pasta, spinach, calculus and the notion of zero (without which computers could not have developed). Arabic translations of otherwise forgotten ancient Greek authors stimulated the flow of ideas in philosophy, medicine, mathematics and astronomy in Western Europe. Without the influence of the Arabs, Christopher Columbus could not have found his way to the New World.

A turning point in history need not be a conflict or a confrontation; it can be a natural disaster. Time and again, history shows that the task of civilization is to insulate us against natural shocks. In 1347 a disease against which there was no defence swept across Asia and Western Europe: the Black Death. Living and dying were never the same again, and modern life could never again be complacent or certain. So much learning died with the monks who treated the sick and so contracted the disease; the rural economy changed irrevocably, and the established foundations of religious faith were rocked. The bacterium responsible, *Yersinia pestis*, disappeared as mysteriously as it had arrived, a silent reminder of the power of disease and the vulnerability of man.

The plague began without warning and ended unexpectedly. Are beginnings and endings predictable? The Renaissance statesman Machiavelli knew that wars begin when you wish but do not end as you please. When in 1453 the fine city of Constantinople fell, the once powerful Byzantine Empire had been ended by an extraordinary combination of religious zeal, military technology and force of will. The Turkish Sultan, Mehmet II, had been as determined to take the city as the Emperor Constantine had been to defend it.

Eighty years later, another old empire died and a new one was born when Spaniards reached South America. The Incas in Peru lacked horses and sufficiently sophisticated weapons technology to counter the surprise attack by the Spanish explorer and adventurer Francisco Pizarro in 1532. Modelling himself on Hernán Cortés, the great *conquistadore* who had imposed Spanish rule on the Aztecs in Mexico in 1522, he was – like all great men – skilled at making himself equal to the task required of him. His legacy was the Latin cultural presence in South America.

Were men like Pizarro and Cortés products of the times they lived in? Can individuals rise above their culture and background? In 1614 the Native American princess Pocahontas defied her father and her tribe, the Powhatan of Virginia, to marry the English colonist, John Rolfe. Can love alter history? Can it conquer racial and cultural differences? In those seven years of peace after the union of Pocahontas with John Rolfe, the English gained a firm foothold in North America.

The future of North America was again in question in 1759 when the British defeated the French at Quebec and won effective control of the continent. Two of the greatest military tacticians of their generation faced each other at Quebec. In a daring tactical coup, the British general James Wolfe outwitted the Marquis de Montcalm and emerged as the man who changed the future of all Canadians.

Another struggle, which took place in 1879 high on the South African veldt at Isandlwana, found the British Empire defeated and embarrassed by the Zulus. In their fury, the British then sought to erase the Zulu people from South African politics. It was the relationship between two men, a British administrator and an ambitious Zulu king, which led to the foundation of apartheid. Were they aware of the consequences their actions would have for generations to come?

History teaches that those who do not apply new remedies must expect new evils. In the nineteenth century, Japan cast off its feudal Samurai past and began an unprecedented programme of modernization in its quest to become a world power within a generation. One of the architects of this success was the Japanese admiral, Heihachiro Togo. His approach was thorough and uncompromising, modelled on the best thinking and technology of his day and exploiting British shipbuilding technology and the battle tactics of Admiral Nelson. His subsequent successes resulted in the annihilation of the Russian Atlantic fleet at Tsushima in 1905, a battle which heralded the rise of Japan as a new force in world politics.

Do leaders look into the glass of history and find the image of great men and women in the past? It was the teaching and example of his idols, Karl Marx and Maximilien Robespierre, which in 1917 inspired Lenin and his Bolshevik party to overthrow the Russian Provisional Government. That moment in history began seventy years of Communist rule.

The final turning point we have chosen here, the dropping of the atomic bomb on Hiroshima in 1945, ended one military age and began another. Could the scientists who tested the first atomic bomb have known what they had created? The nuclear age was born in the cold dawn over Hiroshima. Did the people of that city die in vain? Would their sacrifice at least hold back the awful powers unleashed by scientific advance?

We have drawn together a wide range of sources and expertise to bring these thirteen turning points into focus and so help us to see what they mean to us now. How often is history the clash of great personalities? Do we ever realize the significance of our actions? Does nothing happen by chance and does nothing happen wholly by design? And how can we sense that our own lives are passing through a moment which will become a turning point in history.

REVEL GUEST AND
ANDREW ST GEORGE
July 1995, London

· 1 ·
Clash
OF THE TITANS

THE GREEKS EXPEL THE PERSIANS AT SALAMIS BAY
AND THE GOLDEN AGE OF GREECE BEGINS.

> A king sate on the rocky brow
> Which looks o'er sea-born Salamis;
> And ships, by thousands, lay below,
> And men in nations; – all were his!
> He counted them at break of day –
> And when the sun set, where were they?
> (Byron, *The Isles of Greece*)

O**N 23 SEPTEMBER 480 BC** the Persian king Xerxes came to Salamis Bay in the Aegean Sea off Athens. He led the Persian fleet against the Greeks in a battle which would decide the fate of both nations. It was an encounter of will and might, a test of military nerve and prowess, a fight for liberty and independence.

The battle became famous as the first recorded in history. For its chronicler Herodotus (*c.* 484–*c.* 420 BC), dubbed 'the father of history' by the first-century BC Roman statesman and philosopher Cicero, the battle represented a clash of ideals between the democracy of Europe and the despotism of Asia. In his account of the wars between Greece and Persia, Herodotus set the pattern for the writing of history. Composing a connected and systematic prose work, he organized it into sections, provided precise descriptions, weighed testimony and analysed evidence. He wrote as impartially as he could, freeing himself from racial prejudice. Even so, some Greeks, resenting such a display called him 'the father of lies'.

Herodotus' story of the battle is the first and best account. But another work of literature, by the first and greatest Greek tragedian, Aeschylus (524/5–456 BC), came out of the battle. He wrote at least eighty plays, and the seven which survive form the backbone of Greek tragedy. One of them, *The Persians*, is the story of the battle at Salamis. Aeschylus had fought there and at Marathon, and his vivid account gives the distant events a mythic status in history and literature.

OPPOSITE: *Persian noblemen depicted on a relief from Xerxes' palace at Persepolis.*
BELOW: *Herodotus, 'The Father of History'.*

The Greeks and the Persians

In the fifth century BC, Greece was a confederation of squabbling city-states, the most important of which were Athens and Sparta. Their great military and political leader, the orator Pericles (*c.* 490–429 BC), was to speak for all Athenians who had long been proud of their democratic tradition, fifty years later, when he said that his country's government 'cannot envy the laws of our neighbours – for it hath served as a model to others, but is original at Athens. And this our form, as committed not to a few but to the whole body of the people, is called a democracy.'

To the east, the Persian Empire was the greatest the world had seen. It had started as a small region of south-western Persia in 559 BC when Cyprus the Great (d. 529 BC) began his conquest of Asia Minor; his son, Cambyses, took Egypt (d. 522 BC). The Empire expanded not by destruction but by assimilation, with the Persians ruling by local consent. In 522 BC King Darius the Great (548–486 BC) began to recognize it, putting down small revolts and consolidating what Cyrus and Cambyses had so rapidly won, himself adding the Indus Valley and Thrace. Over the next ten years he strengthened the structure of the Empire by introducing coinage and a unified legal system.

Darius ruled from the capitals of Susa in Elam and Ecbatana in Media, his empire covering the ancient territories of Asia Minor, Syria, Egypt, Palestine, Arabia, Persia, Mesopotamia, and what is now Afghanistan, Armenia, Azerbaijan, Turkestan, Uzbekistan, western Pakistan and also parts of modern Kirgiziya. The Empire was divided into twenty administrative districts (satrapies), run by a tightly knit group of seven great Persian families and protected by an army consisting of 10,000 Persian spearmen and cavalry together with mercenaries and recruits from the satrapies. There was a common currency, a common market and an extensive network of trade routes which gave the Empire continuing vigour for over 200 years.

Ruins of the once luxurious palace at one of the Persian capitals, Persepolis.

Relief from Persepolis at the height of the Persian Empire: tribute-bearers from every province mounted the great stairs every New Year with gifts for the Persian king.

Xerxes, King of Kings

In 486 BC, after reigning for thirty-six years, the great Darius died, and was succeeded by his son Xerxes (519–465 BC). Xerxes himself placed the crown on his head, becoming King of Kings, since no mere mortal could perform the ceremony. His first concerns were his rebellious subjects in Egypt. Having successfully quelled the uprisings there, he turned his attention to the third Persian capital, Persepolis, forty miles north-east of Shiraz, determined that it should become the most splendid city of the ancient world. He had magnificent palaces built, richly decorated in glass and inlaid stones and approached by great avenues. Tributes and gifts of subjugation arrived from all over the Empire and neighbouring states: horses from Assyria, camels from Egypt, antelope and ivory tusks from Africa, caskets of gold dust and bales of rich cloth from Asia Minor. But there were major omissions: nothing came from Athens or Sparta. The democratic Athenians were especially opposed to the despotism and extravagance of the Persian Empire although, despite the long-running antagonism that existed between the Persians and the Greeks, the Persian court itself was often used as a haven by those Greeks who had been exiled from their own cities and hoped to be restored to power by the Persians.

These omissions so angered Xerxes that, motivated as much by revenge as by a zeal for conquest (so far he had only suppressed rebellions) he vowed to expand the Persian dominions to the west, beyond the Aegean. 'If we crush the Athenians,' he declared, 'we shall extend the empire of Persia that its boundaries will be God's own sky, so the sun will not look down upon any land beyond the boundaries of what is our own.'

But Athens had inflicted other insults. In 490 BC the Greeks had defeated Darius' army at the famous Battle of Marathon. (The story that Pheidippides, the famous runner, had

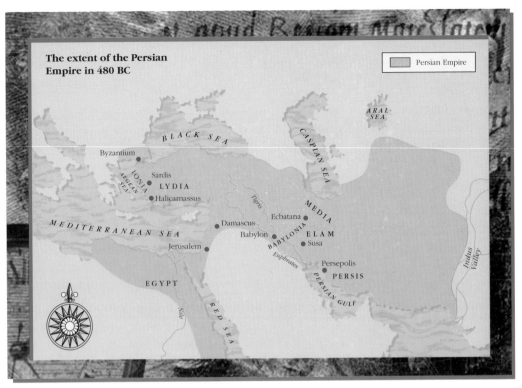

The extent of the Persian
Empire in 480 BC

Persian Empire

carried news of the victory to the Greek command – the distance he reputedly covered
some twenty-six miles – is the basis for the modern Olympic Marathon.) Nine years before
that, the Athenians had also burnt the town of Sardis, the capital of Lydia, as part of the
Ionian revolt against Persian rule. Xerxes' fury became a cold mission of revenge:

> I will not rest until I have taken Athens and burnt it to the ground in revenge for the
> injury the Athenians without provocation once did to me and my father. [They] came
> to Sardis . . . and burnt the temples, and the trees that grew about them. (Herodotus)

It took Xerxes five years to raise and equip the army he needed for the invasion of Greece.
This was to be the greatest fighting force ever seen. He had begun his detailed planning
in the spring of 481 BC. During this period of preparation, he devoted himself completely
to the cause, and travelled the Persian Empire to raise more men and money to crush the
Greeks.

Herodotus' history is filled with accounts of incidents which give an insight into Xerxes'
driven character. He described him not as the Asiatic despot of history but as a complex
figure who was by turns generous, vain and cruel. In the town of Celaenae a rich Lydian
called Pythius offered Xerxes his entire fortune of 2,000 talents of silver and 3,993,000 of
gold Darics as his contribution to the campaign. Moved by this show of loyalty, Xerxes
unexpectedly gave Pythius the extra 7,000 gold Darics to make up an even four million,
and then told him to keep his fortune. But when the same man came to him soon afterwards to beg the favour that the eldest of his five sons be excused military service, Xerxes
was furious:

> He at once gave orders that the men to whom such duties fell should find Pythius'
> eldest son and cut him in half and put the two halves on each side of the road, for
> the army to march out between them. The order was performed. And now between
> the halves of the young man's body the advance of the army began. (Herodotus)

The Great March

Satisfied that his army was complete, Xerxes set out in the spring of 480 BC for Abydos, where the Hellespont divides Asia from Europe. On the way, the army passed near Troy. Xerxes wished to see the once great city, home of King Priam, where the Greeks and Trojans had fought for ten years over Helen, the wife of Menelaus, King of Sparta. There were two qualities which Herodotus valued in Xerxes: respect for others' gods, and a reverence for the past:

> [Xerxes] . . . went up to the citadel, and when he had seen what he wanted to see and heard the story of the place from the people there, he sacrificed a thousand oxen to the Trojan [goddess] Athene, and the Magi [priests] made libations of wine to the spirits of the great men of old. (Herodotus)

The prow of a Greek trireme, reinforced for ramming other ships and decorated for war.

When the army reached Abydos, Xerxes gave orders for a military review of all his land and sea forces. 'There was not a nation in Asia that he did not take with him against Greece,' Herodotus wrote; 'save for the great rivers there was not a stream his army drank from that was not drunk dry.' On a whim, Xerxes ordered a rowing-match to be held among the various nations which composed his army. To Xerxes' delight it was won by the Phoenicians of Sidon. But, as he watched the spectacle – the Hellespont packed with ships, the beaches of Abydos crowded with men – he began to weep. 'I was thinking,' he said, 'and it came into my mind how pitifully short human life is – for of all of these thousands of men not one will be alive in a hundred years' time.'

If the Persian army was to pass from Asia into Europe, the Hellespont had to be bridged at Abydos. Xerxes commanded his architects and engineers to start building. A structure of papyrus and flax cables was strung out over the sea, but it was destroyed in a violent storm – the first of several setbacks for the Persians. Xerxes reacted violently. He put the hapless architects to death and gave orders that the Hellespont should receive 300 lashes and have a pair of fetters thrown into it, to punish the sea-god Poseidon. 'And I have heard', Herodotus reported,

> that he also sent people to brand it with hot irons. He certainly instructed the men
> with the whips to utter, as they wielded them, the following words: 'You salt and
> bitter stream, your master lays this punishment upon you for injuring him, who never
> injured you. But Xerxes the King will cross you, with or without your permission.

A new team of architects tried a different method. Taking 674 galleys and triremes, the Persians lashed them together and used them to support the superstructure of a bridge. It was a tremendous undertaking. To ensure their safe crossing, the Persians laid boughs of myrtle on the bridge; at dawn, Xerxes poured wine into the sea from a golden goblet and prayed to the sun that nothing should prevent him from taking Europe or turn him back before he reached its utmost limits. Herodotus wrote:

> His prayer ended, he flung the cup into the Hellespont and with it a golden bowl
> and a Persian short sword. I cannot say for certain if he intended the things he threw
> into the water to be an offering to the Sun-god; perhaps they were – or it may be
> that they were a gift to the Hellespont itself, to show he was sorry for having caused
> it to be lashed with whips.

Most Persians, who lived far from the sea, had not lost their awe and fear of large bodies of open water. Their uneasy relationship with the sea was to prove crucial when they encountered the Greeks, who were expert seamen. Most of the Persians, moreover, could not swim. So they tried, through prayer and persuasion, to placate the wind and the sea. When at last the waters were calm, the army began to cross into Europe. So numerous were Xerxes' soldiers that it took two days for the entire army to pass over the pontoon bridge. He then exhorted his troops: 'Persians, I have brought you together because I wish you to act bravely . . . if we conquer these Greeks, no one in the world will try to withstand our arms.'

The invading Persian army then struck west into Macedonia as far as the River Strymon. Here they stopped so that the Magi could make sacrifices and practise their magic in the hope of winning the river's favour:

> They crossed it by the bridges which they found at Nine Ways . . . and when they
> learnt that Nine Ways was the name of the place, they took nine native boys and nine
> girls and buried them alive there.

OPPOSITE: *The magnificent temple of the Parthenon on the Acropolis, the centre of the fortified city of Athens.*

Burying people alive, explained Herodotus, was a Persian custom. Now Xerxes did all he could to provoke war with Greece. Early in 480 BC, the Persians had demanded and gained symbolic tributes of earth and water from those they considered the subjects of their Empire. But the Athenians and the Spartans alone stood out; they had thrown the Persian envoys into pits and wells, telling them that they would find their earth and water there. Xerxes redoubled his efforts to punish them.

Themistocles at Athens

The Athenians received the reports of Xerxes' advance with alarm. They turned to the oracle of Apollo at Delphi, which was open only nine days each year (the times when Apollo chose to speak to mortals), though ambassadors from the Greek states were given priority over private citizens. The Athenian envoys were accompanied by a prophetes, who led them through the rituals of the sanctuary. They duly sacrificed a goat, and received the following advice from the oracle's priestess as she was seated on a bronze tripod:

> Why sit you, doomed ones? Fly to the world's end leaving
> Home and the heights your city circles like a wheel.   (Herodotus)

The Athenians begged for more wisdom, and received this strange reply:

> The wooden wall only shall not fall, but help you and your children.
> But await not the host of horse and foot coming from Asia,
> Nor be still, but turn your back and withdraw from the foe.
> Truly a day will come when you will meet him face to face.
> Divine Salamis, you will bring death to women's sons
> When the corn is scattered, or the harvest gathered in.   (Herodotus)

The Athenians wanted to rouse the other Greek city-states and fight the Persians together, but when the envoys returned to Athens, the professional interpreters of the oracle advised the Athenians to flee rather than resist the mighty Persians. One man alone spoke up in favour of fighting. His name was Themistocles.

Themistocles was born in about 528 BC. A statesman and military commander, he stood at the centre of Athenian politics in the early part of the fifth century and was renowned for his ruthlessness. The general Miltiades, although he had won the Battle of Marathon for the Greeks in 490 BC, was arraigned on Themistocles' instructions after his military failure against the island of Paros the following year and thrown into prison. He died there when gangrene infected a wound he had received on Paros. Themistocles was one of the main contenders for Miltiades' position as leader of the Athenian army, and this was his unscrupulous way of obtaining the position.

The fact that Themistocles was confident of his popular support is borne out by his subsequent challenges to his political rivals under the legal device known as ostracism (the word comes from the potsherds or voting tiles, *ostraka*). According to this system, 6,000 public votes could ban someone from Athens for ten years if their presence was felt to be a threat to the *polis* or city. He and the liberal party he led made use of all that Greek cunning and good luck could provide by taking advantage of this institution to remove all opposition.

Exploiting his rhetorical skills and political influence he persuaded the Athenians in 480 BC to join the other Greek city-states in fighting the Persians not on land but at sea.

He interpreted the 'wooden walls' of the oracle as ships, and Salamis as the site of a Greek victory. Why else would the oracle have called the island 'divine'?

Themistocles planned not only for his own future but for that of his country, understanding that sea power would make or break his country. Earlier, he had urged the Athenian assembly to build a navy with the profits from the government-owned Laurium silver mines, instead of sharing them out among the citizens. Two hundred newly designed warships called triremes were immediately contracted for construction at Piraeus. The trireme had originally been intended for a naval war against the island of Aegina. It was a piece of luck, wrote Herodotus, that 'the outbreak of this war at that moment saved Greece by forcing Athens to become a maritime power'. The trireme was a long, streamlined warship made of oak and propelled by oars arranged on three decks, with enough space on each level for 170 oarsmen. Manoeuvrable and strong, it was ideal for ramming other ships. The triremes' prows were painted with warlike symbols.

As news of the Persian advance reached the Greek confederation, the squabbles between its constituent city-states were forgotten in the face of this new threat from the east. By 480 BC, Xerxes' army had subdued the northern cities of Greece, and his vast fleet had reached the promontory of land that was overlooked by Mount Athos, close to Athens.

A Persian naval force had earlier been wrecked trying to sail around the promontory. Xerxes immediately ordered a canal to be cut across the isthmus. This was so enormous an undertaking that Xerxes had to force teams of men to work under the lash. As Herodotus observed, it would have been quicker to haul the boats overland. But Xerxes was not to be deterred, and his navy at last arrived at Sepias, north of Artemisium. Herodotus listed the Persian fleet at 1,207 ships and over 500,000 men. Xerxes' army meanwhile reached Thermopylae in central Greece; his troops, servants, and camp followers (excluding eunuchs) numbered, according to Herodotus, an improbable 5,230,320. (More likely estimates range from 100,000 to 500,000 men.)

The Corinth Canal, a classic example of Roman engineering.

At any rate, the Greek forces (of probably 70,000 or so) were certainly outnumbered. But weather was on their side when the Persian fleet reached Cape Sepias. At least 400 Persian ships were lost in a storm, a 'Hellespontian'. 'It raised a confused sea like a pot on the boil,' wrote Herodotus:

> The storm lasted three days, after which the Magi brought it to an end by sacrificial offerings, and by putting spells on the wind, and by further offerings to Thetis and the sea-nymphs – or, of course, it may be that the wind just dropped naturally.

Still Xerxes persisted. The two armies clashed at Thermopylae, where the Greeks held the mountain pass between Thessaly and Locris for two days before being overwhelmed by the Persians' superior numbers. Xerxes was so outraged by the valour of the Greek commander, King Leonidas of Sparta, who had died in the battle, that he ordered his corpse to be decapitated and the head fixed on a stake. Herodotus later wrote of Xerxes' unusual and extreme reaction: 'normally the Persians, more than any other nation I know of, honour men who distinguish themselves in war'. The Greek lyric poet Simonides penned a famous two-line epitaph to the Greeks who fell at Thermopylae:

> Go now, and tell the Spartans, passer-by,
> That here obedient to their laws we lie.

From Thermopylae, Xerxes directed his army towards Athens. As the advancing forces approached, Themistocles ordered an evacuation of the city, and the women and children fled to the island of Salamis just off the coast. By the time Xerxes attacked, only a few Athenians remained in the Acropolis, hurling boulders at the Persians. They were soon overcome and the Acropolis, the symbol of Athenian pride and power, was burnt to the ground. Xerxes then set his soldiers loose to loot and pillage the city. The Athenians had lost everything.

Meanwhile, the Persian fleet at Artemisium finally engaged the Greek forces, Spartan and Athenian together numbering 271 ships. There was a messy, costly and inconclusive battle off the Euboean coast, the ships tangling with each other's oars and rigging. After sustaining heavy losses, the Athenians withdrew to regroup. The army's defeat at Thermopylae, the loss of Athens and now this naval setback forced the Greek fleet to retreat to Salamis, which had always been their choice of battleground. It was there that Themistocles would make his stand against the Persians. He told the Greek council of war:

> Let a man lay his plans with due regard to common sense, and he will usually succeed; otherwise he will find that God is unlikely to favour human designs.
> (Herodotus)

Themistocles' wisdom had a counterpart in Xerxes' camp. This was the daring of Princess Artemisia, a bold and exceptional woman, who, like Herodotus, was from Halicarnassus, a Persian-controlled Greek city in Asia Minor where women were treated as men's equals. She was fighting for the Persians, at the head of the Halicarnassus fleet. She saw the danger of fighting the Greeks at Salamis:

> Spare your ships and do not fight at sea, for the Greeks are infinitely superior to us in naval matters – the difference between men and women is hardly greater. In any case, what pressing need have you to risk further actions at sea? Have you not taken Athens, the main objective of the war? Is not the rest of Greece in your power? (Herodotus)

Xerxes ignored her. He marched his army from Athens to support his fleet at Salamis. Themistocles and the Greeks watched and waited.

Salamis Bay, 23 September 480 BC

The small Bay of Salamis separates Attica from the island of Salamis, to the south-west of Athens. It was here, in the narrow straits between the island and the mainland, that Themistocles had decided to fight:

> If we fight in a narrow sea with few ships against many, we shall gain a great victory;
> for to fight in a narrow space is favourable to us – in an open sea, to them . . . the
> whole fortune of the war depends on our ships. (Herodotus)

The prophecy of the oracle at Delphi seemed to have come true: all Athenian territory on the mainland had been overrun by the Persians. Only the 'wooden wall' of ships could save Greece now.

All Xerxes' military planning of the last five years converged on this moment. He woke on the morning of 23 September at Salamis Bay having slept little. He had been busy during the night with the disposition of his fleet, which had been at sea and on the alert since dusk. As dawn broke, from his vantage point near the sacked city of Athens he could see that his ships outnumbered those of the Greek confederation by three to one. He had successfully trapped the Greek fleet, now 380 strong, in the narrow straits between the mainland and Salamis, his own fleet blockading the south-eastern and the western exits. Now all he had to do was wait for the Greeks.

Since his ships were outnumbered and could be outrun by the larger Persian ships in the open sea, Themistocles knew that his best chance lay in fighting the battle in a confined space. He had learnt from the engagement at Artemisium that in this way the numbers and bulk of the Persian ships could be made to work to his advantage.

He also counted on the Persian crews being tired after spending the night at sea repositioning their ships. In contrast, the Greeks arose rested and refreshed. The longer Themistocles waited before making his attack, the more drained his opponents were becoming. What at first looked like the trapping of the Greek fleet was becoming the reverse, since the Persians were now committed to an arduous blockade of opponents who were the superior seamen. In Aeschylus' play *The Persians*, a Persian messenger announces:

> All night the captains kept the fleet awake;
> And night ran on. No Grecian army set secret sail.

The Greeks waited patiently for the wind to turn to their advantage. When it at last shifted to the south, it began to blow Xerxes' ships towards them, and the Persians realized that they had been out-thought by their enemy. As soon as the wind had changed, the Greek fleet put to sea. Aeschylus gave an eyewitness account, from the Persian viewpoint, of what happened next:

> First the floods of Persians held the line,
> But when the narrows choked them, and rescue hopeless
> Smitten by prows, their bronze jaws gaping,
> Shattered entire was our fleet of oars.

In the midst of the battle the ship of the Halicarnassus Princess Artemisia seemed doomed, about to be run down by an Athenian trireme. She was surrounded on all sides; the only escape route she could see was to turn and ram one of her own ships; so she

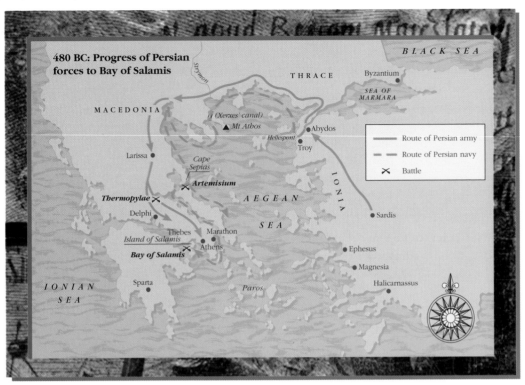

bore down on a Persian trireme, rammed and sank it with the loss of all on board. This caused even greater panic and confusion among her allies. The Greeks thought she had changed sides, and renewed their efforts; Xerxes believed she had struck a Greek ship. Herodotus remarked drily, 'she was, indeed, lucky in every way'.

The confusion continued. Jammed in the narrow waters and slow to move, the Persian ships were sitting targets for the Greeks; some of them therefore fled, but others, commanded by men eager to impress Xerxes, moved to the thick of the battle: 'the greatest destruction took place when the ships which had been first engaged turned tail; for those astern fell foul of them in their attempt to press forward and do some service for their king'.

While the Persian fleet lost all direction, Themistocles' smaller force was more organized:

The Grecian warships, calculating, dashed
Round, and encircled us; ships showed their belly:
No longer could we see the water, charged
With ships' wrecks and men's blood.
Corpses glutted beaches and the rocks.
Every warship urged its own anarchic
Rout; and all who survived that expedition,
Like mackerel or some catch of fish,
Were stunned and slaughtered, boned with broken oars
And splintered wrecks: lamentations, cries
Possessed the open sea, until the black
Eye of evening, closing, hushed them. The sum
Of troubles, even if I should rehearse them
For ten days, I could not exhaust. Rest
Content: never in a single day
So great a number died.
(Aeschylus' *Persae*)

Many men died, either by drowning or in the fierce hand-to-hand fighting between the ships. Luckily for the Greeks, they could swim, so they lost fewer men by drowning. Over 200 Persian ships were sunk, while the Greeks lost only forty. Control of the sea was now in Greek hands. In a single day they had overcome the might of the Persian Empire. Greece was saved.

Xerxes quickly retreated, fearing that the Greeks would beat him to his bridge over the Hellespont and destroy it before he could cross back into Asia. In a shrewd move which was to serve him well later, Themistocles sent his slave Sicinnus after Xerxes to reassure him that he and he alone had stopped the Greeks from pursuing him and destroying the bridges. Knowing that he might become unpopular in the precarious world of Athenian politics after his victory, Themistocles was insuring his future. It was an act which Xerxes was never to forget.

It took Xerxes forty-five days' hard marching to reach the Hellespont, and he arrived there with only a fraction of his army intact. He crossed the water safely, and retreated to Asia. The Persian threat had evaporated.

Fifth-century BC Grecian urn depicting a Greek warrior defeating a Persian in battle.

After Salamis Bay

The Battle of Salamis was recounted by two of the greatest writers of the ancient world, Herodotus and Aeschylus. They set the pattern not only for the way this battle was described, but for the ways in which any conflict could be seen. They depicted the struggle for liberty against despotism, independence against colonialism, and East against West.

Aeschylus made the massacre of superior numbers seem more appalling than the massacre of inferior numbers. His play *The Persians*, produced in Athens in 472 BC, related the Battle of Salamis from the enemy's point of view, a testimony not only to his own humanity but to the love of rationality which made Athens celebrated in the fifth century BC. Herodotus summed up the battle as 'a confused struggle in the narrows'. Yet he had set the conflict in context, and was the first to write sustained, connected and comprehensive prose about a military campaign. He declared: 'I, Herodotus of Halicarnassus, publish this research to preserve the memories of the great and wonderful actions of the Greeks and the Barbarians.'

Socrates, one of the most famous philosophers of Ancient Greece.

One year after Salamis, in 479 BC, Xerxes' reformed army was destroyed at the Battle of Plataea by a Greek army with sounder armour, longer spears and finer training. In the same year Xerxes lost the bulk of his navy at Mount Mycale. The territories of Macedon, Thrace and Cyrenaica broke from the Persian yoke.

Their victory at Salamis encouraged the Greeks in 478 BC to form a pact – the Delian League – to liberate the remaining Greek city-states from Persian control. The League was run by the prime element in the victory at Salamis, the Athenians, who leased 100 ships to their allies to create a force of 300 ships and 60,000 men. The League's army then liberated the Greek cities of the Aegean; the regained territory was to become, in essence, an Athenian empire.

Themistocles was prominent in the Delian League but was disliked for his high-handedness. Other Athenians were jealous of his success and, in due course, he fell victim to his own voting system of *ostraka*. He was accused of non-cooperation with Sparta, and voted out of Athens as a threat to the *polis*. This was not enough for the Spartans who insisted that he should be condemned to death for pro-Persian sympathies. This sentence was passed in his absence. He was banished from Athens and also condemned to death throughout the Greek confederation.

As he had once feared, he had to flee his country. He made for Asia Minor and an audience with his old adversary, King Xerxes:

> O, King, I am the Athenian who has done you most harm and the most good. If you destroy me, you will be destroying an enemy of the Greeks. (Herodotus)

It was one of the most notable moments in military history when Xerxes, remembering Themistocles' act after the Battle of Salamis, welcomed his former enemy. He allowed him to end his days in honour and comfort in Magnesia. Over 2,000 years later, another formidable military commander, Napoleon Bonaparte, compared himself to Themistocles in his letter of surrender to the English. He put himself entirely in English hands just as Themistocles had given himself over to the Persians.

Greece grew to greatness during the fifth century BC. Politics, philosophy, literature and architecture flourished. In politics the speeches of Pericles of Athens, and the formation of the political system known as democracy, though not quite in its twentieth-century sense, helped shape the ideas of the next 2,000 years. Athens was to become the centre of philosophical and political thought in the Western world. Ideas from Classical Greece influenced the West for the next two and a half millennia.

Fifth-century Athens produced the great tragedians Aeschylus, Sophocles and Euripides, as Greek tragedy became a model of man's experience. Greek comedy flourished with Aristophanes, history with Herodotus and Thucydides, philosophy with Socrates, medicine and science with Hippocrates and Democritus, and sculpture with Phidias. Greek architecture, channelled through the ideas of Vitruvius and Palladio, became a model of public building and retained a hold on design into the twentieth century.

The glory of Athens, born of Salamis, was short-lived. The small Athenian Empire fell with Athens' defeat by Sparta in 404 BC; and 142 years later in the fourth century BC Philip II of Macedonia, the father of Alexander the Great, crushed the Greeks at Chaironea in 338 BC – a defeat which finally ended the independence of Athens and other city-states. This fateful change became a lesson in the vicissitudes of life which had been taught by Heraclitus, one of the greatest of all Greek philosophers: his theory of history, society and physics was simply that everything must change.

皇始帝

· 2 ·

Absolute
POWER

THE FIRST EMPEROR, 'THE TIGER OF CH'IN',
COMPLETES THE GREAT WALL AND CHINA IS UNITED.

Give up wisdom, abandon knowledge,
And the people will benefit a hundredfold.
Give up benevolence, abandon righteousness,
And the people will go back to natural affection.
(Lao Tzu, *c.* 500 BC)

I N THE THIRD CENTURY BC the land known to its inhabitants as 'All Under Heaven', which would become modern China, was a region at war with itself. From the latter part of the second millennium BC in this expansive country, a powerful culture was developing. This culture evolved and survived over a continuous span of time longer than that of any other in the world.

Imperial China emerged at the end of the third century BC ruled by a remarkable dynasty under the control of the brutal despot, King Cheng of Ch'in, China's First Emperor. His imperial system was to endure over 2,000 years, and he left behind the world's greatest structure, the Great Wall, to protect it.

OPPOSITE: *King Cheng of Ch'in, Sovereign and First Emperor of China.*

'All Under Heaven'

Man has been in northern and central China since Neolithic times, and discoveries in western Honan, south of the Yellow River, show that the early ancestors of the Chinese were nomadic food-producers who lived in small, temporary villages. This ancient civilization is known as the Yang-shao period, dating from around 5000 BC. These nomads grew millet and wheat, and kept domestic animals, probably pigs and sheep. As well as developing techniques of hunting and fishing, the Yang-shao culture had learnt how to make silk, destined to be one of China's most important producers over the next 3,000 years.

The Yang-shao culture evolved into the more advanced Lung-shan culture (dating from 3000 BC), which, according to archaeological traces at a site in Shantung, added rice to the staple crops and was based in larger and more sophisticated villages. There is evidence of armour, shields and weapons, not only for hunting but for combat; war-chariots were drawn by horses, which were not yet ridden. The subsequent Shang culture, based around the Yellow River in northern central China, developed a writing system of over 2,000 characters.

While conventional Chinese history dates from 1650 BC, the beginning of the Shang dynasty, the 'annals of the bamboo books', a record of astronomical observations of this early period which were discovered in AD 281, date the earliest start of the Shang period from 1766 BC, more than 1,000 years before the Iron Age in China. The Shang dynasty lasted until it was overthrown by the great Chou dynasty in 1027 BC, which was itself crushed by the rising Ch'in dynasty in 256 BC.

The years between 256 BC and 206 BC were crucial to Chinese history, and were to shape the future of the country. Two men – Cheng, who later became Ch'in Shih-Huang-ti, the first Emperor of China, and his adviser and senior scribe Li Ssu, were to set about creating and securing one of the world's greatest and longest-lasting empires.

They lived during the last period of the powerful Chou dynasty, 403–221 BC, known as the Age of the Warring States, when the art of war itself became professional and every citizen had to serve in the army. Until 500 BC, such conflict had been essentially ritualistic, with an agreed suspension of hostilities in the harvest season. The seven provinces or states, Ch'i, Yen, Chao, Han, Wei, Ch'in and Ch'u, were ruled by kings and feudal lords, princes and ministers, all competing for power. Typically, one peripheral state would claim sovereignty over a central state and defend it against its rivals. Their private armies consisted of ill-armoured and expendable infantry, charioteers and bowmen using the crossbow invented in the fourth century BC (well before the same design was developed in the West). In times of peace, the large standing armies, sometimes numbering many hundreds of thousands of men, turned to civil and public projects.

Cheng and Li Ssu were part of a violent and unforgiving world. Crimes were punishable by branding, castration, slitting of the nose or tendons, chopping off of toes or feet, or breaking of kneecaps. However, the seven states made up an expanding society in which artists, intellectuals, technicians and administrators had the means and scope to prosper. Intellectuals such as Han Fei Tzu in the third century BC directed their thinking to practical rather than abstract ends. Strategists and planners like Li Ssu were much in demand.

The Chinese made formidable tacticians and warriors, and would have been more than a match for any Western army of the same period. Military discipline was of the highest strictness. The sixth-century Chinese military historian and theorist, Sun Tzu, wrote in his book *The Art of War*:

> When, for example, Ch'u fought against Ch'in there was an officer who before the battle was unable to control his ardour. He advanced and took a pair of heads and returned. The Ch'u general ordered his execution. Though it was pointed out how brave and talented the officer was, the general said: 'I am confident he is an officer of ability, but he is disobedient.' Thereupon he beheaded him.

By the third century BC, after centuries of fighting, the disciplined armies of Ch'in had finally gained supremacy, perhaps by using the new military technology of long iron swords originated in Ch'u by a new metallurgical process developed in the fourth century BC.

In 273 BC the Ch'in defeated the Wei, and in 260 BC they were triumphant over the Chao, allegedly slaughtering tens of thousands of defeated soldiers. Then in 256 BC the once mighty Chou dynasty fell to the forces of the Ch'in. In the turbulent years that followed, both Cheng and Li Ssu saw the opportunity to use the massive, disciplined armies

The young warrior and future Emperor Ch'in: 'He is merciless with a heart of a tiger or wolf'.

of the Ch'in to make a new, unified country which would hold strong against the increasing numbers of nomadic tribesmen from the north and west who had been a threat from the ninth and eighth centuries BC onwards (and whose equine culture had fully developed by the fifth and fourth centuries BC), and also against its own internal divisions. Imperial China would be born amid tumultuous change and epic tragedy.

King Cheng and Li Ssu

Cheng was the son of King Chuang-hsiang and a concubine, and was born into the house of Ch'in in 259 BC. Throughout these troubled times, the Ch'in were at war with the other six states, vying for supremacy. Cheng came to the throne in 246 BC at the age of thirteen. Even as a youth he was cunning and ambitious, but he exercised no real power until eight years later in 238 BC, when he and his adviser, Li Ssu, began to work closely together:

> The king of Qin [Ch'in] has the proboscis of a hornet and large all-seeing eyes. His chest is like that of a bird of prey and his voice is like that of a jackal. He is merciless with the heart of a tiger or a wolf. When he is in trouble, he finds it easy to humble himself, but when he is enjoying success, he finds it easy to devour human beings . . . Should he achieve his goal of conquering the Empire, we shall all become his slaves.
> (L. Cottrell)

Li Ssu was born in 280 BC in Shang-ts'ai in the state of Ch'u. But he had thought the King of Ch'u unworthy of his attention as a politician, and at the age of thirty-three, in 247 BC, left for Ch'in:

Seventh-century statue of the Chinese philosopher, Confucius.

I have heard that to attain the opportune moment one should not be tardy. Now is the time, when 10,000 chariots are at war, and when the travelling politicians control affairs. At present the King of Ch'in desires to swallow up the world and rule with the title of Emperor. This is the time for the commoners to be busy, and is the golden age of the travelling politicians . . . Therefore I intend to go westward to the King of Ch'in. (L. Cottrell)

In Ch'in, Li Ssu was appointed assistant to the Grand Councillor in the court of Cheng's father, King Chuang-hsiang. He had trained as a clerk and studied under the great philosopher Hsun Tzu in Lan-ling, following the teachings of Confucius (551–479 BC). One of the central beliefs of Confucianism was that all people are basically good, and that relations between them should be founded on the idea of equal treatment. In his famous collection of essays, *The Analects*, he wrote:

Tzu-kung asked: 'Is there a single saying which one can act upon until the end of one's life?' The Master said: 'Would it be reciprocity? What you do not wish done to yourself, do not do to others.'

But Li Ssu believed that people were naturally selfish, and – contrary to Confucius – that their selfishness had to be restrained in the interests of the state and their fellow men by strict laws and punishments; consequently, they had to be driven, not led. This was a belief which placed him foremost among a new philosophical school called the Legalists. He quickly allied himself to the powerful statesman Lu Pu-wei (who was later exiled from Ch'in); and he carefully distanced himself from his more traditional schoolmate, Han Fei Tzu, whom he later caused to be imprisoned. Li Ssu was a statesman who had the vision, intelligence and guile to put his ambitious plans into action.

Li Ssu first met Cheng in 246 BC. He petitioned for an audience with him, and then delivered this speech:

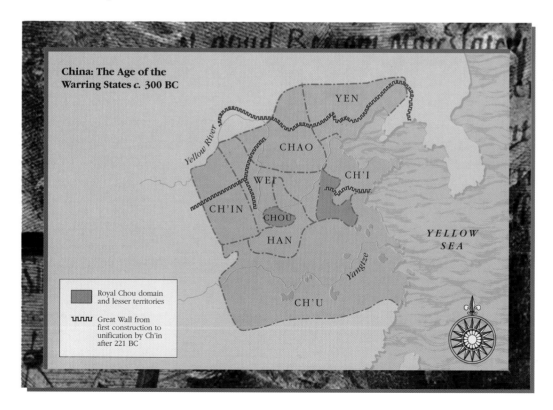

With Ch'in's might and its Great King's ability, the conquest of the other states would be like sweeping the dust from the top of the kitchen stove. Ch'in's power is sufficient to obliterate the feudal lords, bring to reality the imperial heritage and make the world a single unity. This is the time of 10,000 generations. If now you are negligent and do not press to a finish, the feudal lords will return to strength and combine to form north-to-south alliances against you so that, though you have the ability of the Yellow emperor, you would be unable to bring them into unity. (L. Cottrell)

The two men realized that Ch'in's position as the leading state should be strengthened, and that its power offered an opportunity to extend and consolidate its domains. Cheng listened to Li Ssu's plans and at once set about bribing those feudal lords who could be won over by gems and money. The rest would be put to the sword.

Ch'in again went to war, and over the next seventeen years completely subdued the other six states: Han in 230 BC, Chao in 228 BC, Wei in 225 BC, Ch'u in 223 BC, Yen in 222 BC and finally Ch'i in 221 BC. For the first time China was unified under one imperial dynasty. King Cheng declared: 'I have raised troops to punish the rebellious princes, and with the aid of the sacred power of our ancestors have punished them as they deserved, so that the last empire is pacified.' But the Empire needed more than the unity enforced by power of arms. Religion was inexorably entwined with politics, and although King Cheng was a semi-divine being and the 'Son of Heaven', he wanted to be emperor: 'Now unless we create the dignity of a new title, how can we preserve our achievements for posterity?'

The First Emperor of China

In 221 BC at a lavish ceremony in the capital of Ch'in, Hsien-yang, Li Ssu summed up the achievements of King Cheng:

> Your majesty has raised forces of justice to punish tyrants, subjugating all the lands within the four seas; our provinces are everywhere and our law cords are unified. This is something never achieved before. We have consulted learned men and, as long ago, there were Heavenly Sovereign, Earthly Sovereign and Supreme Sovereign. (L. Cottrell)

Cheng replied:

> Let me be called Sovereign Emperor. We are the First Emperor, and our successors shall be known as the Second Emperor, Third Emperor, and so on for endless generations. (L. Cottrell)

King Cheng duly became Ch'in Shih-Huang-ti, the First Emperor. From that moment on, China can be thought of as the location of a single, self-conscious civilization. Thus 221 BC was the most important date in Chinese history before the refounding of the Empire in 581 AD under the Sui and the modern revolutionary ferment of the twentieth century.

To gain an empire was one thing; to hold on to it was quite another. Ch'in became worried that internal enemies as well as the barbarians on his northern borders would take

Emperor Ch'in maintained control by travelling the length and breadth of his new empire.

his new Empire from him. Many attempts were made on his life. He trusted nobody and determined to take measures to avoid a return to the civil strife of the previous twenty years. Hoping to divert his subjects from rebellious thoughts, Ch'in, with Li Ssu's help, set about binding his conquests together with an extraordinary series of civil, social and commercial projects. He lined major rivers, built great canals and developed a standardized writing system. As a symbol of his intent, Ch'in also ordered weapons from the states to be brought and melted down into bells and into twelve metal figures to adorn the palace.

In 221 BC, Ch'in achieved his most important change: he abolished the feudal system, by which the independent kingdoms had ruled through nepotism, and divided his new Empire into thirty-six and later forty-two commanderies or administrative units garrisoned by Ch'in's troops and connected by a network of roads. These units were run by professional administrators, who were to establish a tradition of bureaucracy which persisted through China's imperial era and into the republican culture of the twentieth century. Ch'in then used the bureaucratic elite to impose a standard system of weights and measures, a codified set of laws.

Through this official and administrative class, Chinese tradition and culture was moving towards becoming self-sufficient and self-sustaining, a development which was to occur properly under the Han and later Tang dynasties. The processes of change existed alongside continuity. Official duties were vague, but rested on the annual tasks of compiling the census returns and land registers. To ease communication between parts of the Empire, Ch'in established a written language common to all seven states. Although the spoken dialects differed considerably, in time each of his subjects could recognize the new Chinese characters which would bind his Empire together.

As soon as Ch'in achieved his goal of imperial rule, he ordered the construction of what was and still remains the largest system of inland waterways in the world. He employed large numbers of his subjects on this project, thereby reducing their energy and their opportunity for rebellion. He also revolutionized road transport, introducing a programme of road construction to enable food and manpower to be carried to all corners of the Empire. In particular, he standardized the cart sizes so that taxes due on goods could be easily assessed; carts could also run in the same ruts, making travel quicker.

One reason for the road-building programme was the imperial tour. Unlike previous rulers of the states, who remained in their cities, Ch'in embarked in 219 BC on the first of several journeys throughout the Empire, 'following the path of the sun' through his newly conquered lands, reinforcing his imperial rule by physical presence and imposing his power and omnipotence at first hand. By the end of his reign, there were 270 palaces within seventy miles of the capital, each ready to receive and honour him on his journeys.

Ch'in had control of China, but now he wanted power over death. Even as he contemplated his political victories, he was beginning a search beyond life itself, for the key to immortality. The semi-divine First Emperor saw the world in terms of the five elements of Taoism: earth, wood, metal, fire and water. Taoism, traditionally said to have been founded by the philosopher Lao Tzu (b. *c.* 604 BC), induced a belief in the elixir of life and encouraged alchemistic experiments to unearth the secret of immortality. Since the Emperor was superstitious and his native state relatively undeveloped, he became influenced by magic and shamanism after he had conquered the peoples of Ch'i and Yen. He embarked on a regime of physical and mental hygiene, practising mysticism and sorcery and so strengthening his belief in himself as a semi-divine being.

In 219 BC, Ch'in sent envoys in search of three mystical mountain islands, P'eng-lai, Fang-chang and Ying-chou, where the immortals dwelt, in the hope of discovering the magic potions that would enable him to live forever. The envoys never returned. Four years later, he ordered a second tour of the Empire to hunt for the elixir. Three years after that, he mounted a further search. It became a quest that would fill the rest of his days.

Ch'in building works required money. To raise it, the people of the Empire had to be located, identified and taxed. Ch'in instituted reforms which changed the pattern of farming all over China by preventing the nomadic farmers from moving around the country, and by forcing them to settle. In this way, the census returns could establish a tax base. However, in the northern provinces, the settled farmers were now harassed and threatened by the marauding barbarians. Ch'in acted decisively. He launched a military campaign against the marauders and relocated 120,000 families from that area to the safer and less populated agricultural regions of the south.

In 215 BC Ch'in had defeated his enemies from the vast regions on the northern frontier. The imperial armies under the command of General Meng T'ien, 'Conqueror of the Tartars', had crushed the nomadic tribes, but Ch'in still needed to protect his Empire from future incursions. His successors so far had been both civil and military. An inscription of 215 BC at Mount Chieh-shih commemorated them:

He has been the first to achieve a single peace.
He has demolished the inner and outer walls of cities.
He has cut through the embankments of rivers.
He has levelled the bulwarks at mountain defiles.

But one year later, in 214 BC, Ch'in ordered General Meng T'ien to begin the greatest engineering project the world had seen. He would link the existing border fortifications into one long great wall to keep out his enemies permanently.

The Great Wall

The Great Wall of China was Ch'in Shih-Huang-ti's lasting achievement. It took him twelve years to build, and it remains the only man-made object visible from space, stretching 1,400 miles over mountain, river and plain. He gave his name to the country he created, and his legacy was to endure, despite periods of disunity, in a line of imperial dynasties which stretched for over 2,000 years up to 1912, when the last Emperor of China was deposed and a republic was formed. The wall became a symbol of that dynastic legacy, a psychological boundary of Chinese statehood.

His name lives on in Chinese folklore:

How long did the Emperor take to build the Wall?
No time at all; he rode a strange horse which made the valleys and the hills equal;
    where his horse's hooves trod, the Wall sprang up.
Did he use men to build it?
There were thousands of mouths working there.
How did they get the Wall across the Yellow River?
The water parted for a hundred li, and so the masons did their work.
Has the Wall got any end to it?
No, it is a circle, and the Central Kingdom is surrounded on all sides by the Wall.
What else do you know about the Emperor Ch'in?
Ch'in passed here building the Great Wall but he has never come back. He is going on still.
How do you know that?
There was God-breath in him. (Geil)

Emperor Ch'in's decision to join and strengthen parts of the existing fortifications was a symbol of the vigorous unifying effects of empire. But the cost was enormous. It became known as the 'Wall of Tears', the first Gulag in history, as every class of Chinese society was pressed into service to build it.

But the Emperor and his Grand Councillor faced opposition from Confucian scholars at court who objected to Li Ssu's brutal Legalist measures. They cried out against his relocation of the northern farmers, and condemned Ch'in's increasingly brutal and despotic methods. One source, a Chinese historical work known as the *Shih Chi* and probably a piece of propaganda by Li Ssu, put one side of the argument:

Shih-huang [they said] is a man whose nature is violent, cruel and despotic . . . He thinks that since antiquity there has been nobody to equal him . . . The Emperor delights in showing his intimidating power by means of punishments and executions . . . To such a stage has his thirst for power reached. (A. Cotterell)

Dissenting intellectuals during the Ch'in dynasty were buried alive and decapitated.

Some went further. They unwisely began to call for the Emperor's downfall. Li Ssu explained to Ch'in:

> They study the past to criticize the present, burying reality in their empty arguments and rhetoric. There are those who condemn your laws and your orders, and as soon as they hear that a decree has been issued, they debate its merits according to their own school of thought, opposing it secretly in their hearts at court and disputing it openly in the streets. This lowers the prestige of the sovereign. It must be stopped.
> (L. Cottrell)

Ch'in and Li Ssu acted with calculated violence: 460 of the scholars were taken, buried alive and then decapitated. The Emperor and Li Ssu declared war on the past and set about systematically destroying the scholars' accumulated wisdom. Anyone who sympathized with the scholars was punished. On the advice of Li Ssu, Ch'in banished his eldest son, Fu Su, for siding with the Confucians: he was sent to the Great Wall.

The scholars' 'books' – inscribed wooden strips – were burnt, and the past was reinvented in an extraordinary attempt to rewrite history and to remove all reference to

Confucius and his thought. With Li Ssu, Ch'in realized not only the power of history but also the need to build his Empire with fresh ideas. Many scholars, however, hid their books in bricked-up walls. These Confucian legacies were later discovered and are the foundation of our present understanding of China in those early days.

The burning of the books had a psychological as well as a practical impact. The scholars were silenced and the power of Confucian philosophy replaced by the harsh precepts of Legalism. The most controversial works were kept in the bureau of the academicians, since it was their general discussion which Li Ssu sought to end. Works on medicine and agriculture deemed essential to the running of the Empire were spared, and although Confucius' thinking was taught once more in Chinese government schools by the middle of the first century BC, for over 150 years it was wiped from the curriculum.

Ch'in had rewritten the past. Now he had to shape the future. The Great Wall, uniting past structures and standing as a new symbol of his power, was the focus of his energies. Between 214 and 210 BC, he ordered thousands of scholars who had escaped execution to work building his Wall, joining the conscripted force of 300,000 workmen, peasants, prisoners and soldiers formed into construction teams. The army was sent to guard both the Wall and the workers, a cunning ploy by Ch'in to keep the troops occupied in peacetime.

On the Wall of Tears, thousands died of cold, starvation, exhaustion or disease, and were buried in the foundations of the very structure they were building. The Emperor had heard the prophecy that the Wall would not be finished until 10,000 men had been buried in it; even he found this a shocking statistic. Legend has it that he searched out and found a man called Wan – the name means 10,000 – and buried him in the rampart. The work continued.

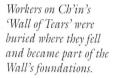

Workers on Ch'in's 'Wall of Tears' were buried where they fell and became part of the Wall's foundations.

Within four years, Ch'in's vision had taken shape. The Wall consisted of a rampart twenty feet high, linking forty-foot towers spaced equally at the range of an archer's arrow. Each tower was provisioned to withstand a four-month siege. Beacon towers every eleven miles could transmit a message across Ch'in's Empire in twenty-four hours, and the Wall itself was used as a road for transporting troops and provisions. To occupy his large army and keep it distant from court intrigues in Hsien-yang, the capital, Ch'in stationed a standing garrison the entire length of the Great Wall.

It stands today as a magnificent feat of civil engineering. Even the great builders of antiquity, the Egyptians or the Romans, would have trusted to nature to keep them safe and would have left the mountains and rivers alone. But Ch'in felt responsible for the guardianship of 'All Under Heaven' and took the whole task upon himself. However, it is an irony of history that contemporary chronicles made little mention of the Great Wall; the credit was given to General Meng T'ien, Conqueror of the Tartars:

> He . . . built a great wall, constructing its defiles and passes in accordance with the configuration of the terrain. It started at Lin-t'ao and extended to Liao-tung, reaching a distance of more than ten thousand li. After crossing the [Yellow] River, it wound northward, touching the Yang mountains. (A. Cotterell)

The End of the Ch'in Dynasty

In the years after his enthronement the First Emperor survived no fewer than fifteen assassination attempts. He continued to search for the elixir of immortality, but, even as he dreamt of living forever, he began to prepare for his own death. As early as 246 BC, Ch'in had planned a sumptuous tomb. It is mentioned again in documents dating from 221 BC. By 212 BC, when the first extant reports of its construction appear, the tomb had become a symbol of his power. A workforce of 700,000 men had been allocated to the great project at Mount Li in the northern province of Shensi.

The tomb was enormous. The mound covering the mausoleum was 300 feet high, and the total circumference of the interior was eight miles. In death Ch'in was to be placed within a central sanctum of palaces and gardens, which was protected by an army of 7,000 terracotta warriors in battle formation. The tomb was filled with priceless objects of gold and silver, and surrounded by subterranean rivers of mercury flowing across an image of Ch'in's Empire under a painted vault of stars.

This marked the height of Ch'in's power. Only five years later, his dynasty would disappear forever. Li Ssu's strong sense of the changeability of things is evident from an address he gave to a royal banquet in 212 BC:

> Things should not be allowed to become too flourishing. I was a commoner of Shang-t'sai, an ordinary man from the village . . . Among the Ministerial posts at the present time there is none higher than mine, which may indeed be called the peak of wealth and honour. But when things have reached their peak they decline. I do not know yet where I shall unharness. (L. Cottrell)

Li Ssu accompanied Ch'in on each one of the imperial progresses. The fifth began in 211 BC, a journey south-east from Xianyang to Mount K'uai-chi, north to Lang-yeh and Chih-fu and then west to Xianyang. In July/August of 210 BC, the First Emperor's procession

The Great Wall of China, completed by Ch'in in 210 BC. It stretches 1,400 miles over the country's terrain and is the only human construction that can be seen on the earth's surface from space.

reached Sha-ch'iu in southern Hopei. There, Ch'in Shih-Huang-ti suddenly died. In all probability, he was killed by an overdose of one of the potions for immortality containing the virulent toxins mercury or phosphorus. He was forty-nine years old, in the thirty-seventh year of his reign, his twelfth as emperor.

By due succession, the imperial crown would pass to Ch'in's eldest son, the exiled Fu Su. But Li Ssu and the eunuch Chao Kao, who had together arranged for Fu Su's exile to the Great Wall two years before, wanted to see the throne pass to the impressionable second son, Hu Hai. They immediately realized that they had to take the Emperor's body back to the capital, and that his death should be kept secret as long as possible in order for them to start their plotting. Afraid that the decomposing corpse would arouse suspicion, Li Ssu and Chao Kao disguised the smell by burying it in a cart of fish.

After they had reached Xianyang, Li Ssu and Chao Kao forged the Emperor's signature on a document ordering Fu Su and General Mien T'ien, Ch'in's most powerful ally, to commit suicide (which they duly did). They even provided the swords. They took over the government of the Empire through the weak younger son, Hu Hai. A turbulent period followed, with peasant uprisings and a bloody war of succession. Li Ssu, imprisoned by Chao Kao in 209 BC, was executed after torture the following year. In 207 BC, Chao Kao, who next tried to take over the throne, was himself killed. A year later, the Ch'in dynasty finally fell, and a new power, the Han dynasty, founded by the illiterate peasant Liu Pang, rose in China. Liu Pang was proclaimed emperor in 206 BC.

The Han dynasty ruled until AD 9, imposing a monopoly of coining and a standardized currency. It was a much gentler regime. Perhaps benefiting from the harshness of the First Emperor, Liu Pang's successor, Hwei-ti, appointed a commission to restore as far as possible the texts which had been destroyed. Much of this restoration was done by memory. It rescinded Ch'in's book-burning edict in 191 BC, and made the Confucian texts canonical, as well as the ethical basis of Chinese culture. In AD 58, sacrifices to Confucius were ordered in China's government schools.

The Great Legacy

The First Emperor left much more than the Great Wall. He had unified the people of seven states into a country which became one of the world's greatest empires, and he unleashed a period of cultural and material expansion. He had unified the language, the system of weights and measures, and the law; he had standardized travel through road and canal, which he used to bind his Empire together; having subdued his enemies, he achieved a remarkable disarmament while at the same time maintaining a standing army. To posterity he left the Great Wall and his extravagant tomb at Mount Li, discovered in 1974 and still under excavation.

Ch'in abolished the feudal system and replaced it with an appointed bureaucracy. He also established the imperial persona in China, a semi-divine figure who had the power of life and death over the subjects of the Empire. He achieved this by using political and military power with brutal effect. The tactics of Sun Yat-sen in the 1920s and Mao Tse-tung and his revolutionaries in the 1930s were drawn directly from the example of the First Emperor.

Mao's theory of combat was learnt from the tactician Sun Tzu, who had studied Ch'in and his military successes. Reflecting on tactics, Mao wrote: 'We must not belittle the saying in the book of Sun Wu Tzu, the great military expert of ancient China. Know your enemy and know yourself and you can fight a hundred battles without disaster.'

The First Emperor set the example for control of intellectual life in China by killing the most vocal dissidents and sending the remaining ones to build the Great Wall. This despotic leader applied military tactics to dissident poets and thinkers. If his government could control, as he did, the sum of available history and scholarship, then he could also control what people thought. In an age when learning provided social mobility, he would control that too. The Cultural Revolution of Mao in 1966–9 was a similar intellectual purge, designed to revitalize Maoist Communist doctrine. Mao treated the bureaucrats with comparable cruelty, forcing them to work on the land.

In building the Great Wall, Ch'in recognized the central fact about China's sense of itself: the country stayed remote and safe behind its physical and psychological barrier, and it was advanced enough from the fifth century BC onward to rival anything that fifth-century Athens or Persia could produce. Yet the soul of China has always been its image of the past rather than its hope for the future. The First Emperor knew it, and Mao knew it – and, knowing it, both attempted to rewrite history. The imperial legacy of Ch'in lasted over 2,000 years; its successor, the Republic of China, survived from 1912 to 1949, and was replaced by the People's Republic of China. Each leader, from the time of the First Emperor to the present, has fought the battle for China's history.

The army of terracotta warriors built to guard the tomb of the First Emperor at Mount Li.

· 3 ·

Roman POWER

OCTAVIAN CAESAR DEFEATS ANTONY AND CLEOPATRA,
AND THE GREAT ROMAN EMPIRE IS FOUNDED.

To the historian, looking back from the vantage-ground of two thousand years, Actium seems like the undrawing of a curtain and the letting in of daylight on the world. He knows that it meant two centuries of peace, and many more of ordered government and established law. But, to contemporaries, it seemed as if things were still on a razor edge; one great fear had been laid, but others remained . . . The world could draw breath for a moment, but its nerves were still quivering. It had lived so long among catastrophes that it scarcely dared to hope. (John Buchan, *Augustus*)

THE BATTLE OF ACTIUM on 2 September 31 BC was one of the most decisive turning points in world history. It marked the undisputed leadership of Rome's most successful empire-builder, Augustus Caesar. It began an age of power and success for the Romans which carried down the centuries through the reigns of the Caesars Tiberius, Claudius, Caligula, Nero and their successors. If the battle itself made history, the aftermath was history in the making.

The protagonists facing each other across the Bay of Actium were on one side the great Roman senator and orator Marc Antony and Egypt's Queen Cleopatra, and on the other the much younger Octavius and his wily general Agrippa. It was clear that the winners at Actium would win more than a sea victory; they would win an empire, and they would win the right to tell their version of history to succeeding generations. Nations which fight not only have to win the war; they have to win the subsequent peace.

OPPOSITE: *Roman onyx cameo of the Emperor Augustus: the goatskin breastplate was considered to have divine power.*

The Ides of March: 44 BC

The story began in Apollonia, a town on the Illyrian shore, in the spring of 44 BC. Gaius Octavius Thurinus – known as Octavius – had been studying in Apollonia for six months. Born in Rome nineteen years before to a family originating from the town of Velitrae in the Alban Hills, south of Rome, Octavius was slightly built, with a delicate frame, steady grey eyes, a pale complexion and a studious air. His father had governed Macedonia, and had married into Roman nobility, taking as his wife Atia, the niece of the most powerful

Marc Antony mourns the death of Julius Caesar in a powerful oration over his funeral pyre. (Painting after Benjamin West.)

Roman alive, Julius Caesar. This made Octavius a great-nephew of the dictator of Rome, a relationship rendered much closer by Caesar's lack of other heirs. As a result he was thought to be an intimate of the great and was sedulously courted. He responded to this treatment warily, knowing the danger of making enemies; he gave no promises. In December 45 BC, before leaving for Apollonia, he had bade farewell to Caesar. It was the last time he saw him.

In Apollonia, Octavius had two close friends. These men were to influence the Battle of Actium and its aftermath: Gaius Cilnius Maecenas (d. 8 BC) and Marcus Vipsanius Agrippa (63–12 BC). Maecenas was to become one of the first great exponents of propaganda in the struggle for political power. He was a striking figure: hollow-eyed, strong and rugged but with a contrastingly effeminate manner. He always spoke candidly and was known to be a loyal friend and adviser. Octavius had met him on arrival in Apollonia. Agrippa he had known even longer. They had studied together at school. Agrippa was one of the most astute commanders Rome had produced, the supreme example of a man whose loyalty and devotion to his leader confined him to a supporting role. He was a firm friend and trusted ally of Octavius for thirty years.

In late March 44 BC, Octavius received a letter from his mother Atia. Dated 15 March, it reported that Julius Caesar had been stabbed to death that day in the Senate House in Rome. 'The time has come', his mother wrote, 'when you must play the man, decide, and act, for no one can tell the things that may come forth' (Buchan). Octavius acted quickly, immediately setting sail for Rome. As a sign of mourning he let his beard grow. He resolved to keep his own counsel and bide his time.

When he landed, he learnt of the developments since Julius Caesar's death. The dictator had been killed by a group of senators led by Gaius Cassius and Marcus Brutus, all of them anxious to stop him taking total power in Rome. Afterwards they had declared their action a triumph of liberty over tyranny. Caesar's close friend and fellow Consul for the year (two Consuls were elected every year in Rome), Marc Antony, had taken charge of the city. He had called a meeting of the Senate for 17 March at which he had pronounced an amnesty for the murderers and had promised to enact the last few decrees which Caesar had made or intended to make. Rome had been in uproar; and at Caesar's funeral on 20 March a pyre had been built in the forum and Caesar's body had been burnt in a frenzy of mourning and lamentation never before seen in Rome. Antony had roused the enormous crowds with a moving oration, delivered over Caesar's body as he held the dead man's bloodstained toga. Rioting had followed. Brutus and Cassius had fled, together with the statesman Cicero and a number of senators and nobles. Caesar's mistress, Cleopatra, had also fled from Rome back to Egypt. By the time that Octavius entered the city, Marc Antony was in charge.

Marcus Antonius was born in the early 80s BC and had led a raffish and profligate youth, but he had risen to become commander-in-chief and later governor in Italy; now approaching his fortieth year, he was vigorous, handsome, direct and a charismatic leader.

> There was a noble dignity about Antony's appearance. His forehead broad, his nose aquiline, and these gave him a certain bold and masculine look . . . this swaggering air, his ribald talk, his taking of his food while standing at the common mess-table . . . made his troops delight in his company. (Plutarch)

Marc Antony, the charismatic leader of Rome.

Marc Antony now had the use of Caesar's money, and was able to use the late Emperor's name to pass decrees, although many were believed to be forgeries. But when Caesar's will was read in public, the young Octavius was named as heir to Caesar's vast wealth and name: from that point, he was called Gaius Julius Caesar Octavianus – or Octavian in modern historical accounts. Marc Antony angrily dubbed him 'the youth who owed everything to his name' (Cicero). To Antony, Octavian seemed no more than a boy who had done nothing for Rome.

As Antony consolidated his power base in Rome, Octavian was travelling the Appian way to Puteoli and then to Rome. He had decided to confront Antony. *En route*, he stopped to meet the statesman Cicero, by now sixty-two years old and the wise man of Roman politics. He declared to Cicero: 'May I succeed in attaining the honour and position of my father to which I am entitled' (Cicero). Cicero wrote of him:

> I see clearly that he has brains and spirit, and is as well disposed to our heroes as we could desire. But we must carefully consider the degree of reliance that can be placed on him, taking into account his age, his name, his position as Caesar's heir, and his upbringing. He must be trained, and above all he must be alienated from Antony . . . He has an excellent disposition, if it only lasts.

Octavian at last arrived in Rome at the end of May. But Antony was not there. He had snubbed Octavian by departing in April for Campania to recruit a bodyguard of veterans and Syrians. When he returned and they met for the first time, he ignored and then humiliated the young man, leaving him waiting in the ante-room of the former house of Caesar's late rival Pompey. Antony determined to deny him access to Caesar's legacy.

The only tactic open to Octavian was a policy of covert and subtle undermining of Antony's power base. With Maecenas' help, he began a campaign of rumour and political lobbying; in July of 44 BC, he scored a popular triumph by arranging that the public games be dedicated to Julius Caesar's victories. In addition, he petitioned the senate to declare Caesar a god, thus keeping Caesar's name and his own cause in the public eye. Realizing that Octavian had a following among Caesar's supporters, Antony saw that he would have to compromise.

Octavian was slowly building his own power base. He continued his campaign to ridicule Antony, drawing support from those who approved of him as Julius Caesar's heir and from those who were on Antony's side against Caesar's murderers, Cassius and Brutus, who had called themselves 'liberators'. In a delicate and poised campaign, he gradually strengthened his following in Rome. Now he needed military support. He travelled to Campania, approached the veterans settled there and raised 3,000 men. He wrote (in *Res Gestae*):

> At the age of nineteen years, on my own authority and at my own cost, I raised the army
> by means of which I liberated the republic from the oppression of a tyrannical faction.

Octavian's army provided an attractive alternative for the troops which made up Antony's legions. Eventually Octavian prised the bulk of the army from Antony's control by offering the troops more money; moreover, some legionaries were incensed that Antony had not acted more quickly to avenge Julius Caesar's death, and joined Octavian on principle.

Octavian brought his forces to Rome on 10 November; Antony arrived with full military pomp on 20 November and summoned Octavian to a meeting of the Senate four days later. But the meeting never took place. When he received news that still more legions had joined Octavian, Antony left Rome, heading north. In his absence, Cicero launched a series of attacks against Antony in the Senate, pledging his support for Octavian. 'What god', he said in a Senate debate, 'has given to the Roman people this god-like youth?'

Antony realized that he had underrated his young rival. He had calculated that, in order to regain the initiative and popularity with the Senate, he needed to leave Rome in search of Julius Caesar's murderers, who were then in northern Italy. While Antony was away from Rome, Octavian lobbied for support and convinced enough senators of Antony's political ambitions and the danger he posed to their safety. Using Julius Caesar's money, Octavian reinforced his army and raced after Antony.

In April 43 BC, his army caught up with Antony's at Modena. The encounter turned into a rout, with Antony's troops unwilling to fight their former comrades. Antony himself surrendered, and was declared a public enemy. The victorious Octavian demanded election to the consulship, and when the Senate refused, he marched on Rome with his troops, and was finally elected Consul on 19 August 43 BC.

In a short time, Octavian had achieved extraordinary success: he had adroitly handled a volatile and complex political situation, he had made his enemies his tools, and he had shown self-restraint and self-confidence; he was now 'lifted high on the consciousness of himself' as Aulus Gellius said. His adoption of Caesar's name was now finally confirmed by a law passed by the popular assembly. From then on, Gaius Julius Caesar Octavianus became Caesar's officially acknowledged heir.

A late example of an Imperial triumphal arch, in Rome, traditionally built to celebrate great victories.

The Triumvirate

Within weeks of the march on Rome, in November 43 BC, Antony and Octavian made peace. Both men understood that only by acting together could they avoid a new civil war. Together with Antony's ally, Marcus Aemilius Lepidus, a Triumvirate was formed to reconstitute the new republic and to bring Julius Caesar's murderers to justice. This arrangement placed full political power in the hands of these three men. But once it became clear that Lepidus was ineffective, the alliance was based on the axis between Antony and Octavian alone.

Octavian, Antony and Lepidus decided to rid Rome of all who had supported Caesar's assassins. Accordingly they embarked on a brutal programme of executions called proscriptions, carried out under an emergency military law passed on 27 November 43 BC. Over 400 senators and 2,000 knights were listed for execution, among them Octavian's close friend and mentor Cicero. His name headed the list of those to die, his head fixed by Antony above the Rostra in Rome. This cruel but effective action devastated opposition to the Triumvirate. At this time, Octavian believed he was reshaping the Empire. He was moved by a desire to avenge Julius Caesar, by a rational urge to bring order out of chaos, and by a belief in his own destiny.

In October 42 BC, with the capital now quiet, Antony and Octavian moved against the armies of Brutus and Cassius, catching and defeating them in a ferocious battle at Philippi in northern Greece. It was a close-run thing. At one point Brutus' troops overran Octavian's camp, but by pure chance Octavian had just left it and was saved. Brutus and Cassius themselves committed suicide. The republican cause they represented was rapidly dying with them.

Bust of a Ptolomaic woman once thought to be Cleopatra, Queen of Egypt.

During the next few years, the 100,000 troops of the Triumvirate were disbanded and settled on lands found for them in Italy, an arrangement that was later to prove crucial in binding them to Octavian. This was a time during which Octavian was away from Rome; Antony's wife Fulvia and his brother Lucius, the Consul of 41 BC, took all possible steps to obstruct Octavian's highly unpopular land distributions. They made the mistake of trying to raise a force against Octavian; but he learnt of their plan and trapped them at Perusia (Perugia). Although he allowed them to go free, he burnt the town.

Now Italy belonged to Octavian. The strengthening of his position owed much to the machinations and political skills of his old friend Maecenas. In October of 40 BC, with Fulvia now conveniently dead, an important political liaison was effected: Antony was married to Octavian's sister Octavia to cement relations between the families. The ineffectual Lepidus, third member of the Triumvirate, was dispatched to run the Empire in Africa.

The Roman Empire was now effectively divided between Octavian based in Rome in the West and Antony based in Athens in the East. Since the Battle of Philippi, Antony had been on a triumphal progress through Syria and Palestine, meeting the client monarchs and consolidating his hold on the eastern part of the Empire. In Bithynia, he met Herod of Judaea, and at Tarsus, in Cilicia, Queen Cleopatra VII of Egypt.

Antony and Cleopatra

Cleopatra, Queen of Egypt, was descended from the Greek Ptolomaic conquerors of Egypt. The fire of her forefather, Alexander the Great, burned bright within her. She had been Julius Caesar's mistress for the last few years of his life, and was the mother of Caesar's son, Caesarion. She was twenty-nine years old, half Greek and half Macedonian. 'Her own beauty, so we are told, was not of that incomparable kind,' the historian Plutarch wrote, 'but the charm of her presence was irresistible.' She had an extraordinary magnetic vitality and sexual allure, which she used coolly and rationally. Cleopatra was politic, astute, intelligent and educated, ambitious for power and status. She posed a real threat to the security of Rome; Cleopatra (and earlier, Hannibal) in the 800 years of empire had been one of the few who had succeeded in alarming the Romans.

Her charms and abilities captivated Antony, ravishing his imagination and his intellect. As Plutarch wrote: 'Plato speaks of four kinds of flattery, Cleopatra knew a thousand.' She also knew she had to make herself indispensable to Antony if she was to succeed. During the winter of 41–40 BC she indulged his approaches for friendship and co-operation, but gave him nothing, neither her money nor her love. She knew he would eventually pay her price. She knew that Egypt was the key to Rome's survival: with most of Italy and what is now France covered in forest or too difficult to cultivate, the fertile Nile delta provided the grain to feed the expanding provinces of the Empire. As long as the rulers of Egypt remained under Roman influence, Rome felt secure.

Nineteenth-century engraving of Cleopatra embarking on the Cydnus.

Cleopatra knew that her ambitions could be realized with Antony's help. She saw herself founding a new Greek-Roman dynasty and rebuilding the empire of Alexander the Great. But she would need Antony to help her. In 41 BC, she travelled to him at Tarsus on her elaborate pleasure boat. It was a meeting that changed the course of Roman history.

Through her son Caesarion, she had her own claim to the legacy of Caesar. Through Antony, by now her lover, she had the means to make it a reality. In 37 BC she persuaded him to acknowledge her twins as his; in 34 BC she succeeded in making him recognize her son Caesarion as legitimate heir to Julius Caesar. Antony declared Cleopatra 'Queen of Kings' and Caesarion 'King of Kings'. For him, here was all the wealth and power of Egypt for the taking, and here too was Caesar's own son.

It was a challenge which Octavian could not ignore. In 33 BC the Triumvirate was dissolved. The Roman Empire was now divided between two men, Antony and Octavian. With Antony in thrall to Cleopatra and subject to her ambitions for Egypt, a confrontation between the two Roman leaders became inevitable. Their rivalry no longer had the look of a civil war. Octavian understood this, and determined to alter the way Antony was perceived in Rome. Aware of the importance of public support, he devised and with Maecenas' help staged a propaganda campaign to manipulate the image and undermine the popular support of his charismatic opponent.

Antony was careless about his public image. When he had arrived at Athens, he had identified himself with Dionysus, the god of sex and revelry, and had laid himself open to charges of Dionysiac excesses. After the break with Octavian the accusations became harsher: Antony was soft, godless and entirely in Cleopatra's power. Worse, he had adopted the vile eastern gods of Egypt. The historian Cassius Dio wrote:

> He appeared in public either on a kline [bed], as Dionysus, or on a golden throne, like a king. He commissioned paintings and statues of himself with Cleopatra, he as Osiris or Dionysus, she as Silene or Isis. More than anything else this created the impression that she had cast some kind of spell over him.

Antony still had a faction in Rome which supported him, and which, according to Plutarch, 'accepted his luxurious life-style and decadence, his excesses and egocentrism, as gaiety and good fellowship and even commended it as a dazzling display of power and good fortune' (Plutarch). But Octavian and the astute propagandist Maecenas worked to silence Antony's supporters in Rome. Within weeks, they had the crowds baying for a war against Egypt before the Roman Empire was destroyed by the half-human demons worshipped in the East. Egypt's vast treasury only increased Octavian's appetite for conquest.

Octavian knew he would have to confront and defeat Antony. He could call on the diplomatic and propaganda skills of Maecenas to handle the approach and aftermath of a war with Antony, and he could exploit the military skills of Agrippa to win that war. He waited for the right moment.

It came in 31 BC, the year of Octavian's third consulship. Antony and Cleopatra had established a base at Ephesus in Asia Minor. The combined powers of Antony in Athens and Cleopatra in Alexandria posed too great a threat to Imperial Rome: the future of the Empire was now at stake. If Antony and Cleopatra were to overthrow Octavian, the Roman Empire would move to Alexandria, in any case commercially and strategically a better site. As yet, neither had invaded the other's territory. The sea between them would decide the future of the Roman Empire.

The Battle of Actium

Antony had the first move. In the summer of 32 BC he had deployed his army and navy in bases on the western coast of Greece. Antony and Cleopatra had 500 ships, many of them constructed in Athens and Alexandria to match or even outclass Octavian's Sicilian fleet. They were built by the Ptolomies of Egypt, one of the greatest ship-building cultures of all time; their ships, it was felt, would deliver a victory at sea. On land, too, Antony and Cleopatra were formidable. They had 75,000 legionaries, 25,000 light infantry and 12,000 cavalry, although some estimates give Antony 60,000 legionaries and 80,000 Asiatic horse and foot.

Against them, Octavian had a fleet already trained and which had proved successful in action against Sextus Pompeius, who had turned Sicily into a centre of opposition against Octavian. Five years earlier, in 36 BC, in a specially built harbour on the bay of Naples, within the protection of Lake Avernus, Octavian and Agrippa had constructed and trained the greatest fleet Rome would ever have. Thus prepared, Octavian launched one of the most effective propaganda campaigns in history. He held spectacular games in the public stadiums, using them to denounce his rival, Antony. Coins were struck that depicted Octavian as a wise hero, while graffiti critical of Antony turned up all over Rome. Most important of all, Octavian cultivated the friendship of the poets and playwrights of Rome – he understood that it would be artists like Horace, Virgil and Livy who would write the Empire's official history. Within weeks he had the crowds in Rome demanding that he declare war on Egypt. Antony's supporters, including half of the Senate, fled to Alexandria.

A Roman trireme which was fitted with three banks of oars.

In the autumn of 32 BC, Antony and Cleopatra moved to Patras, west of Athens, stationing the fleet along the coast from Corfu to Crete. When the winter came Octavian declared war on Egypt. His forces amounted to 80,000 infantry, 12,000 cavalry and 400 fast, light ships, whose value Agrippa had learnt from sea battles off Sicily.

Leaving Maecenas in charge in Rome, Octavian went to war in Greece. In March 31 BC he ordered Agrippa to attack Antony's western supply lines at Methone on the western edge of the Peloponnese. The result was that Antony's vast and hungry land army could not rely on seaborne supplies from the south. In one action, just off Actium on the Gulf of Ambracia, Antony lost nearly a quarter of his fleet to Agrippa.

Octavian himself landed on the Greek mainland and marched south until he reached Actium where Antony's fleet was anchored in a sheltered harbour, his chosen place for the inevitable battle. When all of Antony's land army arrived, he tried to force an engagement, crossing the narrow strait and setting up camp two miles from Octavian. He tried an outflanking cavalry manoeuvre, but it failed and he was forced to retreat to Actium. There he found himself penned in by Octavian on land and by Agrippa's ships, which had by now established a blockade.

Each day, Antony's forces declined in strength. He was encamped in a swampy, malarial area. His supply lines had been disrupted by Agrippa. Disease and desertion diminished his army. Cleopatra advised fighting at sea, using their larger ships to burst through Agrippa's blockade. If they won, they could sail on to Rome; if not, they could flee to Egypt in their fast ships, regroup, and begin the campaign again. Antony's land commanders advised him to use his forces where they were strongest. Their counsel was immortalized by Shakespeare in *Antony and Cleopatra*:

> O noble emperor, do not fight by sea:
> Trust not to rotten planks . . .
> Let the Egyptians and the Phoenicians go a ducking:
> We have used to conquer standing on the earth.

Antony ignored them, allowing Cleopatra to prevail in her advice to fight at sea. Octavian learnt of Antony's plans to fight or flee on water. Instinctively he wanted to avoid a battle, knowing that the sight of Antony escaping to Egypt with Cleopatra would strengthen his propaganda campaign and dishearten Antony's troops. Agrippa, however, knew that Antony had ships which could outrun his, whether retreating to Egypt or advancing on Rome. He urged war.

All through late August, the weather was stormy, and the winds inauspicious for Antony. But he prepared carefully, rigging and manning 170 ships alongside Cleopatra's squadron of 60, readying them for battle. Of his original 500 ships, many had been lost in skirmishes along the coast. Desertions had depleted his crews, and he was left with more ships than sailors to man them. These superfluous vessels he was forced to burn. Agrippa's fleet, on the other hand, was constant at 400 ships.

Although Antony's ships, according to Horace, were larger and faster, Agrippa's smaller craft were more effective because they were more manoeuvrable in action. Most historians drawing on Roman sources have supposed that Antony's fleet contained a greater number of larger ships than Agrippa's; in fact, according to other sources, both fleets had large and small ships. It suited Octavian, in the after-history of the battle, to emphasize the power and might of Antony's navy.

Antony was waiting for the weather to change. At last it did, and 2 September dawned clear and fine. Antony now waited for the afternoon shift in the wind from the north-

Victorian engraving of the Battle of Actium.

west which would separate the enemy fleet from the land, or, if he had failed at sea, speed his retreat. Antony's great land army looked on, annoyed that Cleopatra had persuaded Antony to fight at sea.

In the early afternoon the two fleets joined in battle. Just as on land, arrows and cata-pult shots filled the air, while the ships steered to grapple with each other, standing to side by side to form fighting platforms, their oars and sails often tangling. 'The fighting was carried on with wicker shields, spears, poles, and flaming missiles, while Antony's soldiers also shot with catapults from wooden towers' (Plutarch). Before long, Agrippa's ships were inflicting heavy losses on Antony's fleet.

Midway through the fierce and confused action, Cleopatra took the opportunity of a sudden breeze and sailed off to the south. Antony followed her with sixty or seventy fast ships, leaving his men to fight alone. Cleopatra's flight was, it seems, part of a coolly planned manoeuvre which made use of the fresh afternoon breeze, and was not promoted by panic. Nonetheless, their departure demoralized Antony's fleet, and its resistance broke. According to Plutarch's often disputed records there were 5,000 of Antony's men killed and 300 of his ships captured during the battle, but he is probably referring not just to the Battle of Actium but to the campaign as a whole. Both figures are too high for Actium alone.

Antony's retreat left a huge and undefeated land army under his military commander Canidius Crassus to fend for itself. It took only a week of sporadic resistance before these nineteen legions (of approximately 5,000 men each) surrendered to Octavian. The poet Virgil, writing between 29 and 19 BC, immortalized the scene in the *Aeneid*:

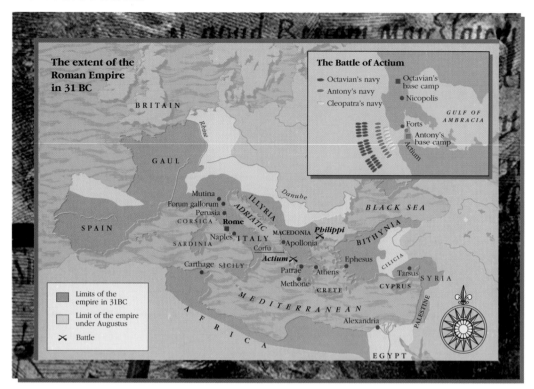

Looking thereon, Actian Apollo above drew his bow; with the terror of it all Egypt and India, every Arab and Sabaean, turned back in flight. The Queen herself seemed to call the winds and spread her sails, and even now let her sheets run slack. Her the Lord of Fire had fashioned amid the carnage, wan with the shadow of death, borne along by the waves and the north-west wind; and over gainst her the vast bulk of mourning Nile, opening out its folds and calling with all his raiment the conquered people into his blue lap and the coverture of his streams.

Triumphant, Octavian arrived at Cleopatra's capital Alexandria in July of 30 BC. Here he found Antony deserted by his legions and fallen into a profound depression. Before Octavian had time to decide what to do with him, events took their own course. Antony, thinking Cleopatra dead, and ashamed of facing his victorious adversary, killed himself, falling on his sword and, in the event, dying in Cleopatra's arms. He had done Octavian's work for him.

Even though she was a prisoner in her own palace, Cleopatra came before Octavian and offered an alliance with him. When he refused, all she could do was to plead for her sons' lives. But Caesarion, her son by Julius Caesar, posed too great a threat to Octavian, and he was killed. Antyllus, Antony's son by Fulvia, was also put to death. All of Cleopatra's dreams of power and her ambitions for empire had come to nothing. Knowing that Octavian would parade her through Rome as a spoil of war from Egypt, the crocodile kingdom, she too killed herself, and in so doing, conveniently solved another of Octavian's problems. He allowed that her body be buried next to Antony at her mausoleum at Alexandria.

Octavian and Agrippa had won the war. Octavian recorded his version of the battle in his *Memoirs*, published between 25 and 22 BC; only two dozen fragments remain, but it was the source for the battle's historians, Plutarch and Cassius Dio. From now on, Actium was a matter for the image-makers, the hidden persuaders. The poet Propertius wrote in 'The Battle of Actium':

The wide sea here at Actium never troubles
The sailors' prayers, and preserves the memory
Of Caesar's warships.
Here came the world for battle; vast structures of wood
Towered on the sea, but different the fates of their oars.

One fleet had been doomed by Rome's founder God, and there
Our spears were held – what shame! – in a woman's hand;
But Augustus' ships carried sils that Jove had blest,
And standards already taught to conquer
On behalf of their country.

Propertius' poem was commissioned for the quinquennial festivities established in honour of Octavian's victory and first celebrated in 28 BC. The man who asked him to write it was Maecenas, the patron also of Horace and Virgil.

After Actium

Octavian and Maecenas immediately began to heal the wounds of civil war. Together after 31 BC they evolved a new visual language, a 'cultural programme', designed to bring about not only a cultural but a moral revival. This included works of art, poetry and buildings, state ceremony and public ritual. Octavian and Maecenas understood the effect of images on public opinion. Vitruvius, who wrote the classic account of ancient architecture, *The Ten Books of Architecture* (20 BC), dedicated it to Octavian; and the poet, Horace, wrote in his ninth *Epode:*

Ruin at Delphi: a site of both Greek and Roman worship.

My bless'd Maecenas, when shall you and I,
In your lofty palace, rejoicing in
Caesar's triumph, as is grateful to Jove,
Drink the Caecuban put up for special feasts,
While the lyre propounds the Dorian mode
In consort with exotic pipes?
. . .
Boy! bring larger goblets
And Chain or Lesbian wine, or measure out
Caecuban to settle our seasick stomachs:
It is sweet to disperse with Bacchus' aid
Our anxious concern for Caesar's affairs.

And Maecenas is directly addressed by Propertius in his poems:

Maecenas, Knight of the blood of Tuscan kings –
You who do not aspire to a loftier rank –
Why launch me on such a vast poetic ocean?
Such spread of sail does not suit my ship.
. . .
My powers will rise to your high commands.
Let my theme be the chariots, victors from East and West,
The Parthians' bows, undrawn in pretended fights,
Pelusium's stronghold toppled by Roman steel,
And the death-heavy hands of Antony, armed
For his own destruction.
Take the reins, meanwhile; grant kindly aid to my youth
On its chosen course; cheer on my speeding wheels.
This measure of praise, Maecenas, you allow me;
And to you it is due that men will say
Where you led I followed.

Octavian and Maecenas used Actium as the foundation of a secular miracle, the start of a new imperial imagery, clear and simple. They believed that the way to heal civil wounds was to present Actium not as a battle lost or won, but rather as the moment when peace could begin. Instead of the obvious victorious images, at the sanctuary to Apollo at Actium on the Palatine Hill in Rome Octavian depicted the god as a peace-giver, and joined in the general feeling of goodwill. Glorification of peace and subtle self-glorification marched hand in hand. Octavian wrote:

The statues of myself in the city, whether standing or on horseback or in a quadriga, numbering eighty in all and all of silver, I had removed, and from this money I dedicated golden offerings in the Temple of Apollo, in my own name and in the names of those who had honoured me with these statues. (*Res Gestae*)

The wealth of monuments celebrating Actium were a lesson in how to mark a victory without referring to the defeated enemy. Octavian knew that to do so would not be in his interests. Antony had been a great Roman figure, and many of the defeated 'enemy' were themselves Roman citizens. Therefore the language of victory told not of military conquest but of the gentler sea-images of Actium: this was a language of seascapes, ships, Tritons and dolphins, all of which Romans used on their private seals.

From Octavian to Augustus

Octavian returned to Rome in 29 BC to celebrate the Triumph of Actium. Virgil wrote of his entry into Rome 'in triple triumph', he 'dedicated his vowed offering to the gods to stand forever, three hundred stately shrines all about the city'. After Actium, Octavian was the most powerful Roman in the Empire. Realizing that Julius Caesar had been murdered because he had flaunted his power and influence, Octavian's tactic was to appear to restore power to the Roman people. He decided to keep the trappings of a republic in place, with the Senate and its consuls seen to be running the Empire.

Through Maecenas and Agrippa, Octavian presented himself to the Romans as a peacemaker whose job of uniting the Empire was not yet done: Virgil and Horace urged him to complete the work. The historian Suetonius recorded Octavian as declaring in 29 BC:

> May it be my privilege to establish the state firm and secure and to reap the fruit of my toil, so that I may be called the author of the best possible government, and bear with me when I die the hope that the foundations which I have laid will remain unshaken.

The secret of his success was his preservation of the ancient magistracies; in 29 and 28 BC he acquired these powers for himself without seeming to hold the offices. During the war with Antony he had preserved the state from destruction by his assumption of emergency powers; now he gave the impression that he was ready to hand those powers back to the Roman people. In fact he drew the citizens of the Empire under one rule – his own – exercising absolute power. But the binding image of the time was the *pax Romana*, the great Roman peace. This golden age of Rome and Empire lasted 400 years, and Latin culture rather than Greek–Egyptian was consolidated in the West.

In 28 BC Octavian adopted the title of 'Princeps civitatis sua' – first citizen. (He considered calling himself Romulus, but this would carry with it the aura of kingship.) On 13 January that year he fully restored power to the Senate and the people; three days later the Senate named him Augustus, meaning 'stately', 'dignified', and 'holy'. It also renamed one of the summer months 'Augustus' in tribute. In this way he was immortalized in the calendar. He died in AD 14, and it was said of him that he arrived in Rome to a city of brick and left it a city of marble.

Following Julius Caesar's murder, the ensuing thirteen years of civil war and the Battle of Actium, a new Roman age dawned. History had been rewritten, and within it the age of Augustus Caesar was secure. For the Romans the blue shores of Actium became the place where the Empire was reborn. It was also the end of a nightmare of civil war. The love poet Propertius could recall those days with a shudder as he lay at peace in the arms of his beloved:

> In such a night could any of us become a god. If only we all wished to live such a life and to stretch out our limbs heavy with wine and recline. Then there would be no dread sword, no ships of war, and the sea at Actium would not roll over the bones of our comrades. And Rome would not have to loosen her hair in perpetual mourning for the triumphs won at her own expense.

· 4 ·
Arabian
CONQUERORS

THE ISLAMIC CONQUEST OF SPAIN
BRINGS 800 YEARS OF ENLIGHTENMENT.

[In 732] A victorious march had been prolonged above a thousand miles from the
Rock of Gibraltar to the banks of the Loire; the repetition of an equal space would
have carried the Saracens to the confines of Poland and the highlands of Scotland;
the Rhine is not more impassable than the Nile or the Euphrates, and the Arabian
fleet might have sailed without a naval combat into the mouth of the Thomas.
Perhaps the interpretation of the Koran would now be taught in the schools of
Oxford, and her pulpits might demonstrate . . . the sanctity and truth of the
Revelation of Mahommet.

(Edward Gibbon, *The Decline and Fall of the Roman Empire*)

*I*N SPAIN, modern history began in 711 when a new culture swept into
Europe from North Africa. It was to bring extraordinary discoveries in science, philosophy, architecture, literature, and medicine. It was to carry the
torch of Greek learning into the European Renaissance, continuing the
influence of Classical Greece that the Romans had absorbed and spread.
And it was to usher in a society of eight centuries of coexistence (albeit uneasy) between
Muslim, Christian and Jew. When Arab Muslims and Berbers from North Africa set foot
on the Rock of Gibraltar on the southern tip of Spain, the continent of Europe had
reached a turning point which changed its history forever.

OPPOSITE:
*Muhammad, the
Prophet of Islam (whose
face is always veiled),
rides his miraculous
steed, Al Burak, on his
'Night Journey' through
the sky from Mecca to
Jerusalem.*

The Visigoths

The first people the Muslims encountered in Spain were the Visigoths. The Visigoths
were a Germanic people, then known as the Theruingi, who by the third century had settled in an area north west of the Black Sea. But in the early 370s, fierce attacks from the
Huns broke up their hegemony and forced them to flee along the Danube, to the Roman
frontier. In 376, they were admitted to the Roman Empire by the Emperor Valens to
strengthen the Roman military, which by then had diminished to such a degree that their

The Visigothic crown of Reccesuinth. Visigothic kings often donated a liturgical crown to the Church.

once great legions were too weak to withstand the continuous onslaughts from other barbarian tribes. The local Roman commanders in the Balkans treated them badly, exploiting their military skills but withholding essential food supplies which the Visigoths depended on as a result of their move to a new and unfamiliar land.

The Visigoths finally rebelled in 378 and inflicted a major defeat on the Roman army at the Battle of Adrianople. After this change in the balance of power, there was a period of uneasy alliance between the Visigoths and the Romans. The Visigoths needed to supply their huge army and the Romans used this bargaining power to force them to serve in the Emperors' wars. The Visigoths lived in garrisons like the Roman soldiers, and this similarity of lifestyle eventually began to influence the habits and outlook of the Visigoths themselves. But their urgent desire for a territory of their own and a regular source of supplies created suspicion on both sides.

In 408 the Visigoths marched into Italy to put pressure on the Western government of Rome to give them the support that the Eastern government, centred on Constantinople, had denied them. In desperation, they sacked Rome in 410, the Visigoth leaders hoping that the chance to loot the city would boost the morale of their troops and make up for all the broken promises made to them for glory and wealth. After their show of military power, they served as mercenaries for the Roman Western government and increasingly, as the Western government weakened, the Visigoths went their own way, eventually settling around Toulouse. In 476 they controlled most of western France. At this time, they also expanded into Spain as the allies of Rome. In the west of the Empire, the Emperor Justinian tried to reconquer the Mediterranean shores between 530 and 550, but the Roman Empire was effectively at an end.

At the beginning of the sixth century, the Visigoths had been forced out of France by the Franks and made Spain their main territory for the next 200 years. During this period they had no real threat to their security, other than minor raids from the Franks. They were quite unprepared for the Arab invasion in 711.

The Church of San Juan de Banõs, near Palencia, one of the few surviving examples of Visigothic architecture in Spain.

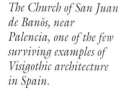

Under the Visigoths, Spain was loosely united under Roman language and law, and Christian religion. The country became a patchwork of alliances between local ruling families, never fully united, yet avoiding the chaos of disunity. Only the Basque region stayed consistently separate in language and culture, albeit under Visigothic control. The Visigoths brought together for an extraordinary moment in history influences from a variety of cultures: Germanic, Byzantine and Hispanic–Roman. But influences alone cannot make an empire. Visigothic culture acquired its strength by being concentrated in its cities, Mérida and Toledo, centres of administration both for the Roman Christian Church and for the emerging Visigothic state, which co-operated closely with the Church. The Christian Church had a powerful presence in Spain, and to maintain uniformity against the threat of heretical variants on the Christian faith as well as its physical safety, it supported the Visigoths. In return, the Visigothic kings adopted the Roman Christian faith and were keen to have the Church's support for their taxes and laws. It was a culture that had much in common with Mediterranean and northern states of the same period: its administration was organized locally rather than centrally, its legal system was closer to that of the Roman Empire than any of the successor states in the West, and it was intolerant of deviant forms of Christianity, or any form of Judaism trying to impose religious uniformity.

Visigothic Spain's intolerance of non-Christian faiths throughout the seventh century resulted in a series of edicts promulgated in Toledo which reduced the Jewish population to virtual slavery, and declared that every Jewish child was to be forcibly taken from its parents and given a Christian upbringing. The Jews thus lost their freedom, their property and – through their children – their future. Their situation was bleak. But it was to change suddenly after the Muslim invasion in 711.

In the seventh century the Visigothic kings achieved a more even pattern of succession as Kings Ervig, Egica and Wittiza followed one another without bloodshed. Although, unlike the Franks, they had no ruling dynasty (indeed, they had lost their ruling dynasty in 507), there was a consensus among the ruling noble families to elect a king, and it was the custom for sons to follow their fathers in taking up the throne, a practice which made for more consistent leadership. However, when in 710 there was a sudden succession crisis, there began a period of civil strife as rivals fought for the crown. Nobles were fearful of a change of dynasty with new supporters who would expect to be given the most important administrative positions. By 711 the Visigoths had already become weakened. Eventually, after a bitter struggle with another king, Achila, who had been created in the north-east, a new king, Roderic, had come to the throne. He was crowned at Toledo and staked his claim to the whole kingdom.

At this point, history comes to us from the literary fiction that the Arabs developed in later years to explain their conquest of the Visigothic kingdom. With a metaphoric force not unlike the Christian account of the fall of man or the opening of Pandora's box in Greek mythology, it produced a startling image of knowledge and power. This was the moment that signalled the end of a kingdom. The story, as told by later Arab legend, is simple. By tradition, Roderic, as a newly crowned king, had to visit the House of Wisdom in Toledo, where the secrets of the Visigoths had been locked in a chamber, and to add a new lock, as every new king before him had done. But Roderic, insisting that he should know what lay inside the chamber, broke open the door and dared to look inside the casket within. What he found was a parchment. It read:

> When this House and this casket which have been so wisely locked shall be opened, then shall the nation shown upon the casket enter the Island of Andalus, and its kingdom shall be blotted out.

Arab tribesmen spread the word of Islam throughout North Africa.

Roderic wept, and indeed it was as if he had released the collective unconscious of a nation. Later Arab accounts of the Visigoths suggest that they became embroiled in civil war, and the casket myth may be no more than an expression of their anxiety. Roderic was then suddenly called north to quell a Basque rebellion in 711, but to leave for the north was exactly the wrong thing for him to have done.

The Muslim Invaders

As the Visigoths declined in strength, a rising Arab power lay waiting in North Africa. And behind that power was Europe's newest, most formidable and fastest-growing religion: Islam. When this great tide of religious fervour washed against the Rock of Gibraltar, Visigothic Spain would be swept away.

The Muslim faith, Islam, was young and full of vigour. It remains a dominant religion, strong in the Middle East and widely practised in Asia, Africa and Europe. Muhammad, the Prophet of Islam and the spiritual leader of his peoples, was born around the year 570. The son of a poor merchant, he belonged to the Quraysh tribe in and around the town of Mecca, a centre of trade in the coastal plain of western Arabia.

In about 610, he experienced the first of many visions in which the Archangel Gabriel appeared to him, convincing him that he was God's messenger. From these experiences of divine insight, Muhammad developed a religious doctrine and practice and used these ideas to attract an increasing number of followers.

In Medina, Muhammad's ideas became more worldly, and at the head of an expanding body of adherents he grew in stature as a secular and military leader, waging war against

ARABIAN CONQUERORS • 65

the Meccans in particular. Eight years after his move, he conquered Mecca, and the whole of the Arabian peninsular soon converted to Islam. Muhammad himself died in 632, but within five years Syria, Iraq and the southern parts of Persia and of the Byzantine Empire had likewise fallen. Jerusalem fell in 637; Egypt followed in 642. After one decade nomadic Arab tribesmen, inspired by the Islamic faith, had subdued a variety of sophisticated societies north of the Caucasus and into Persia.

The Empire was given added unity by special ties of loyalty, the outlying commanders coming from trusted families who were in turn clients of powerful Arab governors. At the centre of this network of family and personal relationships were the caliphs, Muhammad's successors, who during the Ummayad dynasty (661–750) ruled from Damascus.

Islam was and is a faith which requires a belief in the oneness of God, in the divine origins of the Koran (which had been dictated to scribes by Muhammad), in the day of final judgement, and in the truth of the Prophet's Mission. According to its doctrine, Muhammad, Allah's messenger, is wholly human and makes no claim to the divine. Within the five Pillars of Islam, duties for believers comprise the profession of faith (*sha-hada*), fasting (*sawm*), charity (*zakat*), a visit to Mecca (*hajj*) and daily prayers (*salat*). Islam was confident, clear and aggressive. Its empire expanded by holy war, *jihad*, which increased the territories under its sway and the numbers of the faithful. Nevertheless Islam in the seventh and eighth centuries was a system, which allowed to conquered peoples their religion, provided they were practitioners of the 'religion of the Book', that is, Jews and Christians.

In North Africa, the Muslims took Tunisia in 670, and by 710, under the command of Musa ibn Nusayr, whose family were clients of the Caliph Walid I (705–15), had reached the north-west tip of the continent. During that advance, the Arab Muslims subdued the Berbers (their name comes from the Latin *barbarus* or barbarian) and henceforth were able to make use of Berber armies and commanders for further conquest. The Berbers, who were the indigenous population of North Africa, had been subjugated by Rome.

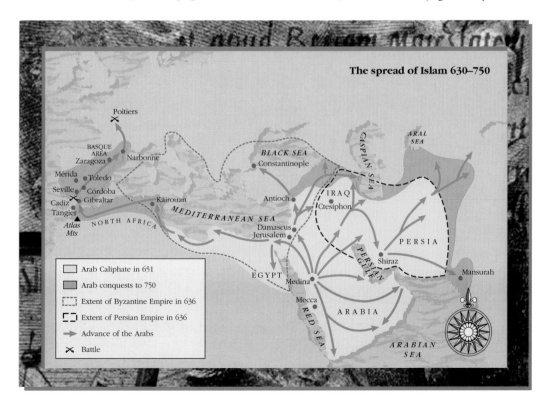

Following the Arab conquest of North Africa which was achieved by 698, the Berbers converted to Islam and would fight alongside the Arabs when they invaded Spain in 711. The relations between the Arabs and the Berbers were nonetheless frequently acrimonious since the Berbers retained their own language and culture and the Arabs treated them with detached superiority and contempt.

According to some Arab sources, in 710 an expeditionary force of Muslim Berbers landed on the southern shores of Spain. Its commander, a former slave called Tarifa, returned to Tangiers and reported to Tariq ibn Ziyad, the Governor. What is said to have happened is that the following year Tariq himself on Musa's instructions sailed north across the twelve-mile-wide Straits of Gibraltar with 1,700 men to explore the land beyond North Africa. That summer he landed at Jabal al Tariq (Tariq's rock, later corrupted to 'Gibraltar'); meeting little resistance, he established a base there on the small peninsula, and called the land Al-Andalus. He would subdue Spain and make it Muslim for the next 800 years. Perhaps the Arabs knew of the near-civil war that was brewing in Spain and they were always prone to attack at their opponent's weakest moment.

The Battle for Spain

While Tariq established himself in the south of Spain, the Visigoths were still distracted by the Basques in the north. When he heard of the invasion, Roderic hurried south with his Royal Household troops, having neither the time nor feeling the need to raise a larger force from other Visigothic nobility. So, according to Arab sources, on 19 July 711 he met Tariq's army in the Guadalquivir valley near Medina Sidonia. Little documentation concerning the battle survives. One of the earliest accounts occurs in the *Chronicle of 754*:

> Mustering his forces [Roderic] directed his armies against the Arabs and the Moors sent by Musa, that is against Tariq ibn Ziyad and the others, who had long been raiding the province consigned to them and simultaneously devastating many cities. In the fifth year of Justinian's rule, the ninety-third of the Arabs, and the sixth of Walid [Caliph Walid I] in the era 712, Roderic headed for the Transductine mountains to fight them and in that battle the entire army of the Goths, which had come with him fraudulently and in the rivalry out of ambition for the kingship, fled and he was killed. Thus Roderic wretchedly lost not only his rule but his homeland, his rivals also being killed, as Walid was completing his sixth year of rule.

History was to repeat itself three and a half centuries later in the Norman conquest of Britain in 1066: in both cases, the defenders had to travel a great distance to engage the enemy, and one battle decided all. In the battle with the Muslims, the Royal Household troops were routed and Roderic either killed or put to flight. The Visigoths dispersed like sand in the wind. Tariq pressed forward to Córdoba and Toledo, encountering no resistance. Visigothic Spain had fallen to Islam.

Tariq immediately reported to Musa, who in turn arrived with a larger army, said to have been of between 15,000 and 20,000 Arab and Berber troops, and there is also evidence from Arab sources to suggest that he started his military operations around Cádiz. He soon took Seville, the provincial capital of Beatica, but was delayed by stiff resistance at Mérida, Roderic's stronghold. The siege lasted sixteen months; when it was over, the surviving males of the city were put to death, the women and children enslaved.

In 713 Musa combined forces with Tariq, who had lately taken Toledo, to produce an army that was both swift and powerful. They advanced north to Zaragoza. There, however, tensions between the two commanders began to surface. Feeling that he needed to assert his authority over Tariq, Musa publicly humiliated him by requiring him to kiss his feet. A third Muslim commander, Abd al-Aziz, who was one of Musa's sons, claimed the south-east of Spain, taking Málaga and Elvira (later Granada).

The ensuing history of these three men was brutish and short. Musa and Tariq were recalled to Damascus, where they lost the confidence of Sulayman, brother of the ruling Caliph Walid I and later his successor after Walid died in 715. It was the caliphal system which sustained the Empire as Islam under the Umayyads became more secular, political and military. The Umayyad dynasty lasted until 750, and was crucial in forming and consolidating the Empire. This process involved strict control not only of the new subjects, but of the new, successful Muslim commanders. The *Chronicle of 754* explains:

> Musa, after fifteen months had elapsed, was summoned by order of the princes and, leaving his son Abd al-Aziz in his place, he returned to his homeland and presented himself to the king Walid in the last year of his reign. Musa brought with him from Spain some noblemen who had escaped the sword; gold, silver, assayed with zeal by the bankers; a large quantity of valuable ornaments, precious stones, and pearls; ointments to kindle women's desire; and many other things from the length and breadth of Spain that would be tedious to record. When he arrived, by God's will he found Walid [Sulayman] angry. Musa was ignominiously removed from the prince's presence and paraded with a rope around his neck.

Musa escaped execution by paying two million solidi to Sulayman. He later died in poverty. Tariq vanished into obscurity. Abd al-Aziz was murdered in Seville in 716 by order of the Caliph.

The Muslims continued their advance north through Spain for the next twenty years, and by 732 reached Poitiers, where they were repelled by the Frankish leader Charles Martel. That was the extent of their ambition. They concentrated their efforts in Spain, and there they built a fine, learned and sophisticated culture which changed the future of Europe.

Life in Islamic Spain

The Muslim discovery of Europe brought innumerable benefits. The Islamic conquerors were few in number, and had no national culture to impose. The first Muslims, traders from Mecca and merchants from Medina, succeeded because they were part of a larger empire, and since Islam was an empire not of nation but of belief, they readily absorbed other cultures, at the same time subduing them by conversion.

In Islam there were four strata: the Arab Muslims, the non-Arab Muslims, the non-Muslim subjects (including Christians, Jews, Berbers and Hindus) and finally slaves (such as Greeks, Turks, Armenians, Kurds, Berbers and Negroes). Non-Muslims were subject to taxes. Islam had a clear vision of the world and a strong culture which carried within it the capacity to learn, adapt and build. It was the adaptability of Islam in the eighth and ninth centuries and its handling of other cultures which made it so potent. Islamic armies worked successfully with the local, indigenous administrations to consolidate their new empire.

Islam under the early Umayyad and, from 750 to 1258, the Abbasid Caliphates maintained an empire which nurtured itself, passing knowledge and learning along its length and breadth. It had a unified religion and a common language to offer. Arabic, the language of the Prophet Muhammad and of the Koran, and so perceived as the key to divine knowledge and learning, became (as Arab chroniclers tell us) the official language of the Empire in 696. It thus gradually replaced the languages of the constituent peoples, especially Aramaic, Greek and Latin, and came to be used foreveryday speech. Arabic also shaped the development of other Muslim languages such as Turkish and Persian, which adopted its script and literature. Arabic numerals – including the all-important zero (from Arabic *sifr*: cypher) – were introduced to Europe through Spain.

In 800 the Arabs who had learnt paper-making from the Chinese fifty years before, built a paper mill in Baghdad and spread its use westwards through Syria and North Africa to Spain. With the creation of a much larger Arab empire, the Muslims were able to foster trade throughout the Empire, and Spain was soon producing luxury goods such as ceramics and textiles. Arab expertise in navigation, cartography and ship design helped transport them.

Since its emergence in Arabia in the seventh century, Islam had been in continuous conflict with Christendom, expressed through the original Muslim conquests and Christian reconquests, through each culture's version of the holy war, *jihad* and crusade, through Turkish advance and European expansion. But the Muslim conquest of Spain ushered in a period of religious coexistence. In some ways, Muslims were much more tolerant of Christianity than Christians were of Islam. For Muslims, Christ was a precursor of Muhammad, whereas for Christians Muhammad was an imposter. Early Islam was a community of religion rather than race, and the Muslims allowed the subjugated peoples to become converts (*muwallads*). In Spain, the conquered Visigoths either converted or were left to their own faith, governed by local administrations and subject to a series of taxes imposed by the Muslims. Those who resisted were enslaved. In essence, while Visigothic culture was monolithic and formed from one creed, Islamic culture embraced a variety of races, creeds and cultures.

Although the Muslims contemplated abandoning their Spanish territories in 718, they gradually consolidated their cultural and administrative hold on the country. Establishing their capital in Córdoba, they turned it into Europe's most magnificent city, possibly twenty times larger than any other western European capital and, with 500,000 inhabitants. It remained the capital of Muslim Spain from the eighth to the eleventh century. The secret of making crystal was discovered and developed here in the ninth century; and it was here that ceramics were decorated using techniques from the east of the Empire. Precious metals were worked with a skill to rival the Byzantine goldsmiths and silversmiths.

The mosque at Córdoba, built between the eighth and tenth centuries, is now a cathedral – a wonder of 450 marble columns and double tiers of receding arches, vivid in red and white. But outside Córdoba is the most striking of the Muslims' achievements: the palace of the Caliph Abd al-Rahman al-Nasir III (891–961), started in 936. (The Caliph was one of the Spanish Umayyads, a dynasty set up in 756 by a survivor of the Abbasid revolution.)

The palace was sited five kilometres north-west of Córdoba in the lush green countryside, 'a concubine in the arms of a black eunuch' according to one Arab poet, calling up

OPPOSITE: *The reconstructed Arabic waterwheel at Córdoba. The Arabs brought improved irrigation techniques to Spain, allowing once infertile land to be cultivated.*

an image of cultural dissonance. It was an entire city in itself, apparently housing at least 20,000 people. Six thousand women lived in the women's quarter, and the whole palace was run by 4,000 slaves. The court included Jewish physicians and Christian bishops; foreign ambassadors, emissaries and dignitaries would arrive escorted from Córdoba by troops bearing silken hangings. One chronicler, exaggerating to make a point, reported that 12,000 loaves of bread each day went to the fish in the Caliph's fishponds.

This elaborate microcosm, and other projects like it, encouraged an influx of learning which had been fostered in other parts of Islam. The wealth of knowledge across the Empire was vast. In 765 a school of medicine was founded in Baghdad, joining the law schools founded by Abu Hanifa and Malik ibn Anas. Jurisprudence and religious and legal culture governed all aspects of Muslim life, providing both a code of law and a pattern of conduct. The Muslims in due course introduced a local government of civil servants and police. The various parts of the Empire stayed in touch by means of a signalling system of light and mirrors: chroniclers claimed that it took only twenty-four hours for a message to travel between Egypt and Spain (2,300 miles).

Later, during the ninth century, Islam evolved an enormous and important translation movement, and learning flourished as never before. This was the time of Kindi, the first Arab philosopher; of Hunayn ibn Ishaq, the great translator of Greek works; and, as the ninth century became the tenth, of Rhazes, the physician and scientist; of Firdawsi, the Persian poet; of Pharibius, the philosopher, and of Al Biruni, the physician, physicist, mathematician, geographer and astronomer. The Arab invasion became the channel for Greek and Arabian manuscripts that shaped the future of Western mathematics, physics and astronomy. In mathematics, Arab culture produced algorithms, algebra, trigonometry (including spherical trigonometry), geometry, fractions and square roots. To this end, the Arabs drew on Greek and Indian sources, not merely transmitting them, but keeping them alive by contributing and adding to them.

In 1068 the Muslim Said ibn Ahmad, the Qadi (or magistrate) of Toledo, wrote a book of philosophy and geography, dividing the human race into those who concern themselves with science and learning and those who concentrate instead on crafts and skills. In the former, he included the Indians, Persians, Greeks, Romans, Arabs and Jews; and in the latter the Turks and Chinese. The rest were barbarians and infidels:

> The other peoples of this group who have not cultivated the sciences are more like beasts than like men. For those of them who live furthest to the north, between the last or [sic] the seven climates and the limits of the inhabited world, the excessive distance of the sun in relation to the zenith line makes the air cold and the sky cloudy. Their temperaments are therefore frigid, their humours raw, their bellies gross, their colour pale, their hair long and lank. Thus they lack keenness of understanding and clarity of intelligence, and are overcome by ignorance and apathy, lack of discernment and stupidity . . .

This was typical of the Muslim view of the world at that time. Islam saw itself as the centre of the civilized world. North lay the Franks and to the south were African tribes; east of Persia the Chinese had achieved a different form of civilization; and the lands to the west lay undiscovered.

Science and learning were vital to the Muslims' image and identity, their culture absorbing others' knowledge and developing its own. In science, Arab culture produced ideas and terms now long familiar in the West: zenith and nadir in astronomy; alkali, alcohol and alchemy; syrup and soda in medicine (the interest in medicine was clinical and surgical rather than theoretical). Toothpaste was introduced by Ziryab, a ninth-century Muslim courtier at Cordoba. The works of Ibn Sina, the philosopher-physician known to history as Avicenna (980–1037), were translated into Latin in Spain, and helped form Graeco-Arab medical thought.

The greatest Islamic philosopher was the Spanish Arab, Ibn Rushd (called Averroes, 1126–98) who wrote an important commentary on the Arabic translation of the Greek philosopher Aristotle's works, which in turn were translated into Hebrew and Latin. In agriculture and botany, the Muslims introduced spinach, rice, sugar cane, limes, lemons,

Abu Walid Mohammed Rushd, twelfth-century philosopher.

The Court of Lions at the Alhambra palace, Granada.

oranges, hard wheat (for pasta); pomegranates and watermelons; aubergines, artichokes and the methods of cultivating them. The Muslims farmed and cultivated not only for subsistence, but for profit. They were magnificent agricultural engineers, and developed waterwheels, sluices, cisterns, ditches, drains and pipes to irrigate the crops. They also cultivated herbs for medicines, creating gardens specifically for different types of botanically derived medicine.

Even after the Muslims had at last been driven out of Seville and Cordoba in the thirteenth century, the growth in learning continued. For the Muslims had established ways of thinking and a culture of intellectual endeavour which were to persist for centuries. In twelfth-century Toledo, after the Christian reconquest (*reconquista* – see below) in 1085, the new Castilian kings had allowed the Muslims to remain in their kingdom under virtually the same conditions as the Muslims themselves had allowed their Christian subjects. In Toledo, Arab culture continued to absorb elements of Greek, Persian and Indian learning. Texts were translated from Arabic by Jewish scholars, who in turn collaborated with Christian scholars to produce Latin translations. In the twelfth and thirteenth centuries, the city became a centre for scholars from many parts of western Europe, and in the following century Michael Scotus and Hermannus Alemannus translated Ibn Rushd's commentary on Aristotle. By the mid-thirteenth century Aristotle was taught in Paris, and the debate between him and Plato fuelled intellectual life for half a century.

The Muslims left behind them a wealth of architecture inspired by Syrian Arab culture. Arab architects in Spain built libraries, mosques, palaces and public baths as well as feats of civil engineering in the form of bridges, gardens, fountains and terracing. One of the finest examples of Muslim culture was Granada, the capital of an independent Muslim kingdom and one of the most important centres of Jewish population in the medieval world; tolerated by the Spanish, it outlasted the rest of Muslim Spain by 250 years, and was not brought into the kingdom of Castile until 1492. It was here that the Muslims built the great Alhambra Palace, completed in 1353. It remains the greatest Moorish monument in Spain, a glittering tribute to the centuries of Muslim culture and achievement.

711 and 1492

The Muslim conquest of Spain in some respects brought about the birth of a modern age, a medieval enlightenment. After the initial conquest, successive Islamic dynasties (Umayyads, Almoravids, Almohads) ruled Spain. But by the eleventh century the Islamic Empire had become over-extended, fragmentary and hard to manage.

The Christian *reconquista* began slowly in the eighth century, with the establishment of a Christian kingdom in the Asturias in 718. Another Christian kingdom came into being around Pamplona in the early ninth century, and the Franks took Barcelona in 801. Small Christian principalities in northern Spain began to extend their territories, and later, in the eleventh century, they used French troops to help reinforce their expansion. By 1250, only Granada remained Islamic. The reconquest of Portugal was completed in 1267, and the Portuguese pressed south to take Ceuta on the north coast of Morocco. The *reconquista* faltered in the fourteenth century as a result of the Black Death (see Chapter 5), which caused a crisis of manpower. But then in 1453, when Constantinople fell to the Muslim Turks (see Chapter 6), the idea of reconquering Spain and making it wholly Christian turned the *reconquista* into a religious war. The

Castilians resumed in earnest in 1455 under Henry IV. On 19 October 1469 Ferdinand, heir to the throne of Aragon, and Isabella, heir to the throne of Castile, married to unite the two most powerful kingdoms in Spain.

In history, one of the rewards of conquering or simply outlasting one's enemies is the opportunity to tell a particular kind of truth, a version of events. The Christian *reconquista* began this process by destroying thousands of manuscripts and documentary records in Muslim Spain. Nonetheless, the great cities of Toledo and Granada will provide more information as archaeologists uncover further remains, and there are many unexcavated Spanish Muslim sites. For 800 years Spain had absorbed the remarkable civilization which had prospered for nine centuries in the Middle East, Persia, Central Asia, India, North Africa and Sicily and which had brought to Spain the benefits of empire without the disadvantages of subjugation. Islamic Spain created the bridge between the middle ages and the modern era, enabling the learning of the East to inspire the Renaissance in the Eest.

In the 1480s the pace of the *reconquista* increased, and on 6 January 1492 Ferdinand and Isabella, now monarchs of a new unified Spain, made their triumphal entry into Granada. The terms of that kingdom's surrender were generous. The Muslims were allowed to keep their property and their weapons, and their faith and customs were safeguarded. But the Jews fared worse. Already expelled from England in 1290, Normandy in 1296, France in 1306 and 1394, in Spain they had enjoyed favourable conditions under Aragon and Castile, evolving and strengthening the distinctive branch of Jewish culture called Sephardic Judaism. These were the cultural middlemen of Europe: thinkers, writers, translators, scientists, courtiers, financiers, diplomats and physicians. Now, in 1492, they were evicted from Spain.

The *reconquista* was complete. Spain turned away from the East and started to look towards Europe. But Islam, which had shaped its culture for 800 years, would always remain an important influence. For the future, the western horizon beckoned. On 3 August 1492, Christopher Columbus set sail from Palos for the New World.

· 5 ·

The BLACK DEATH

A PLAGUE RAVAGES EUROPE AND
A THIRD OF ITS POPULATION DIES.

Some say that it descended upon the human race through the influence of
the heavenly bodies, others that it was a punishment signifying God's
righteous anger at our iniquitous way of life. But, whatever its cause, it had
originated some years earlier in the East, where it had claimed countless
lives before it unhappily spread westward, growing in strength as it swept
relentlessly on from one place to the next.   (Boccaccio, *Decameron*)

FOR THE FOURTEENTH-CENTURY Florentine Giovanni Boccaccio it
was a 'deadly pestilence'; for his contemporary, the English writer Geoffrey
Chaucer, it was 'the privee theef men clepeth Deeth'; and for King Edward
III of England (1312–77) it was a signal of even greater calamities to come.
It killed around a third of the population of Europe. It was a microscopic
bacillus called *Yersinia pestis*: the Black Death. It is still alive today.

One kind of history speaks of battles, another of conquests, yet another of society or politics. This is the history of an epidemic, of the fear and suffering produced by the Black Death
as it swept across Europe between 1347 and 1352, five years that changed the continent
forever. The outbreak of the Black Death in 1347 was a turning point in world history. It
rocked the feudal foundations of the medieval world and questioned the traditional structure
of religious belief which had supported the institution of the Christian Church. The effects
of the Black Death were more destructive and more widespread than those of any war that
has been fought, more terrifying than those of any known disease. Perhaps only the virulent
epidemics of smallpox in sixteenth- and seventeenth-century South America (see Chapter 7)
or the twentieth-century spread of malaria in Africa match the scope and terror of the plague.

The mid-fourteenth century saw humankind confronted for the first time in its history
with an implacable, undiscriminating opponent in the form of *Yersinia pestis* and the disease that the bacillus caused. It was part of the struggle for existence between two different forms of life, just one battle (albeit the most brutal) in the never ending war between
species and species. Other battles have been fought between human and virus as infectious diseases, including syphilis, influenza, smallpox, scarlet fever, typhus, measles and

OPPOSITE: *The
plague influenced many
works of art which
depicted man as the
object of God's wrath
and divine retribution.
(Fifteenth-century
manuscript.)*

diphtheria, have devastated whole nations. Some of these diseases have been brought under control, but the modern era still faces others, such as Lyme disease, Legionnaires' disease, malaria and AIDS.

Death from disease of epidemic proportions was nothing new in the fourteenth century, and plague epidemics were to kill people in China in the late nineteenth century and in India in the late twentieth. In fact, according to recent estimates, from 243 BC to 1911 there were at least 290 epidemics of the plague in China. The West, too, had suffered an early experience of the plague. Two and a half thousand years ago, in the Athens of the fifth century BC, a form of plague was described, from personal experience, by the historian Thucydides:

> First, overwhelming fever in the head and redness . . . of the eyes came over them; the throat and tongue became blood red . . . From these beginnings there ensued sneezing and hoarseness, and in short the distress settled in the chest with a violent cough . . . there followed the emesis [vomiting] of every kind of bile . . . the skin . . . was flushed, livid and broken out with small blisters and open sores . . . the patient burned with fever . . . consumed by unceasing thirst . . . most perished of the fever on the ninth or the seventh day . . . If they survived this stage, the disease settled in the bowels, eventuating in . . . watery diarrhoea . . . Loss of memory was also a sequel.
>
> (Quoted in *New England Journal of Medicine* (1985), 313)

What made the Black Death of the 1340s different from previous epidemics was the scale and scope of the disease: it stretched from China to India, Persia, Syria, Egypt and Asia Minor. Its arrival in Western Europe in 1347 produced the greatest natural disaster ever to hit the continent, one which remains branded in popular memory. Even the children's

Ghengis Khan, leader of the Mongol army, in battle, 1201. (From a Persian history completed in 1596.)

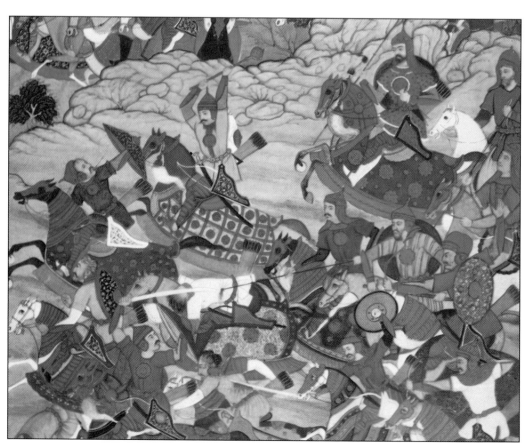

nursery rhyme – 'A ring, a ring o' roses, a pocketful of posies. Atishoo! Atishoo! We all fall down' – evokes the fatal pattern: bubo (or, rather, the subcutaneous bleeding), scent to ward off the stench, the sneeze (another symptom) and death.

The Origins of the Black Death

The deadliest virus ever known, *Yersinia pestis*, began in the remote parts of Central Asia. Two creatures were initially its hosts: *Rattus rattus*, the common black rat, and *Xenopsylla cheopis*, the oriental rat flea. In 1338, some natural calamity – either an earthquake or a drought – disturbed the delicate balance which had prevailed between these three actors and unleashed the terrifying pestilence.

The disease caused by *Yersinia pestis* operates simply and efficiently. The flea bites an infected rat and ingests the bacilli. These are rod-shaped bacteria first identified in 1894, over 500 years after its greatest known outbreak, by the Swiss-French bacteriologist Alexandre Yersin (1863–1943). That year, 1894, marked the last major outbreak of the plague, this time in China. Not until this final epidemic was it at last discovered that fleas and rats were the main carriers of the plague bacillus.

The bacilli multiply in the flea's digestive tract, and form a solid mass which prevents the flea from digesting; the flea becomes insatiably hungry, and repeatedly bites its animal or human host, each time injecting the virus into the host's bloodstream. As the rats die of the virus, the fleas move on to domestic animals and humans. The fleas can survive for between six months and a year without a human or animal host, and can travel on clothing or in produce. They thrive in temperatures of at least 68–77°F (20–25°C) and in humid conditions. For an outbreak to occur among humans, there must first be an outbreak among animals.

The disease develops rapidly. Once infected, the patient experiences large and painful swellings of the lymph nodes in the armpit, groin or neck. These can be substantial enough to distend the body. The swellings are accompanied by high fever (102–105°F or 38.9–40.6°C), thirst and black blotches, which are the result of internal or epidermal haemorrhage. As the disease gains ground, the swellings – or buboes – grow larger and more painful until they burst. The pain in the later stages is excruciating. Even unconscious patients can be roused to an agonized frenzy when the buboes burst.

In 1347, this type of plague, the bubonic plague, was the most widespread. Transmitted by fleas, the disease killed three-quarters of those it infected, the victim usually dying within five days, frequently sooner. Another form, pneumonic plague, which probably affected about five per cent of victims, was passed by droplets of moisture from the lungs of an infected patient. Thereafter the disease developed rapidly: the victims spat and coughed blood, and died within days. A third variety, but the most rare, was the septicemic plague in which the infection took hold in the bloodstream. This variety resulted in massive haemorrhaging, septic shock and rapid death.

The plague's great chronicler, Gabriele de' Mussis (who died in 1356), wrote from Piacenza in Italy in 1348, giving an account similar to that of Thucydides:

> Those of both sexes who were in health, and in no fear of death, were struck by four savage blows to the flesh. First, out of the blue, a kind of chilly stiffness troubled their bodies. They felt a tingling sensation, as if they were pricked by the points of arrows. The next stage was a fearsome attack which took the form of an extremely hard, solid

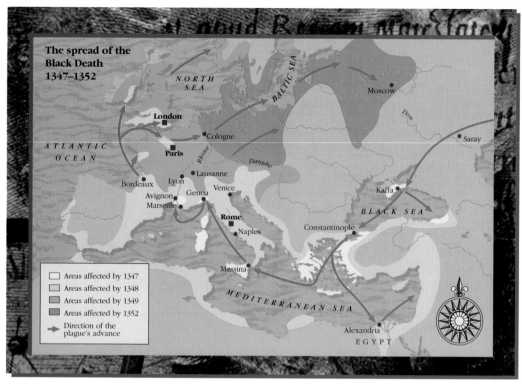

The spread of the
Black Death
1347–1352

NORTH
SEA

BALTIC SEA

Moscow

London

Cologne

Don

Saray

ATLANTIC
OCEAN

Paris

Rhine

Danube

Lausanne

Bordeaux

Lyon

Avignon

Genoa

Venice

Kaffa

Marseille

BLACK SEA

Rome

Constantinople

Naples

Messina

MEDITERRANEAN SEA

☐ Areas affected by 1347
☐ Areas affected by 1348
☐ Areas affected by 1349
☐ Areas affected by 1352
→ Direction of the
plague's advance

Alexandria
EGYPT

boil. In some people this developed under the armpit and in others in the groin between the scrotum and the body. As it grew more solid, its burning heat caused the patients to fall into an acute and putrid fever, with severe headaches. As it intensified its extreme bitterness could have various effects. In some cases it gave rise to an intolerable stench. In others it brought vomiting of blood, or swellings near the place from which the corrupt humour arose: on the back, across the chest, near the thigh. Some people lay as if in a drunken stupor and could not be roused. (Horrox)

Medieval domestic and city culture was perfect for the spread of the disease in this way: little sanitation, no knowledge of preventative measures, and the proximity of animals and humans. Houses were often of single-storey construction, with a thatched straw roof, perfect for rats' nests and the fleas which could have fallen from them on to the humans below. If the medieval city was a fine nursery for the disease, the medieval ship was the perfect cradle. There, men and rats lived in constant proximity: when the humans slept, the rats roamed over the ship, above, below and around the sleeping sailors, amid the cargo and along the ropes. The fleas transferred quickly from rat to human.

The Black Death spread along the trade routes from Central Asia, the infected fleas harboured by dying rats or by marmot furs. Marmots were a popular and ready source of fur; trappers passed the pelts (and the fleas which still lived in them) to traders, and they in turn bundled the pelts together and sent them west along the Silk Road to Astrakhan and Saray. From there it is thought the plague travelled down the Don River to the forti-fied town of Kaffa (Fedosia), one of the busiest ports on the Black Sea. There, in 1346, *Yersinia pestis* found a critical mass of living rats and humans, and was rapidly able to consolidate its hold on the human population.

Kaffa was under siege. A group of Italian merchants – most of them probably Genoese – had been expelled from their trading depot at Tana and had taken refuge in the city. Tensions between the Christian merchants and the local Muslim citizens had provoked a street brawl which escalated into a full-scale war, until the Muslims sought help from their Khan to lay siege to the Italians inside the city. The forces of the Mongol Prince Janibeg accordingly surrounded the port and prepared to wait. After the siege had lasted a whole year, the plague erupted among the Mongols.

The Mongol Prince soon realized the infectious nature of the disease, and in an inspired example of germ warfare he ordered that the putrefying corpses of plague victims be catapulted into the city. Before long, rotting bodies littered the streets of the citadel. The terrified merchants gathered them up, carried them to the harbour and dropped them in the sea. Gabriele de' Mussis wrote:

> What seemed like mountains of dead were thrown into the city, and the Christians could not hide or flee or escape from them, although they dumped as many of the bodies as they could into the sea. And soon the rotting corpses tainted the air and poisoned the water supply, and the stench was so overwhelming that hardly one in several thousand was in a position to flee the remains of the Tartar [Mongol] army. Moreover, one infected man could carry the poison to others, and infect people and places with the disease by look alone. No one knew, or could discover, a means of defence. (Horrox)

As the plague gripped the city, the Italians fled and took to their boats. So did the rats.

The Plague Arrives in Europe

As their flotilla of galleys sailed south into the Mediterranean, bound for Genoa and Venice, the Italians did not know they carried death in their holds. But soon, when it became clear that the sailors were dying of a mysterious disease, no port would let them dock. They had stopped briefly at Pera, a port on the edge of the great trading city of Constantinople, the gateway between Europe and the East. They left the plague there. One of the survivors, Nicepheros Gregoras, wrote:

> The calamity affected men as well as women, rich and poor, old and young . . . It did not destroy men only, but many animals living with and domesticated by men. I speak of dogs and horses and all species of birds, even the rats that happened to live within the walls of the houses . . . Sputum suffused with blood was brought up and disgusting and stinking breath from within. The throat and the tongue, parched from the heat, were black and congested with blood. Great abscesses were formed on the legs or the arms, from which, when cut, a large quantity of foul-smelling pus flowed . . . Whenever people felt sick there was no hope left for recovery. (Horrox)

The city was crippled. But the plague, having gathered strength, spread from Constantinople throughout the Greek islands.

The Black Death finally reached the Mediterranean in October 1347 when Genoese galleys landed at Messina in Sicily. Within a week, the plague spread through the city. One man chronicled the progress of the pestilence. His name was Michele da Piazza, a Franciscan friar typical of the many thousands of literate mendicants and monks who were confronted with the uncertainties of the plague. In a sense, Piazza represented the Church which people looked to first for comfort and then, as the disease spread, for an explanation. He also represented the practical approach of those clerics who tended the sick and buried the dead. He left an invaluable account of the plague in Sicily:

The Franciscan friar, Michele da Piazza, was typical of many monks who witnessed the plague and tended the victims.

The people of Messina, realising that the death racing through them was linked with the arrival of the Genoese galleys, expelled the Genoese from the city and harbour with all speed. But the illness remained in the city and subsequently caused enormous mortality. It bred such loathing that if a son fell ill of the disease his father flatly refused to stay with him, or, if he did dare to come near him, was infected in turn and was sure to die himself after three days. (Horrox)

The plague thus overturned family values and the rule of law. The same breakdown in law occurred and was described by the political writer Niccolo Machiavelli (1469–1527) in his history of Florence, which charted the outbreaks of plague in the fourteenth century. Rapid marriage, incest and all manner of sexual excess became commonplace as people spent their final days in drunken orgies and dedicated hedonism. Others opted for the pious approach, and sequestered themselves. The rich fled.

As the plague spread across Europe, everyone wanted to know what caused it and how it was passed from one person to another. But there was no easy explanation. The terror arrived invisibly and then unfolded in a graphic and increasingly familiar way:

It seemed as if the victim was struck all at once by the affliction and was, so to speak, shattered by it. This shattering impact, together with the inhaled infection, caused the eruption of a sort of boil, the size of a lentil, on the thigh or arm, which so infected and invaded the body that the victims violently coughed up blood, and after three days' incessant vomiting, for which there was no remedy, they died – and with them died not only anyone who had talked with them, but also anyone who had acquired or touched or laid hands on their belongings. (Horrox)

So much for the transmission. As to the fundamental causes, a multitude of theories was used to explain the eruption of the plague, ranging from environmental imbalances to divine retribution. Some attributed the pestilence to infected air or water; some blamed earthquakes or believed in pestilential rains (sometimes of frogs or snakes). Some blamed indecent clothing which was thought to have incurred God's punishment; and others blamed religious minorities.

Burying the dead at Tournai, France. Many people refused to go near their own families and some resorted to paying porters to carry the plague victims off to mass graves.

Flagellants at Doornik in 1349 (from a miniature in the Chronicle of Aegidius Li Muisis): this extreme penitent sect was convinced that the only way to rid mankind of sin was by physical self-abasement.

In Germany, which still had a Jewish population (unlike England and France, where they had been expelled during the previous fifty years), the Jews were linked with the arrival of the plague: they were butchered and burnt in their thousands. One French chronicler wrote: 'When Jews were being burnt mothers would throw their own children into the flames rather than risk them being baptised, and would hurl themselves into the fire after them, to burn with their husbands and children' (Horrox). A further record, from a Franciscan friar, reads:

> God, the lord of vengeance, has not suffered the malice of the Jews to go unpunished. Throughout Germany, in all but a few places, they were burnt . . . in a number of regions many people, noble and humble alike, have laid plans against them and their defenders which they will never abandon until the whole Jewish race has been destroyed. (Horrox)

During 1348 and 1349 there was a concerted programme of persecution against the Jews in Germany: they were burnt at Stuttgart, Lindau, Freiburg, Eisenach and Dresden; in Lausanne too Jews were burnt or impaled; in Savoy they were tortured and then burnt on the strength of the confessions wrung from them. On 5 July 1348, Pope Clement VI intervened, reissuing the papal bull or edict *Sicut Judeis*, which extended the Catholic Church's protection to the Jews. But many had already left for the relative safety of Poland and eastern Europe. Moreover, the Jews were not the only group to be held responsible for the pestilence: Arabs, pilgrims and lepers were also blamed.

The most common explanation for the plague was that it was an expression of God's will, divine retribution for earthly sins: part punishment and part warning. The common reaction to this was a combination of individual penitence and collective prayer. The Papacy declared 1350 a Jubilee Year in which a pilgrimage to Rome would earn full remission of sins. Several Italian cities formed fraternities of penitents to tend the sick and bury the dead.

In this general atmosphere of penitence, moralists and preachers flourished. But since *Yersinia pestis* made no moral distinction between its hosts, animal or human, the indiscriminate nature of the plague was interpreted as a sign of mankind's innate sinfulness. Some even welcomed the death of clearly good and upright people, seeing their infection by the plague as a blessed short-cut to the afterlife.

One extreme penitent sect, the Flagellants, practising ostentatious self-abasement, gained a large following in the latter stages of the epidemic. They whipped and scourged themselves with studded leather thongs, convinced that self-flagellation was the way to purge mankind of the sin which they believed had caused the plague from God.

The processions sometimes included as many as 1,500 participants, who followed a smaller party of flagellants. The latter walked two by two, naked except for a white cloth covering them from their loins to their ankles, and they sang hymns in their native tongue as they lashed themselves so that their bodies became 'swollen and blue, the blood ran down to the ground and bespattered the walls of the churches . . . occasionally they drove the spikes so deep into the flesh that they could only be pulled out by a second wrench' (Henry of Herford). They also prospered around the papal court at Avignon, and even Clement VI (1291–1352) himself took part in their processions. At first, Clement VI encouraged them, but, as the movement grew, it became more disruptive and subversive, cutting across the traditional forms of Catholic worship. So in October 1349 the Pope denounced the Flagellants for contempt of Church discipline. In any case, despite their best efforts, the plague spread inexorably as *Yersinia pestis* multiplied and flourished.

The Franciscan Michele da Piazza saw the progress of the disease in Sicily at this time, observing its symptoms in victims and the terror which the dying evoked:

> What more is there to say? Corpses lay unattended in their own homes. No priests, sons, fathers or kinsmen dared to enter; instead they paid porters large sums to carry the bodies to burial. The houses of the dead stood open, with all the jewels, money and treasure in full view, and if someone wanted to enter there was nothing to stop them. (Horrox)

The same was true wherever the plague struck. In Florence, Giovanni Boccaccio lamented that in the face of so much affliction and misery all respect for the laws of God and man had virtually broken down: 'For, like everybody else, those ministers and executors of the laws who were not either dead or ill were left with so few subordinates that they were unable to discharge any of their duties. Hence everyone was free to behave as he pleased' (Horrox).

Within a month of the Genoese galleys' arrival, the plague had taken hold in Sicily; it was also developing and gaining ground in ports on the Italian mainland, a grim tribute to the efficacy and scope of fourteenth-century trade. By the end of 1347 the plague had broken out in most of the ports between Kaffa and Genoa. Europe was about to change forever.

The Spread of the Black Death

Following its October 1347 arrival at Messina, the progress of the disease from town to town across Europe, and indeed within each individual victim, was clear to see. The terror was silent, swift and deadly. The Black Death bacillus continued its northern and westward path. That same year *Yersinia pestis* reached France, having probably started at Marseilles, and at St Denis where it was claimed there were 16,000 deaths. In Paris, 800 people died each day, and the death toll there, according to the 'Great Chronicle' kept by the monks of St Denis, was 50,000. At the papal court of Clement VI at Avignon *Yersinia pestis* was challenged by a formidable opponent. His name was Guy de Chauliac (*c.* 1300–68), physician to the Pope.

De Chauliac, friend of the great poet Petrarch, was one of the most influential physicians of the fourteenth century; he was an anatomist and surgeon, and his *Chirurgia*

The famous fourteenth-century physician Guy de Chauliac saved Pope Clement VI from becoming another victim of the Black Death.

Magna of 1363 became the standard medical textbook for nearly 300 years. The chapters on carbuncles, abscesses and tumours draw on his experiences at Avignon in 1348 and during a second epidemic in 1360.

When the plague first arrived, de Chauliac at once agreed to tend the sick, and continued to do so throughout the epidemic: 'as for me, to avoid infamy, I did not dare absent myself, but still I was in continual fear'. He was typical of the physicians of that time: they knew enough about the disease to recognize its symptoms and speculate about methods of prevention or cure, but they lacked the scientific sophistication to fight it. 'The disease', he wrote, 'was most humiliating for doctors, who were unable to help. If they risked visiting their patients, they could do no good and so earned no fees, for almost all the infected died.' Clever doctors, according to a fifteenth-century German source, kept their patients safe with simple advice: 'get out quickly, go a long way away and don't be in a hurry to come back' (Horrox).

Eventually, de Chauliac himself succumbed to the plague, and took to his bed. But he survived, each day for six weeks carefully noting the progress of the disease in his own body. This was brave investigative medicine, which he was able to combine with his more general observations: 'It was of two types. The first, with continuous fever and spitting of blood. From this one died in three days. The second also with continuous fever but with carbuncles on the armpits and groin . . . From this one died in five days.' De Chauliac had identified and distinguished between the bubonic and the pneumonic plague and had actually survived one form of the disease. To treat himself, he resorted to bleeding, using a heated cup to raise his blood to the surface of his skin. Draining off the corrupted blood caused by the plague – if it could be done before vital organs were tainted – was regarded as a way of halting the disease. De Chauliac was convinced the plague was caused by the atmosphere becoming infected and that this was responsible for poisoning the blood itself. He was not alone in this belief. The report of the Paris Medical Faculty of October 1348 reads:

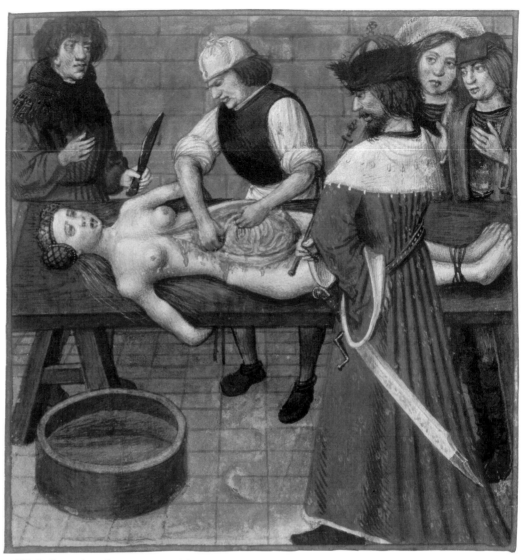

Dissection of a woman. (From a copy of the fifteenth-century manuscript, 'Roman de la Rose'.)

We believe that the present epidemic or plague has arisen from air corrupt in its substance . . . And this corrupted air, when breathed in, necessarily penetrates to the heart and corrupts the substance of the spirit there and rots the surrounding moisture, and the heat thus caused destroys the life force, and this is the immediate cause of the present epidemic. And moreover, these winds, which have become so common here, have carried among us bad, rotten and poisonous vapours from elsewhere: from swamps, lakes and chasms, for instance, and also from unburied and unburnt corpses – which might well have been a cause of the epidemic. (Horrox)

The infected air itself, according to the most popular explanation of the plague, was caused by the conjunction of Mars, Saturn and Jupiter in 1345. Reported the Paris Medical Faculty:

We say that the distant and first cause of this pestilence was and is the configuration of the heavens. In 1345, at one hour after noon on 20 March, there was a major conjunction of three planets in Aquarius. This conjunction, along with other earlier conjunctions and eclipses, by causing a deadly corruption of the air around us, signifies mortality and famine . . . (Horrox)

De Chauliac swiftly found himself in a position to help his most important patient, Clement VI, who had not yet contracted the plague, though it was raging throughout Avignon. To counteract the vapours, de Chauliac borrowed an idea from the writings of Arab philosophers and surrounded the Pope with constantly burning fires. He had struck on a good means of prevention but for the wrong reason: the fires kept the fleas at bay, and the Pope, though he suffered during the heat of the summer, was safe.

So Clement VI survived. But over twenty million Europeans did not. By 1348, the plague had reached the south coast of England. The chronicler Robert of Avesbury, an official of the Archbishop of Canterbury, wrote:

Engraving of Pope Clement VI.

> It began in England in the county of Dorset, about the feast of St Peter in chains [1 August], and immediately progressed without warning from place to place. It killed a great many healthy people, removing them from human concerns in the course of a morning. Those marked for death were scarcely permitted to live longer than three or four days. It showed favour to no one, except for a very few of the wealthy. On the same day 20, 40 or 60 bodies, and on many occasions many more, might be committed for burial together in the same pit. (Horrox)

During its first outbreak, the plague killed a half of the population of England. The records which survive are numerous, and the plague in England is well chronicled by witnesses whose accounts range from sober reporting to fantastical imaginings. But the most chilling descriptions were the plainest. 'This pestilence held such sway in England at that time that there were hardly enough people left alive to bury the dead, or enough burial grounds to hold them,' wrote one chronicler.

The disease spread north to Scotland and west to Ireland (perhaps from Bristol); it probably reached Scandinavia on a ship which left plague-ridden London in May 1349, the fleas hiding in the cargo of wool. It then spread through Denmark and Sweden in 1350 and across the Baltic Sea to Russia by 1352. But by then the worst of the plague was over.

The Black Death returned to cause sporadic epidemics in the 1360s in France, England and Italy; and in the 1370s in Italy once more, prolonging the effects of the 1347–52 outbreak. It remained endemic for three centuries, and in 1665 the Great Plague killed one-quarter of London's inhabitants. But for five years in the mid-fourteenth century, mankind had battled with a clever, adaptable virus which was indiscriminate and ferocious. It is impossible to determine the causes of the plague's decline; one theory is that the bacillus evolved into a milder and less virulent version of itself simply in order to survive.

The Aftermath

The plague not only caused deaths, it changed lives. The social hierarchy may have been reimposed after the disorder provoked by the epidemic, but the world view had altered. The impact of the plague on medieval psychology was immense. Boccaccio wrote from Florence, a city which suffered subsequent outbreaks of the plague in the 1360s, 1370s and 1390s:

> No more respect was accorded to dead people than would nowadays be shown towards dead goats. For it was quite apparent that the one thing which, in normal times, no wise man had ever learned to accept with patient resignation (even though it struck so seldom and unobtrusively), had now been brought home to the feeble-minded as well, but the scale of the calamity caused them to regard it with indifference. (Horrox)

The Triumph of Death
(c. 1562) by Pieter
Bruegel the Elder
(c.1515–69). Art as
well as literature was
profoundly affected by
the psychological impact
of the plague. For
centuries afterwards,
apocalyptic images of
death in paintings often
became fantastical in
response to a new
awareness and fear of
man's mortality.

The Black Death, above all, marked a psychological turning point in the history of Western Europe. The plague seemed part of an apocalyptic drama where the final judgement was imminent.

While the plague challenged, it did not overthrow the underlying social structures of medieval life. Its effects were superimposed on deeper social and economic trends. It struck at a time when Europe's population was at its medieval peak – England's had trebled between 1086 and 1300. The pan-European famines of 1309 and 1315–17 had reduced numbers or at least slowed their growth, but the plague struck again when the population had only just recovered.

The plague's impact was greatest on rural society. Across Europe, whole communities perished or were abandoned; agricultural land was turned over to forestry or sheep farming. The impact of the disease in these areas caused a crisis in labour, even though there is evidence that the rural European population had been too great for the land to support. Initially, mortality within the labour force sent wages soaring. At the same time, the deaths of tenants forced lords to renegotiate rents if they were to fill their empty holdings – something which allowed those peasants who held their land by the performance of labour services for their lord to bargain down their obligations. This dislocation was short-lived. In England, the government introduced legislation to peg wages and prices at pre-plague levels, and lords were often able to pressure their tenants into taking on empty properties. But the cumulative effect of successive outbreaks meant that by the 1380s, wages were again rising, and property rents falling.

Rising wages meant that although the fall in population had brought a national slump in industrial and agricultural output, *per capita* wealth rose for most people, allowing many workers greater leisure and more say in how they chose to spend their time. The labour force became more mobile, and the shortage of workers allowed women a wider range of

Death lay his icy hands on kings . . . This ghoulish illustration from a fourteenth-century manuscript was born in the aftermath of the Black Death when fear, doubt and despair had taken the place of belief – and hope.

possible employment. In the countryside, labour services were gradually abandoned and legal categorisation of many peasants as 'unfree' lost its significance.

But the plague's effects were wider even than this. The deaths of so many clerics – on the front line in the plague – meant that in England, for example, French and Latin came to be less widely taught, and English gained ground as the language of authority. The Church's domination of formal education, which was being challenged before the plague, was further weakened. More education was geared to the needs of laymen and women, and the rising levels of literacy not only allowed laymen a greater role in government and administration but produced congregations which were more willing to question the received wisdom of the Church.

The literature, sculpture, painting and illustration of the time were haunted by death, which had become so much a part of daily living. One anonymous English lyric of the period is typical:

> Take hede un to my fygure here abowne
> And se how sumtyme I was fresche and gay
> Now turned to wormes mete and corrupcion
> Bot fowle erth and stynkyng slyme and clay.
> (*British Library Add. Ms 37049*)

Devils at Hell's mouth (in Winchester Psalter): the fear of Hell was employed as a deterrent against moral chaos, and the Church warned of the return of the plague if sins were unrepented.

After the plague, the fear of hell and the joy of living, coexisted with a new intensity. The bacillus engendered a set of moral attitudes which were difficult to forget. All that had passed for accepted truths became clouded by uncertainty. The plague may have been seen as divine retribution on a sinful earth, but it created conditions in which lawlessness and libidinousness made sense. Daily life was now different.

Whatever the social implications, no moral explanation was apparent for *Yersinia pestis*. At first the Church had seemed to offer a meaning for the visitation of the plague, but nothing by way of prevention or cure. Whilst the plague raged in Europe, prayer proved useless, pilgrimage futile and penitence ineffective. Concern about this moral vacuum was well expressed by Edward III, speaking to the bishops of England in September 1349:

> We have been turning the matter over in our mind with intense concentration, and we are amazed and appalled that the few people who still survive have been so ill-fated, so ungrateful towards God and so stiff-necked that they are not humbled by the terrible judgements and lessons of God. For, if their works are any guide, sinfulness and pride are constantly increasing in the people, and charity has grown more than usually cold in them. (Horrox)

For some, once the plague had ended, the Church offered the only promise of escape from a future epidemic and in the later fourteenth century it sought to strengthen its financial and social position, and to reclaim the hearts and minds of its congregations. It preached the return of the Black Death as punishment for unrepented sins; this in turn reinforced the system of indulgences, which was to become insupportably corrupt in the late fifteenth and early sixteenth centuries. Indeed, the practice of buying indulgences was one of the abuses which provoked the Reformation. For others, the life and death choices brought about by *Yersinia pestis* prompted a scepticism about the power of the Church and its servants.

Those lucky enough to survive the plague had to face a new world shattered by loss of life, a world in which only uncertainty was certain. As the chronicler Gabriele de' Mussis wrote, 'Our hearts have grown hard now that we have no future . . . The survivors can weep if they want.' (Horrox)

· 6 ·

The Jewel
OF THE EAST

In the fall and the sack of great cities an historian is condemned to repeat the tale of
uniform calamity; the same effects must be produced by the same passions; and when
those passions may be indulged without control, small, alas! is the difference
between civilised and savage man.

From the first hour of the memorable twenty-ninth of May [1453], disorder and
rapine prevailed in Constantinople till the eighth hour of the same day, when the
sultan himself passed in triumph through the gate of St Romanus.

(Edward Gibbon, *The Decline and Fall of the Roman Empire*)

THE YEAR WAS 1453. The Christian city of Constantinople, founded as the 'New Rome', fell to the Muslim Turks. 'There had never been and there never will be a more dreadful happening,' wrote one Greek observer. All of Christendom was shocked. The great Roman Empire, already dying, was at an end. The fall of Constantinople was a turning point which closed a thousand years of Greek culture, Roman institution and Christian faith and saw the start of five centuries of Turkish rule in the East. But it also heralded a new power, the Ottoman Empire, which was to remain a mighty force in Europe until the end of the First World War.

OPPOSITE: *Mehmet
II. (Sixteenth-century
painting by Sinan Bey.)*

The city was renamed Istanbul. From that moment, it would belong to the East rather than western Europe. Europe itself, its trade routes to China and Asia now cut off, turned towards the New World in search of trade and opportunity. This momentous division of East from West was achieved by one man, the cruel and brilliant Sultan Mehmet II. It was his tactics which brought the city to its knees.

Constantinople and the Dying Empire

Constantinople was dedicated in 330. By that time it had been a Greek colony – under its original name, Byzantium – for 500 years and a Roman province for 257 years. Its foundation, after a long period of civil war between co-Emperors, was instigated by the Roman Emperor Constantine I, who dedicated it, 'on the command of God', as the capital of his Empire. And although the Empire remained nominally Roman, 330 was later

The fortified walls of Constantinople.

taken to mark its transformation into the Byzantine Empire. Constantinople first rivalled, and then outshone Rome.

For a dramatic period in history, Constantinople thus united the Greek-speaking East and the Latin West, its empire stretching from the Adriatic in the west to the Tigris and Euphrates rivers in the east. On its seven hills, Europe and Asia met. For trade, its location was perfect: it controlled the Silk Road to Asia, and it was the gateway between the cool waters of the Black Sea and the warm promise of the Aegean. Strategically, too, the city's situation was formidable. It occupied a spacious and easily fortified peninsula protected on three sides by water – the Bosphorus and the Hellespont straits. The land border to the west was short and difficult to reach.

Three cultures combined in Constantinople: Greek, Roman and Christian. Other cultures among the millions of imperial subjects in the eastern Mediterranean, the Middle East and North Africa were further ingredients in this cosmopolitan melting-pot. To this cultural richness was rapidly added unparalleled material wealth as the city exploited its position at the centre of world trade. Paradoxically, Christianity flourished here at the same time. Pagan Rome had won converts to this relatively young religion, and Constantine, who had himself become a Christian, in 324 proclaimed it the official religion of his Empire. Christianity was imaginatively adapted to the forms of Greek architecture and its Gospels translated into Coptic, Nubian, Armenian, Gothic and Latin. In effect, in Constantinople, Christianity replaced the old Roman imperial concepts.

But that Empire was very soon under threat, stretched beyond its capacity, unable to police Britain and Spain in the West, Egypt in the south and Armenia in the East. Unaware of the gravity of the dangers that faced them and of the number of their enemies, the Romans were defeated by the Persians in 363, and lost Gaul in 407; Rome itself fell in 410 to the Germanic Visigoths who swept down from the north, and, although it was recaptured, the scars were deep. By the middle of the fifth century, the imperial administration in the East had begun to use Greek rather than Latin; fifty years later little remained of the once mighty Roman Empire in the West, though in the sixth century the great Emperor Justinian (527–65) reconquered the western Mediterranean, which had been lost to the Ostrogoths, another Germanic tribe.

But that was the final period of unity. Thereafter, although Constantinople survived, the Roman Empire declined. In 636, in a battle east of Galilee, the Byzantines suffered their first defeat at the hands of the Arabs, inspired to conquest by Islam, the religion newly founded by Muhammad. In 641 the Arabs conquered Byzantine Egypt, and in 717 they were at the gates of Constantinople itself. The Empire was fighting for its life, its provinces lost, its resources drained and its armies depleted. Rome was finally divided from Constantinople. The city was saved by the Byzantine emperor, Leo III (c. 680–741), and the Byzantines realized that from now on they could expect no help from Rome.

Religious schism followed. In the eighth century, Christendom divided itself, with Catholic Rome in the West and Orthodox Constantinople in the East. For the next 200 years, religious strife predominated, coming to the fore again in 1054 when the Patriarch of the Orthodox

Mosaic depicting Christ, in the Hagia Sophia in modern Istanbul.

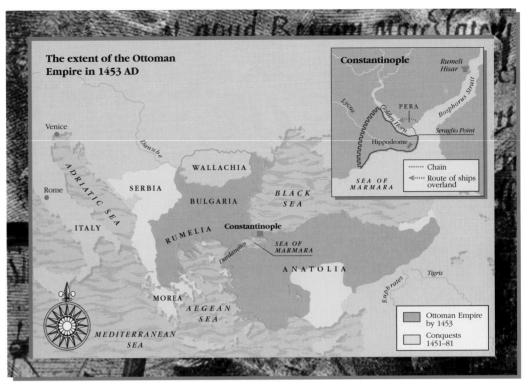

Church at Constantinople was excommunicated by the Pope in Rome. The gulf widened so precipitately that Rome came to see Orthodoxy as more dangerous than Islam. Instead of attacking the Muslims, who were by now occupying the holy city of Jerusalem, the Christian Crusades (the first was launched in 1095) attacked the weaker, and richer, Christian enemy at Constantinople. During the Fourth Crusade in 1204, Roman Catholic Crusaders – spurred on by cynical Venetians jealous of Constantinople's trade – arrived at the gates of the city.

Until then, Constantinople had never fallen, and the attacking troops were awed by its forbidding walls and high battlements. One of the leaders of the Crusade described his reaction:

> Those who had never seen Constantinople marvelled greatly at it, for they could not conceive that the world held so mighty a city, when they saw the height of the walls, the great towers enclosing it all around, the splendid palaces, the lofty churches (the number of which was so great that none could believe it who had not seen it with his own eyes), and the length and breadth of the city that lorded it over all others. And know ye that there was no man so bold that his flesh did not creep thereat, and this was no wonder . . . (Garraty and Gay)

But before long the Crusaders launched the bloodiest of attacks on Constantinople, slaughtering its inhabitants and plundering its religious relics:

> They broke the holy images, beloved of the faithful. They hurled the sacred relics of the martyrs into unmentionable places. They scattered the body and the blood of the saviour. They seized the chalices and paten, tore out their precious stones and ornaments, and drank from them.

OPPOSITE: Sixteenth-century detailed map of the walled city of Constantinople.

An exiled Greek historian, Nicetas Choniates, wrote: 'Even the Saracens [Muslims] are merciful and kind in comparison with these creatures who bear the cross of Christ on their shoulders.' The Crusaders' loot was sent to Venice: four bronze horses from the Hippodrome in Constantinople until recently decorated St Mark's basilica today; other treasures were

dispersed throughout Europe. The imperial administration fled to Nicea, leaving control in the hands of the Crusaders' Latin Empire, but the city itself never recovered.

Constantinople was recaptured by the Greeks in 1261, but the Byzantine Empire was a shadow of its former self: gone now were the kingdom of Serbia and the Empire of Bulgaria in the West and the Sultanate of Iconium in the East. The Emperor was now one among many potentates and princes in the area. His Empire existed only because neighbouring powers allowed it to linger on. The prosperity of Constantinople declined with it, unable to supply the money and men it needed. Over the next 200 years, the city decayed, its population declining from over a million in the twelfth century to fewer than 100,000 in the fifteenth; the Black Death (see Chapter 5), which arrived through the port of Pera in 1347, claimed many lives.

But Constantinople remained a city of mystical allure for East and West alike, the depository of enormous commercial wealth, the site of some of the most magnificent buildings of the middle ages, and the home of fine intellect and high culture. Yet it was bankrupt. The crown jewels were sold to cover loans, and the island of Tenedos, commanding the seaway, was sold for 30,000 ducats. In 1359, Emperor John V was arrested for debt in Venice. By 1400, the once formidable Empire had shrunk to a sliver of land around the Aegean and the Black Sea.

As Byzantium crumbled, a new power was rising in the East: the Ottomans. These were Muslim Turks, named Ottomans (Osmanlis) after their renowned leader, Osman. As early as 674, the Arabs had laid siege to Constantinople, but had been repulsed. In the fifteenth century, they became more insistent. The city may have been bankrupt, but it represented the splendour of the past and, if taken, it promised a new Muslim future. Sultan Murad II besieged Constantinople in 1422, but without success. Thirty years later his son, Mehmet II, would bring the proud old city to its knees.

The Conqueror of Constantinople

Mehmet II was born at Adrianople in 1432 to Sultan Murad II and a slave girl, Huma Hatun. He was the third of Murad's sons, but the first two died, and Mehmet became heir to the throne at the age of eleven. His father summoned the boy to court and, realizing that he had neglected his education, employed an army of tutors. Mehmet received tuition in Greek, Latin, Arabic, Chaldean, Persian and probably Slavonic. His father further instructed him as a commander and a statesman.

When Murad died of apoplexy in February 1451, Mehmet became Sultan. He immediately had his young half-brother Ahmet drowned even as he comforted Murad's widow. He had the good sense to keep Murad's advisers around him, but to make sure they could not conspire to overthrow him, he reduced their powers and divided up their responsibilities. Mehmet was intelligent, nervous, brutal and quick-tempered. His macabre sense of humour led him to appreciate the cruelty of his Black Sea rival Prince Vlad of Walachia (in what is now southern Romania). Known as Vlad the Impaler because he ran stakes through his victims, the Prince on one occasion nailed the turbans of Mehmet's emissaries to their heads because they had refused to remove them in his presence. The Sultan was amused rather than angered.

Mehmet was a strongly built man of middle height, with fine features and quick, piercing eyes. His manner was dignified and distant, except when he gave himself to alcohol, a taste for which he shared with his father. He trusted no one (that much he had learnt from his childhood), and he had the advantage of wanting neither love nor popularity: he wanted glory, to be achieved by expanding the Ottoman Empire. Before him, the Carolingians, the Saxons, the Normans and the Slavs had all looked on Byzantium and dreamed of creating vast empires. For over a hundred years, Christian Constantinople had been surrounded by an Ottoman Empire which stretched from the Danube (bordering Vlad's Walachia) to the Euphrates and included Bosnia, Serbia, Bulgaria and Greece. The Ottomans were poised. The ambitious nineteen-year-old general was determined to have this city as his new capital: 'There is only one thing I want. Give me Constantinople.'

The Last Byzantine Emperor

One man stood in Mehmet's path. His name was Constantine Palaiologos, the last Emperor of the Romans. Born in 1404 to Manuel II and the Empress Helena, Constantine was the most intelligent of six brothers. In 1427 he had fought alongside his elder brother Emperor John VIII in the conquest of Frankish lands in the Peloponnese. At Constantinople, he had often deputized for John, so when his brother died in 1448 it seemed natural for him to take the throne. He was crowned Constantine XI at Mistra in the Peloponnese on 6 January 1449, and arrived at Constantinople on 12 March. Constantine was a man of honour, integrity and practicality, a competent administrator and a fine soldier, respected by his officials.

A Byzantine coin depicting Emperor Constantine's conversion to Christianity.

When Constantine heard of the death of Murad II in 1451, he was at first unconcerned. He would continue to pay tributes to his enemies to keep the peace, as the Byzantines had done. And what harm could the young Mehmet II do to Constantine and Constantinople? After all, Byzantine diplomats had courted Mehmet's closest adviser and most powerful minister, Halil Chandarli, who was known to be a lover of peace. But it soon became clear to Constantine that Mehmet was determined to take Constantinople; reports from spies at the Turkish court warned of imminent danger to the city. Peace had suited Mehmet only while he was preparing to topple Constantinople. The city was running out of money and he saw his chance when Constantine sought to renegotiate the terms. But Mehmet rebuffed him. Throughout 1451, Constantine looked to western monarchs, including Pope Nicholas V in Rome and King Charles VII in France, in an effort to win help. None came.

Mehmet then raised the stakes, and determined to cut off Constantinople's supplies. In the winter of that year, he began to put his plan into action. He ordered stonemasons and labourers to assemble at a small village on the Bosphorus called Khallae (now Bebek), opposite Asia. Local churches and monasteries were demolished for stone, and on 15 April 1452 Mehmet started the construction of a giant fortress, Rumeli Hisar, where the strait is at its narrowest. At once there was panic in Constantinople. All the Turks living in the city were arrested. Constantine sent a deputation to Mehmet asking for reassurance that the building of the fortress was not a prelude to an attack on Constantinople: the Greek ambassadors were imprisoned and decapitated.

Mehmet's castle was completed on 31 August. It commanded not only the Bosphorus, but the Golden Horn, the inlet around which Constantinople is built, and effectively controlled the shipping to and from the city. Grain supplies from the Ukraine were immediately cut off, and any ships which tried to run the blockade were blown out of the water.

Mehmet's next stop was to try to gain control of the seas around the city. In March 1453, he assembled off Gallipoli in the Hellespont a fleet of ships, differing in size: triremes, biremes, fustae and sailing barges. Figures vary wildly, but there were at least 120 ships. At the end of March, the fleet sailed up the Hellespont into the Sea of Marmara. Constantinople was now cut off, surrounded on all sides by the Turkish ships.

At the same time, the Sultan assembled in Thrace an army at least 50,000 strong, to be led by the elite Janissary regiments, which totalled 12,000 men. Muslim converts hand-picked as Christian children from the most warlike regions of Mehmet's Empire (Albania, Serbia and Bosnia), the aggressive Janissaries were waging a holy war against Constantinople. These forces included a rag-bag vanguard of expendable irregulars or 'Bashi-bazouks', the regular trained troops from Anatolia and several thousand camp followers. Altogether, the Muslims outnumbered the defenders of Constantinople by more than ten to one. Only the city's great fortifications, the walls which had always protected it from siege, including that of his father in 1422, stood between Mehmet and the realization of his dream.

The Siege of Constantinople

Around the city of Constantinople soared thirteen miles of walls, the greater part started during the reign of Emperor Theodosius II (408–50). The west wall, on the landward side, was a triple construction: four miles of inner wall, forty feet high; an outer wall of twenty-five feet; and a buttressed wall behind a deep ditch sixty feet wide which could be flooded. Between each wall was an enclosure, forty to sixty feet wide. Along the inner and outer walls stood towers at intervals of fifty to a hundred yards. A series of gates – some public and some military – gave access to the city. When Murad had attacked the city in 1422, the defence had concentrated on the outer wall. The Turks, though they had damaged it, had been unable to breach it. Later, it was repaired and the walls restored to their original strength.

The sea walls, which formed a triangular peninsula at the Seraglio Point in the north-east of the city, ran for eight miles, and were of a single construction. A great chain was stretched across the mouth of the Golden Horn which was reinforced by balks of wood; the imperial fleet of twenty-six ships lay sheltered behind. This was the only entrance to the harbour.

Now, in the spring of 1453, Constantine prepared his city to face the Turkish siege. Mehmet offered him territory in Greece (Morea) and religious freedom for his people if he would give up Constantinople. But Constantine saw no reason to trust the Turks. He wrote Mehmet a final letter:

> As it is clear that thou desirest more war than peace . . . I turn now and look alone to God. However, I release thee from all thy oaths and treaties with me, and closing the gates of my capital, I will defend my people to the last drop of my blood. (Nicol)

The historian Edward Gibbon wrote passionately of the last Byzantine Emperor: 'The nation was indeed pusillanimous and base, but the last Constantine deserves the name of a hero; his noble band of volunteers was inspired with Roman virtue.'

A quarter of Constantinople's 100,000 citizens were able-bodied men liable for military service, but Constantine had managed to raise only 5,000 volunteers. So he did a deal with the old Catholic enemy in Italy and appointed John Giustiniani, a brilliant Genoese general, to lead his land forces. Giustiniani arrived in January 1453 accompanied by 700 professional and well-armed troops, a spectacle that brought hope to the city. But it was not to last long.

On 5 April Mehmet brought his army within sight of Constantinople, pitching his red and gold tent on the eastern slope of a small hill. An eyewitness records:

> On the fifth of the month of April, one hour after daybreak, Mahomet Bey [Mehmet] came before Constantinople with about a hundred and sixty thousand men, and encamped about two and a half miles from the walls of the city . . . On the seventh of this month, he moved with a great part of his forces to within about a quarter of a mile of the walls, and they spread in a long line along the whole length of the walls . . . (Barbaro)

Siege tower contructed by Mehmet's army to breach the city walls.

In accordance with Islamic law, Mehmet sent an ultimatum, offering the Byzantines a last chance to surrender. He still wanted the city intact: 'I will, as the law commands, spare you, the citizens of this great city, harm neither your families nor your belongings, if you voluntarily surrender to me.' His offer was rejected. The Sultan then turned his attention to two castles loyal to Constantine: one at Therapia on the Bosphorus, the other at Studius on the Marmara coast. After two days, both castles surrendered, and the seventy-six survivors were impaled within sight of the walls of Constantinople. But, if terror did not shake the Byzantines, Mehmet's new weapon would.

On 12 April, Mehmet began the first great organized bombardment in history, a fifteenth-century form of *blitzkrieg*. He had drawn up over seventy cannon in fourteen batteries along the walls. At first, these produced more noise than damage. Mehmet understood modern warfare technology, and knew of the enormous destructive power which cannon could bring to bear on a city's defences. But the fortifications of Constantinople were so massive that traditional cannon and artillery tactics could not harm them. The Sultan was advised by his artillery engineers to train the cannon in one place, so that the firepower could have a destabilizing effect on the walls. This tactic likewise failed when the defenders repaired the walls and cleared the outer ditch of rubble.

Principal among Mehmet's artillery was a new type of weapon – a gigantic cannon designed and cast on the battlefield. At twenty-nine feet from muzzle to breech, with a nine-inch bore, they were the largest cannon ever made, firing a half-ton marble cannon-ball at least a mile. Sixty oxen and 400 men were required to operate each one, and each took two hours to load. The metal became so hot that oil had to be poured down the muzzle immediately after firing to prevent the gun cracking or exploding. These great guns were put to use, but still the city held out.

On the 18th, Mehmet ordered an infantry attack on the section of wall at the Mesoteichion, midway along the western boundary where the River Lycus flowed into the city. One of the defenders records:

> This happened at about the second hour of the night, and the skirmish lasted until about the sixth hour of the night, and many Turks died in the fighting. When they came it was dark, and so our men were not expecting their attack; and I cannot describe the cries with which they came at the walls, and the sound of cymbals, so that there seemed to be even more Turks than there really were, and the sound carried as far as Anatolia, twelve miles away from their camp. (Barbaro)

After four hours' struggle, the Turks were repelled, having lost 200 men. This cheered the defenders, who had suffered no fatalities. They were further encouraged by a brief sea skirmish two days later. A trio of Genoese ships, outnumbered by the Turkish fleet, but larger and better organized, made for the protected harbour. All Constantinople watched the action as the Genoese successfully crashed through the Turkish ships towards the safety of the Golden Horn. Turkish morale began to slip.

But the Muslims continued the land bombardment throughout April, their artillery having an attritional effect on the walls and a debilitating impact on the city's defenders. Soon, however, Mehmet grew impatient. He realized that he needed to stretch Constantine's resources of men, and he could not do this if he confined his attacks to one section of the land wall where Constantine could concentrate his men. So he determined to open another front by attacking the northern wall of Constantinople, along the Golden Horn. For this he required command of the harbour. Yet his ships lay at anchor in the Bosphorus, prevented from entering the Golden Horn by the great chain.

The Sultan conceived a bold plan. If he could not enter by sea, he would transport his fleet overland and relaunch it in the Golden Horn behind the chain. On 21 April his project gathered pace. While the artillery fire intensified, the ships were placed on cradles with iron wheels cast in the foundries which had been established for cannon manufacture. When a path had been prepared for the ships, they were that night hauled out of the harbour by pulleys to begin the three-mile journey over a 200-foot ridge to the Golden Horn. By the morning of the 22nd, the strange procession of seventy ships was descending into the harbour. It was a coup for Mehmet. He had proved that, with sufficient time, energy and manpower, he would achieve anything.

As dawn broke, the Turkish war fleet had surrounded the city. Constantinople was in uproar. Six days later, Constantine sent out a spoiling force to set fire to the Turkish fleet; it failed. The forty sailors who survived were butchered in full view of the city. The Emperor retaliated by ordering 260 Turkish prisoners to be executed on the battlements.

The Turks taxed the over-stretched defences by maintaining the artillery barrage against the land walls throughout the next ten days. 'There was no activity on sea or land', wrote Nicoló Barbaro, a Venetian doctor living in Constantinople, 'except for the continual bombardment and skirmishing and much shouting according to the custom of the Turks.' Time was running out for Constantinople: supplies were lacking and morale was low. On 3 May a swift *brigantino* was dispatched to search for the Venetian fleet promised to Constantinople at the start of the siege. It slipped through the Turkish cordon and outran its pursuers, but it returned twenty days later. There was no sign of the fleet.

During this time, it is probable that Constantine attempted to negotiate with Mehmet. The Turkish terms remained the same: unconditional surrender in return for land in Morea, and religious freedom for the people of Constantinople. The disheartened Byzantines urged Constantine to escape. He replied:

> How could I leave the churches of our Lord, and His servants the clergy, and the throne, and my people in such a plight? What would the world say about me? I pray you, my friends, in future do not say to me anything else but, 'Nay, Sire, do not leave us!'   (Nicol)

On saying this, Constantine wept. He knew he would die, and his city would be lost. Yet as the Byzantines grew more desperate, the Turks became more frustrated. Few defenders had been killed, and the city, while showing signs of weakness, was still far from falling.

As May wore on, Mehmet staged more assaults on the walls: on the 7th and 12th, attacks by 30,000 and 50,000 troops were repulsed by the defenders. Always in the front line was Giustiniani, whose cunning and inventiveness helped the Byzantines last longer than they otherwise would have done. Giustiniani disrupted the Turkish efforts by destroying the wooden siege towers placed against the walls and countering the Turkish mines (or explosives) with mines of his own. One chronicler described the effects of a Greek mine:

> It was as if the lightning had struck the place, for the earth shook and with a great crash a greenish whirlwind carried the Turks into the air. Fragments of men and timber fell into the city and into the camp. The besieged ran away from the walls and the besiegers fled back from the ditch.   (Barbaro)

On 24 May, the moon would be at its fullest. Tradition held that Constantinople would not fall while the moon was in the heavens, a tradition that should have cheered the defenders. But that night a full eclipse of the moon brought three hours of darkness to the city. The Byzantines were filled with despair.

The Last Hours of Constantinople

On 27 May, Mehmet determined to launch simultaneous attacks on Constantinople by sea and by land: 'I have decided to engage successively and without halt one body of fresh troops after the other, until harassed and worn out the enemy will be unable further to resist.' He planned the final assault for two days later. As the Byzantines looked on, Mehmet's army worked constantly:

> Under pain of death, all his pashas and their lieutenants, and all the rest of his captains and men of any condition who had Turks as their rulers, should be ready at their post all day, because tomorrow he intended to make a general attack on the wretched city.
>
> [On 28 May] one hour after dark, the Turks in their camp began to light a terrifying number of fires, much greater than they had lit on the two previous nights, but worse than this, it was their shouting which was more than we Christians could bear; and together with their shouting, they fired a great number of cannon and guns, and hurled stones without number, so that to us it seemed to be a very inferno. (Barbaro)

The defenders prepared themselves, in military and spiritual terms, for the onslaught. Shortly after sunset on the 28th, the last Christian service was held in the church of St Sophia. Constantine returned there after midnight to make his peace with God.

The simultaneous attacks started three hours before dawn. Mehmet himself came to the walls. He deployed a force along the landward side, concentrating on the heavily bombarded section in the dip of the Lycus valley. The first wave of irregulars, Bashi-bazouks (many of whom were Christian adventurers), ran forward with scaling ladders. The Turks felt it best that expendable Christians should be the first to be killed, using them both to tire out the defenders and to establish a foothold. Behind the Bashi-bazouks were Mehmet's Janissaries, ready to cut down deserters.

A second attack, at the gate of St Romanus, by Mehmet's regular Anatolian troops at first flourished and then faltered. A ball from one of the great cannon tore down the stock-ade at the inner wall: 300 Anatolians at once rushed forward into the city, but were beaten back in fierce hand-to-hand fighting. The attack was called off. But Mehmet's tactic had been for these two assaults to tire the Byzantines. Now he was ready to send in the Janissaries. Nicoló Barbaro recorded:

> There then approached the third group, their paid soldiers the Janissaries, and their officers and their other principal commanders, all very brave men, and the Turkish Sultan behind them all. This third group attacked the walls of the poor city, not like Turks but like lions . . . they spread fear through the city and took away our courage with their shouting and noise.

The thick of the fighting was at the Porta Xylokerkov, the Gate of the Wooden Circus. The turning point in the battle came when John Giustiniani was wounded by a shot. He begged his men to take him off the wall and although Constantine pleaded with him to stay at his station, his bodyguard carried him through the city and on to a waiting Genoese ship. He escaped to Chios, only to die two days later. The other Genoese retreated, leaving Constantine and the Byzantines alone on the walls. Mehmet saw the confusionin at the small Circus gate, urged on his forces, and in a surprise assault, swept the defenders aside. Turkish flags began to appear on the towers above the walls.

Constantinople had fallen. Mehmet himself entered through the gate of Edirne Kapissi, and made his way to St Sophia. There he dismounted, bent to pick up a handful of earth and poured it over his turban in an act of humility towards God.

The victorious Turks butchered indiscriminately, 'and anyone they found they put to the scimitar, women and men, old and young, of any condition,' Barbaro recorded. ' . . . The blood flowed in the city like rainwater in the gutters after a sudden storm, and the corpses of Turks and Christians were thrown into the Dardanelles, where they floated out to sea like melons along a canal.' Barbaro escaped with the Venetian ships moored against the northern sea walls which broke out through the chain across the Golden Horn; they

The Conquest of Constantinople. *(Sixteenth-century painting by Jacopo Palma.)*

had nothing to fear, for the Turkish sailors had all gone ashore to loot. Barbaro lived to write his siege diary and to check with others the sequence of events: he was the last Christian chronicler of Constantinople.

The gazi historian Oruç described the final moments of the city:

The gazis, entering by force on every side, found a way in through the breaches of the fortress made by the guns and put the infidels in the fortress to the sword. The way was opened to the rest of the soldiers. They came through the trenches and set up ladders. They threw these against the wall of the towers and climbed up them. Mounting on the

Mehmet II rides triumphantly into the Hippodrome in Constantinople. (Sixteenth-century manuscript.)

tower they destroyed the infidels who were inside and entered the city. They looted and plundered. They seized their money and possessions and made their sons and daughters slaves. Sultan Mehmed also gave orders to plunder the houses. In this way what could be taken was taken. The Muslims took so much booty that the wealth gathered in Istanbul since it was built 2400 years before became the portion of the gazis. They plundered for three days, and after three days plunder was forbidden. Istanbul was taken on Tuesday the 21st of Rebi ül-evvel of the year 857 [29 May 1453]. (Lewis)

Constantine probably died fighting, as he had sworn he would. His body was never found, although a headless corpse was discovered, the feet in purple boots embroidered with imperial eagles; many think these were Constantine's remains. His last speech (according to traditional accounts) had been, as Gibbons says, the funeral oration of the Roman Empire:

> You, my comrades in arms, obey the commands of your leaders in the knowledge that this is the day of your glory – a day on which, if you shed but a drop of blood, you will win for yourselves the crowns of martyrdom and eternal fame. (Nicol)

Mehmet left the smoking city on 21 June: ruined, deserted and stripped. 'What a city we have given over to plunder and destruction,' he murmured as he rode through the empty streets. The basilica of St Sophia and the partly ruinous cathedral of the Holy Apostles and some churches survived intact. But Constantinople was no more.

Little now remains of the splendour of the Byzantine Empire. Its capital city, the centre of trade for the ancient world, had seen pass through its gates the richest produce: Asian silk and spices, Egyptian corn, Indian gems. Beauty, wealth and strategic security had for an instant united in one place. It was the cradle of Christian civilization, a city formed by its location as the capital of a great monarchy. There, for 1,100 years, intellectual endeavour and Classical learning had been valued and nurtured. Constantinople had been home to many scholars and thinkers, the last generation of whom had fled before the city fell and taken their learning to Italy and France. Now, all that remains of this once magnificent city are St Sophia, the Chora, some 200 cisterns, several churches and the walls themselves.

Mehmet's Empire was to prosper for nearly 500 years. As it grew, the Ottoman presence in Europe threatened the very survival there of Christianity. After Constantinople had fallen, Christians looked west for fresh conquests in the New World, and also to the east. It was left to the Russians, as they saw it, to inherit the seat of the Orthodox Christian Empire. This sixteenth-century writer addressed the Tsar in Moscow:

> Because the old Rome has collapsed on account of heresy . . . and because the Second Rome which is Constantinople is now in the possession of the godless Turks, thy kingdom, O pious Tsar, is the third Rome. It surpasses in devotion every other, and all Christian kingdoms are now merged in thy realm. Thou art the only Christian sovereign in the world, the master of all faithful Christians . . .
>
> All Christian empires are fallen and in their stead stands alone the Empire of our ruler in accordance with the prophetical books. Two Romes have fallen, but the Third stands, and a fourth there will not be. (Garraty and Gay)

As Mehmet made the journey from the church of St Sophia to the desolate mansion which had housed Constantine's forebears, two lines of Persian poetry came to him: 'the spider has wove his web in the Imperial Palace, and the owl hath sung her watch-song on the towers of Afrasiab.' It was, as Gibbon said, a melancholy reflection on the vicissitudes of human greatness.

Voyage into
THE UNKNOWN

THE SPANISH DEFEAT THE INCAS IN PERU
AND THE FATE OF SOUTH AMERICA IS SEALED.

T HE GREAT SPANISH EXPLORER Francisco Pizarro first saw the Pacific Ocean in September 1513 shining beyond the forests of Panama. It was a sight to match his dreams. The seas on the western shores of the New World opened new routes to the lands which lay south and east, rich with promise. Nearly twenty years later, in November 1532, Pizarro would conquer the great Inca Empire in an extraordinary coup that changed the history of South America. And 200 years later, less than a twentieth of the original Indian population would remain.

In 1492, with the reconquest of Spain from the Moors completed after the surrender of Granada to the Castilian King Ferdinand and Queen Isabella (1452–1516), the Spanish turned their attention westward. That year, Christopher Columbus (1451–1506) sailed west and landed in Cuba and Haiti, and for the next twenty years the Spanish concentrated on establishing themselves there, exploring the Caribbean islands and the north coast of South America. Then in 1519 Hernán Cortés (1485–1547) discovered and, by 1522, sub-dued the Aztec Empire in Mexico. Spain became a ferment of would-be *conquistadores* (conquerors), the riches of the New World providing an irresistible temptation.

During the 1520s, the Spanish based in Panama began to explore the Pacific coast to the south and east. These sorties into the unknown were as much financial ventures as military operations. *Conquistadores* would attract capital from wealthy backers and agree to divide any spoils they might find. The Spanish Crown would also receive a share. In 1522 Pascual de Andagoya sailed south 200 miles to the San Juan river, on the northern border of the Inca Empire, searching for a tribe known as the Birú or Virú. When he returned to Panana, his ships were acquired by three men who were to transform the history of the new continent: Francisco Pizarro, his friend Diego de Almagro and the priest Hernando de Luque.

OPPOSITE: *Machu Picchu, the Lost City of the Incas, was undiscovered by the conquistadores and remained hidden from the West for centuries to come.*

Francisco Pizarro

Pizarro's first journey south took place in November 1524. One of the men with him was his secretary, Francisco de Xeres, who wrote:

> At this time the Captain Francisco Pizarro, son of the Captain Gonzalo Pizarro, a knight of the City of Truxillo, was living in the city of Panama, possessing his house, his farm, and his Indians, as one of the principal people of the land, which indeed he always was, having distinguished himself in the conquest and settling, and in the service of His Majesty. Being at rest and in repose, but full of zeal to continue his labours and to perform other more distinguished services for the royal crown, he sought permission from Pedrarias [the Governor of Panama] to discover that coast of the South Sea to the eastward. He spent a large part of his fortune on a good ship which he built, and on necessary supplies for the voyage, and he set out from the city of Panama on the 14th day of the month of November, in the year 1524.

Why did Pizarro, a wealthy and respected man of (by some accounts) nearly fifty years want to push himself and his men further into the unknown? What drove him?

A clue lies, perhaps, in Pizarro's home in Trujillo, Extremadura, 140 miles south-west of Madrid. Home for Pizarro held no significant ties; it was merely a place to set out from. He was born in about 1478, the illegitimate son of Captain Gonzalo Pizarro and Francisca González. He grew strong and tall for the time – 5 foot 9 inches – tending livestock in the fields, but never learnt to read or write. He first left home when he was nineteen, serving as a soldier in Italy before sailing to Spain's colonies in the New World, where he spent his adult years: from 1502 to 1509, he lived on Hispaniola, and in 1513 he joined the expedition of Vasco Nunez de Balboa, catching his first sight of the Pacific. He had prospered as a professional soldier, showing himself to be brave, cruel and ambitious for himself and his country. Now he wished for more, lured by the romantic promise of the lands to the south, or perhaps by the gambler's instinct he loved to indulge. It seems likely that Francisco Pizarro was driven not only by the Spanish *conquistadore* code of honour, but also by the desire for glory and personal gain.

He made four voyages south from Panama down the continent's Pacific coast. For the first two, in 1524 and 1526–27, he had the permission of the Panamanian Governor Pedrarias Dávila. The 1524 voyage was discouraging: some of his men died of hunger and sickness, and Diego de Almagro lost an eye in a skirmish with the Indians. The survivors returned to Panama in July 1525, just twenty of the 130 Spaniards, blacks and Indians who had set out. But Pizarro persisted, busying himself in Panama, and in 1526 he drew up a contract with his partners and prepared to sail south once more. He fitted out two ships and three large canoes and embarked in November 1526 with 160 men, a number of Indian and black slaves, and a few horses. The expedition split in three as the ships reached the coast of modern Ecuador. Pizarro set up camp at the Rio San Juan, Almagro returned for reinforcements, and the expedition's pilot, the capable Bartolomé Ruiz, sailed south.

As Ruiz crossed the equator in March 1527, he saw a strange and wonderful sight: a raft of balsa with cotton sails, freighted with gold. For the first time, Spanish soldiers came face to face with the Incas:

> They were carrying many pieces of silver and gold for adorning the body . . . crowns and diadems, belts and bracelets, armour for the legs and breastplates . . . mirrors decorated with silver, and cups and other drinking vessels. They carried many wool and cotton mantles, shirts and *aljulas* [tunics] . . . They had some small weights to weigh gold, resembling Roman workmanship. (Porras)

Ruiz captured the raft and kept three Indians for training as interpreters. But it wa the fine gold and jewels which excited him. The Spaniards had glimpsed new wealth that could be theirs. Ruiz rejoined Pizarro and the expedition anchored off the Rio Esmeraldas to wait for the winds that would take them further south down the humid and inhospitable coast of what is now Peru. But this expedition too seemed doomed to fail. Sickness was claiming three or four victims each week, and Pizarro risked losing control over his men. So he drew a line in the sand and declared:

> Comrades and friends, *there* lies the part that represents death, hardship, hunger, nakedness, rains and abandonment; this side represents comfort. Here you return to Panama to be poor; there, you may go forward to Peru to be rich. Choose which best becomes you as good Spaniards! (Hemming)

Twelve men crossed that line and entered history. The rest returned to Panama and a life of easy obscurity. Pizarro and his dozen soldiers moved to a nearby island, safe from the

Hernán Cortés advances on Tenocutitlán, Mexico, in 1519.

Two Precolombian gold beakers from the mid-9th to mid-11th century. These are the sort of gold artefacts that the Incas had amassed as part of their great wealth.

Indian attacks which had troubled them on the mainland. When the winds improved, they sailed south along the coast to Tumbez, in the swampy gulf of Guayaquil. There they saw their first Inca city. It was evidently part of a sophisticated civilization, and though the Spaniards could not conceive of one which was not built around cities and fortified towns, they knew that a great empire must lie to the east. Pizarro read to the Indians of Tumbez the *Requirement*, a proclamation setting out their new obligations under the Spanish Empire:

I, Francisco Pizarro, servant of the high and mighty kings of Castile and León, conquerors of barbarian peoples, and being their messenger and Captain, hereby notify and inform you . . . that God Our Lord, One and Eternal, created heaven and Earth and a man and a woman from whom you and I and all the people of the world are descended . . . Because of the great multitude begotten from these of the past five thousand and some years since the world was made . . . God placed one called Saint Peter in charge over all these peoples . . .

And so I request and require you . . . to recognize the Church as your Mistress and as Governess of the World and Universe, and the High Priest, called the Pope, in Her name, and His Majesty [the King of Spain] in Her place, as Ruler and Lord King . . .

Then, following that devout opening, came the threats:

And if you do not do this . . . with the help of God I shall come mightily against you, and I shall make war on you everywhere and in every way that I can, and I shall subject you to the yoke and obedience of the Church and His Majesty, and I shall seize your women and children, and I shall make them slaves, to sell and dispose of as His Majesty commands, and I shall do all the evil and damage to you that I am able. And I insist that the deaths and destruction that result from this will be your fault.   (Chamberlain)

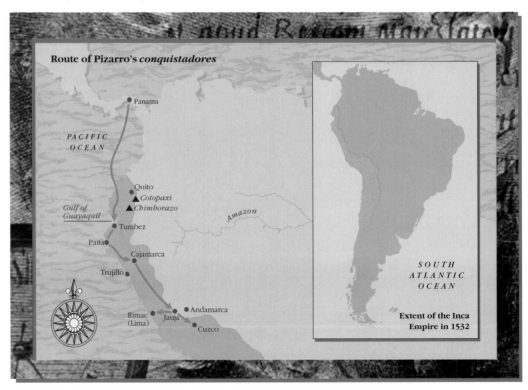

Route of Pizarro's *conquistadores*

PACIFIC OCEAN

Panama

Quito
▲ Cotopaxi
▲ Chimborazo

Gulf of Guayaquil
Tumbez

Amazon

Paita

Cajamarca

Trujillo

Rimac (Lima)
Jauja
Andamarca
Cuzco

SOUTH ATLANTIC OCEAN

Extent of the Inca Empire in 1532

Charles V, the Holy Roman Emperor, grants Francisco Pizarro governor-generalship of Peru.

Pizarro and his men returned to Panama, well pleased with their discovery of the magnificent Inca Empire. But he had displeased the Governor by venturing so far south along the Peruvian coast. For his next trip, he needed higher authority.

In 1528 he sailed east for Toledo and the court of the Holy Roman Emperor Charles V (1500–58), who had succeeded his grandfather Ferdinand as King of Spain. Charles received Pizarro, who passed before the King's eyes all the length of Peru, the quality of the land and its great treasures. He won the applause of all the city of Toledo' (Hemming). He also won royal assent for his great venture. On 26 July 1529 Charles's wife, Queen Isabella, signed a *capitulación* licensing Pizarro to explore and conquer Peru for Spain: Pizarro himself was to be Governor-General of Peru while his partner Almagro was to be Commandant of Tumbez; the priest Luque was appointed Protector of the Indians. Luque, however, was never to join the *conquistadores* in their return voyage to Peru, and instead his orders were passed on to the Dominican friar, Vicente de Valverde.

Few courtiers at Toledo knew of the hardships that had become Pizarro's way of life: disease, famine, shipwreck and warfare seemed a world away from the elegant urban culture of the Spanish court. Likewise, few of the *conquistadores* who sailed west from Spain in the 1520s and 1530s had much idea of what to expect. But the success of Cortés in Mexico in the 1520s had fired their imaginations. Early in 1530, Pizarro's ships sailed from Seville laden with the hopes and ambitions of these young men. Only Pizarro knew what awaited them. He took with him from Trujillo three of his half-brothers, his cousin, and his secretary, Francisco de Xeres, who kept a record of the expedition and helped shape the Old World's view of the New.

Pizarro's third voyage from Panama began on 27 December 1530, his three ships carrying a sickly contingent of 180 men and three dozen horses. He reached the northern coast of Ecuador inside two weeks. Extreme hardship followed. Pizarro and his men trekked south along the coast, fighting their way through dense equatorial jungle, until at last they reached Tumbez. To their astonishment, this once fine city now lay in ruins. They were soon to discover why. The *conquistadores* had as yet seen nothing of the Inca splendour which was to be theirs within two years. They left Tumbez in May 1532, heading south 200 miles to Tangarara, where they founded the settlement of San Miguel. Leaving 60 Spaniards there, Pizarro was joined by the soldier Hernando de Soto and moved east into the interior with reinforcements, 102 soldiers and 62 horsemen, determined to find the heart of the Inca Empire and its renowned king, Atahualpa.

The Inca god-king, Atahualpa. (Seventeenth-century Dutch engraving.)

The Incas

The Incas were at war with themselves. Their empire was scarcely a century old when the Spanish first arrived. It had grown swiftly and now stretched 3,000 miles along the Andes from the volcanic peaks of Chimborazo and Cotopaxi in the north to the Maipó river in the south, and from the Amazon in the east to the Pacific in the west. Latterly, the Incas had been ruled by Emperor Huayna Capac, an ambitious and vigorous soldier who had expanded the Empire to the north, establishing two capitals – the original one at Cuzco in Peru and a new one at Quito in Ecuador. Like the pharaohs of Egypt, he lived as a god-king, since he was thought to be the son of the Sun, the supreme deity in the system of Inca beliefs. During one of his northern campaigns, he heard of the tall strangers from the sea, but he never lived to see a European. He died of an unfamiliar delirious fever which swept through the Inca court and also killed his heir, Ninan Cuyuchi. These deaths proved fatal for the Empire too, because without a single strong leader the Incas were easy prey for the invaders. Meanwhile, this mysterious new disease continued to wreak havoc across the continent.

The disease was smallpox, and it spread through the Inca Empire with terrifying speed. It had probably been brought from Europe with the arrival of the early explorers in Colombia, in 1498. By 1545, the chronicler Cieze de León looked back with horror: 'They say that a great plague of smallpox broke out and spread to all parts of the kingdom . . . In the days of the Incas there was very little arable land . . . that was not under cultivation, and all as thickly settled . . . Now there are few natives . . . their number has diminished to what we now see'. By 1600, less than a tenth of the original population of the Americas remained. It was the most devastating plague in history, claiming 90 million lives. One contemporary remarked that the Indians succumbed so easily to smallpox that the mere sight of a Spaniard was enough to make them give up the ghost (Hemming). God and disease were on the side of the *conquistadores*.

In 1527, following the deaths of Huayna Capac and his heir, a struggle broke out for the Inca leadership. Two men, both of them sons of the late Emperor, were in contention: Huascar in Cuzco and Atahualpa in Quito. For five years a fierce civil war raged, until Atahualpa, who controlled the northern armies, swept south and defeated Huascar at Cuzco. The fighting left towns in ruins and the well-ordered Inca Empire in chaos. As Pizarro's cousin, Pedro, admitted, 'had the country not been divided by the wars between Huascar and Atahualpa, we could neither have invaded nor triumphed – not even if more than a thousand Spaniards had come at once'.

In the spring of 1532, as Pizarro and his band of adventurers moved down the northern coast of Peru, the civil war was drawing to a close. Atahualpa was kept informed of the foreigners' progress, and, although he was still dealing with the after-effects of the battle at Cuzco, he sent an envoy bearing gifts to meet Pizarro at Cajas. There the envoy invited the Spanish leader to meet Atahualpa at the mountain town of Cajamarca, through which the King and his retinue was passing on their march south to join up with the victorious army at Cuzco for Atahualpa's coronation.

The Spanish presented little threat to Atahualpa. His spies told him they were ordinary men who could be enslaved – 'they were lazy robbers, bearded thieves who had come from the sea' (Pizarro). The Inca Emperor had enormous power. He could draw on all the resources of his new empire: a standing army, 14,000 miles of paved roads, a system

of messengers (*chasquis*) carrying coded information in the form of tied and knotted strings (*quipus*), official supply routes, an official language and a policy of ethnic integration. Inca architecture – roads, bridges, temples and fortresses – eclipsed what came before, and remains unique. Vast terraced irrigation schemes in the Andes, which helped to produce the root crops and grains central to the Andean diet, were an extraordinary achievement. Inca cities, whether high in the mountains or down on the sultry Pacific coast, were relatively small – Cuzco, with between 50,000 and 100,000 inhabitants, was the largest. Most Incas, however, lived on the land, grouped together in small villages. The chronicler Cieza de León wrote in 1545: 'It is no small sorrow to reflect that those Incas, even though they were heathens and idolaters, knew how to keep such good order . . . and that we Christians have destroyed so many kingdoms.'

The tremendous resources of the Inca Empire were to prove inadequate against the Spaniards. Atahualpa had inadvertently accelerated his own destruction by inviting Pizarro to Cajamarca. The moment the two men met was the moment which ended the Inca Empire.

Huascar, thirteenth Emperor of the Incas and brother of Atahualpa.

Cajamarca

Cajamarca lies in a flat, lush valley in the Andes, 11,000 feet above sea level. The air is thin and clear, the light bright, and the sun high. Pizarro reached the town on Friday, 15 November 1532. Arranging his men in three squadrons, he rode down with them to the vast stone square in the middle of the town. The 80,000-strong army of the Incas was camped on the hills around them, its myriad fires flickering in the night as if in 'a brilliantly star-studded sky' (Wright). Pizarro's *conquistadores* had seen nothing like this in the Indies. One of Pizarro's men, a tough soldier called Juan Ruiz de Arce, recalled:

> It filled all us Spaniards with fear and confusion. But it was not appropriate to show any fear, far less to turn back. For had they sensed any weakness in us, the very Indians we were bringing with us would have killed us. So, with a show of good spirits, and after having thoroughly observed the town and tents, we descended into the Valley and entered the town of Cajamarca.

The square of Cajamarca where the Spanish lay in ambush for the Incas.

This visceral moment caught all the fear and excitement of two cultures meeting for the first time at the height of their powers. Atahualpa and his retinue were fasting and taking waters at a mountain spring four miles away outside the city, to which it was connected by a paved road. Pizarro sent thirty-five horsemen to visit the Inca Emperor, who greeted them while sitting on a small stool with all the majesty in the world, surrounded by all his women and with many chiefs near him' (Hemming). After welcoming his visitors, Atahualpa invited them forward. Hernando de Soto's horse came so close to the Emperor that the breath from its nostrils stirred the royal insignia. Even then Atahualpa did not flinch. The Spaniards were next given the Incas' customary drink, *chicha* (maize beer), from golden pitchers. But according to Atahualpa's nephew, Titu Kusi Yupanki, the Spaniards behaved badly and angered Atahualpa by throwing away the *chicha* and thrusting a letter at him. It was a strange and telling moment of misunderstanding that stamped itself on South American culture. From then on, South America divided between the invader and the native, the conqueror and the conquered. Those men little knew that they were acting out a model of history which was to remain for hundreds of years.

Atahualpa gave direction for Pizarro and his men to be billeted in some empty buildings which lined the town's *plaza* and agreed to visit them the next day. Although Pizarro had been well treated, he realized that his position was precarious: the Spanish were several days' difficult march from the safety of the coast; they were in the midst of a victorious army in full battle order, and they knew that reports had reached Cajamarca of their violent skirmishes with coastal Indians. They could have no expectation of continued hospitality. That night, few of the Spaniards slept:

> We took many views and opinions among ourselves about what should be done. All were full of fear, for we were so few and were so deep in the land where we could not be reinforced . . . all assembled in the Governor's [Pizarro's] quarters to debate what should be done the following day. (Hemming)

Pizarro decided to take a dangerous gamble. Copying the tactic which had served Cortés so well in Mexico, he determined to kidnap the Emperor, and to do so at a given signal when Atahualpa visited the next day. There were few alternatives. A peaceful outcome was possible if Atahualpa could be persuaded to make an act of political submission; or their friendship could simply be prolonged until something better turned up. The attack on Atahualpa was to be made only if the Incas became hostile, and then only if it looked likely to be successful, 'for the Governor', one Spaniard wrote, 'was afraid to come to grips when there were so many native warriors and we were so few' (Hemming).

At midday, on 16 November, the retinue of Atahualpa began to move down towards Cajamarca, their gold and silver costumes shining in the bright sunlight. Atahualpa himself was richly dressed, wearing a crown and a collar both of emeralds. Carried on a litter supported by eighty Inca chiefs in blue livery and escorted (according to some reports) by 6,000 soldiers, he gave the order to halt when he reached the centre of the square. It was an extraordinary display of power, but there was not a Spaniard to be seen. Atahualpa called out: Where are they?' And from Pizarro's quarters, a Dominican priest Vicente de Valverde emerged, a missal in one hand and a cross in the other.

Valverde invited Atahualpa to Pizarro's lodgings. But the Emperor declined, and instead imperiously demanded that the Spaniards return every object which they had stolen from his kingdom. Valverde read out the famous *Requirement* which Pizarro had proclaimed at Tumbez. He then offered the missal to Atahualpa, only for the Inca leader to throw it to the ground. Valverde cried: 'Come out, Christians! Come at these enemy dogs who reject the things of God!' Pizarro gave the order; a gun was fired, and the Spaniards fell upon the Indians in a frenzy of slaughter. The unarmed Incas panicked, clambering over each other as they tried to flee, many of them suffocating in the process.

Eventually, Atahualpa was captured. But the carnage continued, and after two hours six or seven thousand Incas had been killed, including many nobles, and still more had been horribly wounded. Atahualpa's nephew, Titu Kusi Yupanki, recorded the dreadful scene:

> The Spaniards charged out with great fury into the middle of the square, where there was the high throne of the Inca. They would not let my uncle ascend it. They pulled him from his litter by force, and turned it upside down. They seized his insignia and headband which among us is his crown, and took him prisoner. That square was enclosed by walls and all the Indians were inside like llamas. There were a great many of them and they could not get out, nor did they have any weapons – they had not brought them because of the low opinion they held of the Spaniards . . .
>
> The Spaniards killed them all – with horses, with swords, with guns – just as one might slaughter llamas, for nobody could defend himself. From more than 10,000 men there did not escape 200. And when all were dead they took my uncle Atawallpa [Atahualpa] to a cell, where they kept him bound all night, with a chain around his neck. (Wright)

The Inca Empire was at an end – its power and prosperity, already weakened by civil war and disease, finally laid waste by a small band of Spanish adventurers. The next day, the remaining Inca soldiers surrendered to Hernando de Soto, who relieved them of over 4,000 lbs of gold and silver and returned with it to Pizarro. Atahualpa took this to mean that the Spaniards were merely treasure-seekers, so he offered them a ransom of gold and silver beyond their wildest dreams. In return for his life, he undertook to fill a room full of gold and silver. Pizarro accepted, and every day for two months a file of Indians arrived at the Spanish headquarters to deposit gold and silver ornaments. Pizarro also insisted that the Incas should not impede the Spanish generals in their business of looting the Inca temples. However, he was magnanimous enough to promise that Atahualpa could in due course return to the northern part of the Inca Empire and live in Quito.

On the strength of this arrangement, Atahualpa continued to run his empire from captivity, and was to some extent a willing collaborator. The god-like status of the Inca chief was assurance that his rule, even from captivity, would be unquestioned. One of the Spaniards wrote to Charles V, 'he is the most educated and capable [Indian] that has ever been seen, very fond of learning our customs, to such an extent that he plays chess very well. By having this man in our power the entire land is calm' (Hemming). Atahualpa was a man of about thirty, 'of good appearance and manner, although somewhat thick-set. He spoke with much gravity, as a great ruler' (Hemming). He remained content at Cajamarca while the ransom accumulated. But when he heard of his brother Huascar's impending arrival, he made another mistake, ordering that he be killed by his escort at Andamarca, just south of Cajamarca. By this murderous act he effectively disposed of his Inca rival, but at the same time he removed all hope of an uprising against the Spaniards.

In the meantime, the Spaniards were strengthening and consolidating their position in Peru. In April 1533, Diego de Almagro arrived at Cajamarca with 150 fresh troops. Hernando Pizarro, who had been on a series of reconnaissance missions throughout the early part of the year, returned in May. The balance of power now tipped towards the

The brutal garrotting of Atahualpa.

Spaniards. Virtually none of the priceless and beautiful craftsmanship of the Incas has survived. Pizarro had established a smelting works to cope with the trains of gold and silver arriving daily, and between March and July the nine forges at Cajamarca melted down over eleven tons of gold objects. Another convoy from Cuzco arrived on 13 June with 225 llama-loads amounting to over 25,000 lb of gold. The ransom was achieved that summer and divided among Pizarro's men, with one-fifth going to the King of Spain.

But Atahualpa was not released as he had been promised. With unflinching brutality Pizarro had him strangled at a stake in the square at Cajamarca on Saturday 26 July, Friar Valverde instructing him in a last-minute conversion to Christianity. When news of this betrayal reached Charles V in Spain, he wrote to Pizarro: 'We have been displeased by the death of Atahualpa, since he was a monarch and particularly as it was done in the name of justice.' Pizarro had persistently deceived Atahualpa, lying to him and exploiting him. When he concluded that he could not release him, he had little option but to have him killed. It was time to move on to Cuzco.

After Atahualpa, after Pizarro

During the summer and autumn of 1533, Pizarro and Almagro combined their forces and conducted an effective campaign in Peru, fighting four major battles along the 800-mile road from Cajamarca to Cuzco. On 15 November they at last reached the Inca capital. In a bid to clinch the conquest, Pizarro appointed a puppet king, one of the few surviving sons of Huayna Capac, called Manco. He then ransacked Cuzco for more treasures, torturing Incas for information and forcing them to carry the gold and silver for smelting; this plunder amounted to even more than Atahualpa's ransom. Over the next five years, Inca resistance from Ruminavi in the north and the now rebellious Manco in the south was quashed. But the Spaniards had taken to fighting among themselves: Pizarro's old partner Diego de Almagro, after an insurrection in Cuzco, was defeated and executed by Hernando Pizarro.

The Spanish seize control of the Inca capital, Cuzco, in 1536.

In 1535, Pizarro built a new capital for Peru, choosing a location on the coast, nearly 400 miles from Cuzco, for easy access to the rest of Spanish America. He called it Ciudad de los Reyes, but it became known as Rimac, later corrupted to Lima. Before long, Pizarro himself was to come to a violent end. On 26 July 1541, twelve years to the day after Queen Isabella had licensed him to conquer Peru, eight years to the day after his treacherous execution of Atahualpa, he was cornered in the Governor's palace by followers of Almagro and summarily killed. In 1977, workers repairing the vault in the Cathedral opposite the Plaza de Armas in Lima discovered coffins and a lead box which bore the inscription: 'Here is the head of the Marquis Don Francisco Pizarro, who discovered and won the kingdoms of Peru and brought them under the royal Crown of Castile' (*National Geographic*, February 1992, 121).

The Spanish conquest of what are now Peru, Ecuador, Paraguay, Colombia, Bolivia and Chile was achieved by force of arms and by the effects of diseases unknown in South America before 1492: smallpox, measles, influenza, yellow fever, malaria and cholera. In 1534, Pizarro's lieutenant Simon de Benalcazar founded the municipality of San Francisco in Quito, Ecuador; Asunción in Paraguay was founded in 1537; Bogotá in Colombia and Sucre in Bolivia were established in 1538, and Santiago in Chile in 1541. For more than a century, the wealth of her South American colonies was to fund Spain's imperial ambition.

Today, the indigenous inhabitants of Peru still maintain a traditional way of life in the mountains.

The legacy of Pizarro's in Peru is racial, religious and linguistic. One-third of Peruvians are *mestizos* (of mixed Indian and Spanish blood); in the mountains the indigenous people continue a traditional way of life, and the Spaniards' descendants remain in the cities and towns, retaining their Hispanic culture. The Catholic Church, once represented by an incomprehensible book thrust aside by the last emperor of the Incas, has become the spiritual refuge of many Andean Indians. And the Spanish language is the *lingua franca* of South America. But unlike the empires of the Romans or British, which incorporated the indigenous peoples within a paternalistic administration and coaxed them into gradual acceptance of imperial values, the Spanish conquest of South America was sustained by cruel suppression. The Andean peoples would always remain separate not only from the Spanish system of government but from Spanish society too.

Francisco Pizarro's defeat of the Incas set the pattern for the Spanish presence in South America: violent, unrestrained and inspiring a powerfully romantic tradition. One contemporary said that Pizarro had found more gold and silver than any Spaniard who sailed to the Indies, even more than any commanders there have been in the history of the world' (Hemming). It had been the sight of the Pacific in 1513, far from home, that had led him to explore the inhospitable western seaboard of South America. He was like the times he lived in: urgent, tenacious, quick-thinking and courageous. Poor us,' Pizarro used to say, 'perishing in the struggle to win new kingdoms and empires, not for ourselves or our own children, but for other people's.' The illiterate soldier from Trujillo became the discoverer, conqueror and governor of Peru; his first children, by an Inca princess, were *mestizos.* The transformation of the New World by the Old was unstoppable.

Ætatis suæ 21. Aº. 1616.

atoaks al̇s Rebecka daughter to the mighty Prince
owhatan Emperour of Attanoughkomouck al̇s Virgi
onverted and baptized in the Chriſtian faith, a
Wiſe to the woꝛ:ᵗᵉ Mr Tho: Rolff.

America's
PRINCESS

AN ENGLISHMAN MARRIES AN AMERICAN INDIAN PRINCESS
AND THE ENGLISH COLONY IN VIRGINIA IS SAVED.

O my America! my new-found-land,
My kingdom, safeliest when with one man manned,
My mine of precious stones, my empery,
How blessed am I in this discovering thee!
(John Donne, *Elegie: To His Mistris Going to Bed c.*1600)

THREE ENGLISH SHIPS reached Chesapeake Bay at dawn on 26 April 1607. Their Captain, Christopher Newport, had guided them safely to the New World. The English had come not to explore but to settle. 'Heaven and earth,' wrote one of the men on those ships, 'never better framed a place for man's habitation.' Jamestown, Virginia, was to be the first permanent English-speaking colony in North America. Virginia's subsequent history, and the future of English North America as a whole, were to depend on a fragile union between two peoples, consolidated by the marriage of the Englishman John Rolfe to a Native American Princess named Pocahontas.

OPPOSITE: *Twenty-one-year-old Pocahontas, daughter of the Indian chief, Powhatan. This portrait dates from 1616, the year she came to London after her marriage to the Virginia planter, John Rolfe.*

The Old World and the New

The three ships which had set out from London on 16 December 1606 bound for America were part of England's courageous enterprise to colonize the New World. They were heading for the strip of land allocated to the Virginia Company. The Virginia Company, created by James I's Royal Charter in April 1605, was backed by investors in London, including the great navigator Sir George Somers, the geographer Richard Hakluyt, the soldier Edward Maria Wingfield and the financier Sir Edward Smythe.

The early years of the seventeenth century were a period of great cultural and economic expansion in England. After Sir Walter Raleigh's exploration of America in 1584 and Sir Francis Drake's victory over the Spanish Armada in 1588, England had become the pre-eminent European naval power. It had also developed both the technology and the industry to explore and to colonize westward. In addition, the Protestant English possessed the religious will to extend their influence from the shores of a predominantly Catholic Europe.

NOVA BRITANNIA.

OFFRING MOST

Excellent fruites by Planting in
VIRGINIA.

Exciting all such as be well affected
to further the same.

LONDON

Printed for SAMVEL MACHAM, and are to be sold at
his Shop in Pauls Church-yard, at the
Signe of the Bul-head.
1 6 0 9.

A pamphlet printed in London and aimed to encourage the English settlers to the American colonies.

America was becoming increasingly important to the established European powers. Since the voyages of Cortés and Pizarro earlier in the sixteenth century (see Chapter 7), South America had become the preserve of the Spanish – now under the rule of Philip III – and the Portuguese; the northern continent was now ripe for exploration and conquest in the seventeenth. A seemingly overcrowded England of four million people was perfectly placed to export colonists to and import the riches of the New World.

The English landing place for their first colony in America was to be an island fifty miles up the James River. They named the settlement Jamestown, after King James I. Although initially funded by the private investors of the Virginia Company, Jamestown would have to make its own way. London needed gold to match the riches found by the Spanish in South America, or goods that would make a profit in England. The colonists built a temporary trading post, which they fortified against possible attacks by either the Spanish or the Native Americans.

Princess Pocahontas and the Powhatans

At this time the forests of Virginia were home to Algonquin peoples. More than thirty Native American tribes stretched over an area of 6,000 square miles, in which, according to contemporary estimates, there were around 15,000 Algonquian speakers. A group of these made up the Powhatan confederacy of tribes. The Algonquins had lived in this area since the end of the last ice age. Their agricultural system worked in harmony with nature, of whose seasonal rhythms and balances they had an innate understanding. They grew their own food, fished in the bountiful rivers and hunted in the forests. The Powhatans believed that the land belonged to everyone in the tribe, and that their chiefs were stewards rather than owners.

The lives of the Powhatans centred around their intricate communities, which were united in a complex federation under the strong leadership of the paramount chief, Powhatan. He was a dictator who demanded military support and taxes from all of the constituent tribes. As new tribes were conquered and absorbed into the federation, they added warriors to help protect its boundaries. In such a fluid federation, however, Chief Powhatan's rule was not in practice absolute. New evidence suggests that he exercised less control over the constituent tribes than seventeenth–century English reports assumed.

The Native Americans watched the arrival of the English colonists with some trepidation. Since the Spaniards had landed in Chesapeake Bay in 1559–61, and the English had unsuccessfully attempted to colonize Roanoke Island in the 1580s, Europeans were not new to the Powhatans. Fearing that the white men were planning the settle on their land, a war party of Paspaheghs (part of the Powhatan confederacy) attacked Jamestown within fourteen days of the colonists' arrival, wounding eleven and killing one. This, however, may not have been on Powhatan's orders.

One native American who was not immediately hostile to the newcomers was the apparent favourite of Powhatan's 100 children. She was named Pocahontas, 'the playful one' or 'little wanton'. In 1607 she was a girl of eleven or twelve, and full of 'wit and spirit'. She wore no clothes, and her head was cropped except for a long braid at the back. Pocahontas seems to have been close to her father, often at his side. She heard the news that white men had arrived in his territory and determined to see and speak to them.

The Jamestown Colonists

In order for the English colony to survive, its was essential to attract more men to Jamestown. The unspoilt landscape of Virginia held much promise. The supply ships returned to England with stories of how the rivers of Virginia were teeming with wildlife. But the reality was that the pioneers were ill-prepared to fend for themselves in the harsh, swampy conditions.

They had built a settlement surrounded by 'the boughs of trees cast together in the forme of a halfe moone'. Their church was an outdoor, roughly hewn affair, its pulpit a bar of wood nailed between two trees. But they were forced to leave the safety of their settlement to hunt for food in the surrounding forests. Hunting in these new and strange

A seventeenth-century map of Virginia, based on John Smith's map of 1606.

Pocahontas was the favourite of Chief Powhatan's 100 children.

Captain John Smith, shown here aged 37.

conditions proved difficult. The colonists were hampered by their lack of knowledge of the environment and by their fear of Native American attack.

By the end of 1607, fifty of the first hundred colonists had died of malaria or starvation. Few of the remaining men had the practical skills or the courage to take command of the ailing settlement. But one man, Captain John Smith, a soldier and diplomat, emerged as the natural leader. In his most detailed account of the colony, *Generall Historie of Virginia*, which was published in 1624, Smith explained the seriousness of the colonists' plight:

> As yet we had no houses to cover us, our tents were rotten, and our Cabbins worse than nought . . . Most of our chiefest men either sicke or discontented, the rest being in such despaire, as they would rather starve and rot with idlenes, then [sic] be persuaded to do any thing for their owne reliefe . . .

Smith advocated that a strong line should be taken against the Native Americans. However, he was prepared to make frequent trips into uncharted Native American territory to trade for supplies that would enable the colony to survive. The colonists traded their shovels, hatchets and axes, but the Powhatans loved most of all the easily-made blue glass beads that the English brought. They also loved the metal goods brought from the Old World – copper kettles were immediately cut up, the pieces worn as ornaments. In return, the English received the food they so badly needed.

Smith learned to speak Algonquian and used his newly acquired skills to lie to the Indians, telling them that he and his English comrades had arrived there to escape the Spanish and that they wished to trade, not colonize. Smith remarked:

> They are inconstant in everie thing, but what feare constraineth them to keep. Craftie, timerous [sic] quicke of apprehension and very ingenuous [sic]. Some are of disposition fearefull, some bold, most cautelous [sic], all Savage. Generally covetous of copper, beads, and such like trash. They are soone moved to anger and so malitious, that they seldome forget an injury.

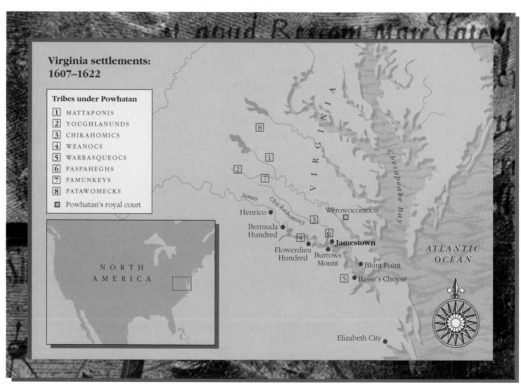

Virginia settlements: 1607–1622

Tribes under Powhatan

1. MATTAPONIS
2. YOUGHLANUNDS
3. CHIKAHOMICS
4. WEANOCS
5. WARRASQUEOCS
6. PASPAHEGHS
7. PAMUNKEYS
8. PATAWOMECKS

☐ Powhatan's royal court

The saving of John Smith by Pocahontas. (Painting of Pocahontas and John Smith *by Victor Nehlig, 1874.)*

The English viewed the Powhatans only as people who could help or hinder their larger imperial aims. Sensing this, the Powhatans mistrusted Smith. In October 1607, a hunting party of Pamunkey Indians encountered Smith on the Chickahominy River, took him prisoner, and paraded him before the Powhatans, 'singing and yelling out such hellish notes and screeches; being strangely painted, every one his quiver of Arrowes, and at his backe a club; on his arme a Fox or an Otters skinne . . . their heads and shoulders painted red . . .'.

After several weeks of captivity, Smith was brought before Powhatan himself at Werowocomoco, the rich royal court. The chief was a tall, well-proportioned man of around sixty, with, according to Smith, 'a sower looke'. A ritual meeting of Powhatan and his chiefs would decide Smith's fate. As Smith himself reported:

> The conclusion was, two great stones were brought before Powhatan: then as many as could layd hands on him [Smith], dragged him to them, and thereon laid his head, and being ready with their clubs, to beate oute his braines . . .

But then (or so the Captain tells us in the *Generall Historie*) Smith was saved from death by a remarkable occurrence. Seeing that the Englishman would be clubbed to death, Pocahontas threw herself between him and his attackers and boldly took his head in her arms in order to save him. Powhatan's heart softened. He spared Smith's life and in doing so probably saved the lives of the English colonists. He also made Smith an honorary member of the tribe and allowed him to return to Jamestown, a day's journey away, on 1 January 1608.

Some historians believe that Smith's own account of his salvation does not stand up to scrutiny. His prescribed form of execution was not one meted out to foreigners; no contemporary of his described Pocahontas as having saved him; and he changed his account twice between the incident in 1607 and the publication of his *Generall Historie* in 1624. He may have exaggerated or manufactured the danger from which he was saved by Pocahontas, or he may have misunderstood the circumstances of his captivity.

However, the myth was strong enough to alter the way the English colonists thought of the Native Americans. The English wanted to believe in Pocahontas, or in a figure like her. During 1608 she became a frequent visitor to the Jamestown settlement, and possibly learnt English and began to copy the customs of the colonists. According to William Strachey's account in *The Historie of Travaile into Virginnia Britannia* in 1612, she would:

> 'gett the boyes forth with her into the markett place and make them wheele, falling on their handes turning their heeles upwardes, whome she would follow, and wheele so her self naked as she was all the Fort over'.

Pacific Overtures

In October 1608 two more ships arrived from England carrying another seventy hopeful colonists and winter supplies for the whole colony. The new colonists, however, were as ill-prepared as their predecessors, and many perished of disease and starvation in the hard winter of 1608–9.

When Pocahontas visited Jamestown in the spring, she learnt that half the colonists had died, and that the remainder could not survive without help. As Smith described it, she immediately ordered gifts of food and supplies to be brought from her father's tribe. It was this act which ultimately saved the English and allowed them to maintain the colony. Smith wrote of Pocahontas: 'She was the instrument that saved this colony from death, famine and utter confusion.'

The remainder of the year was easier for the colonists. Again, Smith's account seems centred only on Pocahontas, although Powhatan himself sent regular supplies of Indian corn either directly or through one of the subordinate tribes; Powhatan also exchanged gifts with Smith, and with this assistance the colonists lasted until the autumn.

But, in helping the white man to such an extent, Pocahontas had angered her father, who, as the year wore on, was growing weary of Smith's lies and broken promises. 'Many do inform me your coming is not for trade,' he complained, 'but to invade my people and possess my country.' By the end of 1608 he concluded that the colonists had no intention of leaving and decided to drive them out. In turn, Smith determined to attack Powhatan at Werowocomoco and seize his provisions. He set out in December and reached the royal stronghold in January 1609. Both Smith and Powhatan planned to ambush each other, and it is probable that Pocahontas warned the English of a potential attack and so saved them from heavy losses.

Both sides prosecuted a scrappy war throughout the spring of 1609, after which an uneasy truce was reached. When hostilities ceased, the English tried hard to learn the Powhatan techniques of hunting and foraging, in order to free themselves from dependence on Powhatan's generosity.

In these early treasure-hunting days, the Virginia Company's London investors expected the colonists to discover wealth or the means to it, to claim possession of the land they discovered, and to make its inhabitants the subjects of King James. With these aims in view, more English colonists set out for the New World. When a new group arrived from London in the summer of 1609, the English tried to dissipate the resulting tension and alleviate the crowding by establishing new settlements. The Powhatans saw this as a breach of the spring truce.

Yet it was not Powhatan who eventually drove Smith from Jamestown. In early October 1609, after returning from a visit to Powhatan's court, he was severely burnt in a powder explosion which:

> tore the flesh from his body and thighes, nine or ten inches square in a most pitifull manner; but to quench the tormenting fire, frying him in his cloathes he leaped over-board in the deepe river, where ere they could recover him he was neere drowned. Mossiker

He set sail for England immediately to have his wounds treated. He said nothing to Pocahontas or the Powhatan girls who had become friends and had often visited Jamestown. When Pocahontas asked for him, the colonists told her that he was dead. He never returned to Virginia.

Without Smith, the colonists were more vulnerable than ever. Powhatan realized this and determined to eliminate them once and for all. He banned all forms of trade with Jamestown, and launched a guerrilla campaign of ambushes and assassinations.

He then dispatched Pocahontas to the northern edge of his territory, where she could be of no help to the English. He knew that the best chance of starving the English off his land would come during the next winter, of 1609–10. The Chief was proved right, and by the following spring, the English had fallen into despair. They lacked leadership, supplies, and the Native American help which had sustained them before. By May, only 100 of the 220 colonists who had settled in Virginia since 1607 were still alive; sixty of them were in Jamestown. The colonists resorted to eating dogs, cats and rats. Some turned to cannibalism:

> Men did things which seem incredible. To dig up corpses out of graves and eat them.
> One of the colony murdered his wife, chopped her in pieces and salted her for food.

English despair meant Spanish rejoicing. Philip III of Spain knew that his colonies to the south were thriving, and that he could profit from the failure of the English at Jamestown. The English in North America were a heartbeat from extinction.

Love and Tobacco

The Jamestown settlement did not perish. On 21 May 1610, two more ships, under Sir Thomas Gates and Sir George Somers, arrived from England. Aboard was John Rolfe, a twenty-eight-year-old gentleman farmer from the east of England. Rolfe noticed that tobacco, a luxury in England, grew wild in Virginia. He began to experiment with new tobacco leaves imported from the West Indies. After two years, he produced a fine leaf perfectly suited to the Virginian soil and climate, 'as pleasant, sweet and strong as any under the sun'. At last the colony had found a product to export.

This good fortune for the English coincided with better winter preparations under their new commander, Lord de la Warr. The colonists survived the winter comfortably, and set about fighting the Powhatans in the early months of 1611. As the English became stronger and better organized, and as their tobacco production took up more

The Marriage of Pocahontas. *(Painting by Henry Brueckner, 1855.)*

and more of his land, Chief Powhatan stepped up his guerrilla campaign. Relations between the Native Americans and the colonists deteriorated, with threats on both sides. Powhatan offered an ultimatum: 'Depart my country, or confine yourselves to Jamestown only. Otherwise I will command my people to kill you.' He refused to sell any more corn to the colonists, and allowed raiding parties to ambush them as they worked in the fields.

The English concluded a 'peace' in December 1612, but continued to explore the land to establish new colonies to follow Henrico, which had already been settled two summers before. Then in April 1613 an English captain, Samuel Argall, struck on a plan to end the conflict with the Native Americans. At Patawomeck, where Pocahontas, now a woman of about eighteen, had arrived to 'exchange some of her fathers commodities for theirs', he lured the Princess aboard his ship, where she was lavishly entertained but held prisoner. She was then taken to Jamestown, and a ransom note was sent to Powhatan demanding the return of English hostages, arms and food in exchange for his daughter. Negotiations lasted a year, but Powhatan knew that Pocahontas would come to no harm.

Meanwhile, the English had been strengthening their position in Virginia, with new settlements at Bermuda Hundred and Elizabeth City. But it was to Henrico that Pocahontas was taken, in the care of a clergyman, Alexander Whitaker. While there, she met John Rolfe. They fell in love. Rolfe wrote to Sir Thomas Dale of:

> Pokanhuntas to whom my hartie and best thought are, and have for a long time been so intangled, and inthralled in so intricate a laborinth, that I was even awearied to unwind myself thereout. (Mossiker)

Rolfe became obsessed by what seemed to him Pocahontas' strange and exotic allure. He struggled not only with these feelings, but with the taboo against relations between English and Native Americans and his sense that Pocahontas was:

> one whose education has bin rude, her manners barbarous, her generation accursed,
> and so discrepant in all nuriture from myself that oftentimes with feare and trembling
> I have ended my private controversie with this: surely these are wicked investigations,
> hatched by him who seeketh and delighteth in man's destruction . . . (Mossiker)

With the help of the Reverend Whitaker, both Rolfe and Pocahontas kept the devil at bay. Whitaker taught Pocahontas the Christian message and European customs. She made an apt student; Rolfe later wrote approvingly of 'her desire to be taught and instructed in the knowledge of God, her capableness of understanding, her aptness and willingness'.

She was baptized into the Church of England in 1614, taking the name Rebecca. With the permission of Sir Thomas Dale, Rolfe and Rebecca were married in Jamestown early in April 1614. Remarkably enough, Powhatan approved of the match, and sent his uncle, Opitchapan, to represent him at the ceremony. He was tired of war with the English, and the marriage promised – as Dale had rightly guessed – a face-saving way for both sides to end the hostilities. At last the English had a period of peace on which to build. It proved vital not only for their agriculture, which they could now concentrate on without harassment, but also for their status in London. For the first time since they had landed seven years before, the English in Virginia looked and felt secure.

Pocahontas in London.

In London, the Virginia Company had lost the financial support of King James, who believed Rolfe's marriage to Pocahontas, the daughter of a savage king and enemy to England, to be an act of treason. The Virginia Company could therefore expect little help from the Crown. Instead, it turned to the Church. More Native Americas could be converted to the Church of England if sufficient funds were made available; Pocahontas' conversion would then be the first of many.

In 1615 a group of Virginia Company officers held a great lottery in the churchyard of St Paul's Cathedral in London to raise money for the 'worthy Christian enterprise'. The lottery was successful, and it encouraged the Virginia Company to plan an even more daring fund-raising scheme: Pocahontas should come to visit England and be brought before the Crown, clergy and commoners. The popular court playwright Ben Jonson and the architect and designer Inigo Jones would conjure a masque for her entertainment: her story would be the story of the new colony of Virginia.

So it was that on 12 June 1616 the twenty-one-year-old Pocahontas arrived at Plymouth with Rolfe and their young son Thomas, *en route* to London. With them they brought ten Native American maids and Pocahontas' brother-in-law, Tomocomo. The couple's fame had gone before them, and all London waited for the Indian Princess.

Pocahontas, now 'Lady Rebecca Rolfe', dressed in fashionable English clothing and sporting her newly learned European manners, was quickly shown off to London society. The Virginia Company lobbied for her presentation at court, urging the colony's first leader, John Smith, to write to Queen Anne in praise of Pocahontas. In Smith's words (in a letter which did not come to light until his *Generall Historie* of 1624), she was:

> the first Christian ever of that nation, the first Virginian ever spake English, or had a
> child in marriage by an Englishman, a matter surely, if my meaning bee truly
> considered and well understood, worthy a Prince's understanding . . . (Mossiker)

King James I of England.

Pocahontas was duly presented to King James and Queen Anne, and she saw the Jonson and Jones masque *The Vision of Delight* in the great Banqueting House at Whitehall on Twelfth Night 1617. Fêted and applauded throughout London, she was entertained at Lambeth Palace by the Bishop of London. Everywhere she went, Rebecca Rolfe bore herself, according to the contemporary Samuel Purchas, 'as a Daughter of a King, and was accordingly respected not only by the great Virginia Company, which allowed provision for herself and her sonne, but of divers particular persons of Honour'.

Away from London, at Brentford, where Pocahontas received a stream of courtiers and dignitaries, she was reunited with John Smith, whom she had thought dead. Smith commented: 'divers courtiers and others of my acquaintance [who] hath gone with me to see her generally concluded that they did think God did have a great hand in her conversion, and they have seen many English ladies worse favored, proportioned, and behaviored'.

The visit lasted seven months. England's most famous colonial family was due to return to Virginia late in March 1617 aboard the *George* from Gravesend. The visit had been successful beyond the avaricious dreams of the Virginia Company. But while English society agreed with Pocahontas, the English climate did not. While waiting at Gravesend, she fell ill, probably with pneumonia or possibly tuberculosis. Her last words to Rolfe were 'All must die. 'Tis enough the child liveth.' She was buried on 21 March 1617 in St George's Church, Gravesend, alone and far from her home. She is listed in the parish register and 'Rebecca Wrolfe, Wyffe of Thomas [John] Wrolfe Gent. A Virginia lady Borne'.

After Pocahontas

The Pocahontas story became the first legend of the English New World. John Rolfe returned to Virginia and worked prodigiously hard at growing tobacco. The new tobacco industry he had founded expanded rapidly, with new plantations along the St James River, and the demand for labour soon outstripped the capacity of the English workforce. The Orinoco tobacco leaf fared particularly well, and by 1617 the streets of Jamestown were planted with it. The tobacco frenzy required more and more land, which the colonists took from the Native Americans.

In 1619 a Dutch ship that put in to Jamestown changed the history of America. On board were the first Africans, 'twenty and odd negroes', to arrive in North America, victims of the Atlantic slave trade, which was flourishing by the early seventeenth century. They were put to work by the English as bound servants – as were many Europeans who arrived between 1620 and 1680 – and were, at least theoretically, able to work their way to freedom. The system of bound servants was impractical and, in essence, slavery had arrived with the first Africans. African manpower was to run the tobacco industry for the next 200 years. Slavery was to be the great issue which set Americans against each other in the American Civil War of 1861–65.

There were other repercussions from the colonization of Jamestown. For the English, it had once been the model colony. The Christian virtues of perseverance and faith had not only prevailed in a foreign land but had begun to convert the foreigners who lived there: Pocahontas, 'Lady Rebecca', was the first Christian or Church of English convert of the New World. She and Rolfe had fired the imagination of a generation of new settlers: the Mayflower, which carried the English puritans to New England, arrived in Plymouth in 1620 on a wave of New World hope.

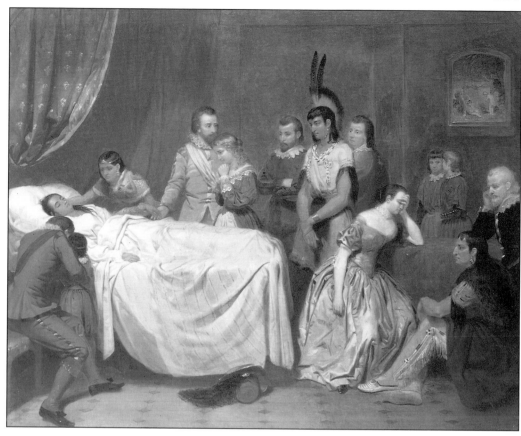

The Death of Pocahontas. *(Painting by Junius Brutus Stearns, 1850.)*

The forgotten participants in this drama were Pocahontas' own people, the Powhatan. In the years between 1607 and 1623 they had seen 5,000 colonists arrive and take their land and its resources. Powhatan died a broken and disappointed man in 1618. His brother Opechancanough became the leader of the Powhatan, and was able to prosecute his policy of fierce and unwavering opposition to all white incursion and to reverse Powhatan's policy of conciliation, an attitude which had given the colonists so much time and leisure to establish themselves.

Under Opechancanough, the Powhatan declared war on the English in 1622. But by then it was too late, for the colonists were well established and, as an economically viable society, were to be supported from London. When the Virginia Company collapsed in 1624 and Virginia became a Crown colony, it was clear that the English had linked their national identity to the success of the Virginia colony and others like it in the New World. From that moment, the colony would receive royal help in defending it against challenges from Native Americans and foreign colonists.

The land which had once belonged to the Native Americans had been taken from them, and that was to be their story until well into the twentieth century. Two hundred years after the first colonists arrived, the Creek Chief, Speckled Snake, said this to his tribe about the white man, the 'great father'. It was the story of John Smith, John Rolfe, Powhatan and Pocahontas in Virginia:

Brothers! I have listened to many talks from our great father. When he first came over the wide waters, he was but a little man . . . very little. His legs were cramped by sitting long in his big boat, and he begged for a little land to light his fire on . . . Brothers! I have listened to a great many talks from our great father. But they always began and ended in this – Get a little further; you are too near me.

· 9 ·
Colonial
RETREAT

THE ANGLO–FRENCH BATTLE IN QUEBEC LEADS TO
FRANCE – AND BRITAIN – LOSING CONTROL OF AMERICA.

W INSTON CHURCHILL called it the first world war. For the eighteenth-century English writer Horace Walpole it was the war that set the world on fire; and for his contemporary the French writer Voltaire, it was a fight for 'a few acres of snow'. It was a personal encounter between four men: two British, one French and one Canadian. It was the battle, on 13 September 1759, for the city of Quebec, the gateway to North America.

Portrait of General James Wolfe (after J.S.C. Schaak).

God, it is said, cannot alter the past. Historians can. The battle of Quebec was, in a sense, also a battle to determine the fate of 'the past'. England and France fought for the right to call America their own, to hear it speak their language and see it adopt their customs – to establish the imprint of their own cultural traditions for future generations. North America was an international battleground as well as a place for peaceful settlement; the English and French had been in conflict there since 1613 when an English squadron attacked French trading posts. Echoes of that battle can be heard today as the French language continues to attempt to find the means to ensure its own survival. But its final phase began in the St Lawrence River in 1759. It was there that four men, plucked for an instant from the tide of world events, emerged to shape the destiny of a nation. They were, on the British side, General James Wolfe and Admiral Charles Saunders; and, on the French side, the Marquis de Montcalm and the Marquis de Vaudreuil. They had come far from Europe to the fierce, bloody encounter at Quebec, and carried with them 200 years of their countries' hopes for a future in the New World. They were to have a sudden awakening.

The British and French Territories

The battle for Quebec between the French and the British altered the history of North America, territory having changed hands several times since the early seventeenth century. This was an age when diplomacy depended on raw power, on armies in the field, on alliances with local inhabitants, on delivery of supplies by sea. The Quebec campaign

An eighteenth-century engraving of Quebec.

would decide the future of a new continent. More than that, the outcome of the battle so altered the status quo that two revolutions followed in its wake: the American War of Independence in 1776 and the French Revolution in 1789.

When Wolfe, Saunders, Montcalm and Vaudreuil came to face each other at Quebec, there was a fifth character in the drama they were about to enact: the St Lawrence River. This river was the key to French North America. It had been explored by two Frenchmen, Jacques Cartier in 1534, who founded Quebec, and Samuel de Champlain in 1608, who developed the city. By the 1750s, the territories of New France stretched from the contested ground of Nova Scotia in the north-east down to the mouth of the Mississippi – around one-third of the present-day United States and part of modern Canada. New France was a river empire, built along the St Lawrence in the north and the Mississippi in the south. In the north-east, French power thought to lay claim to present-day Nova Scotia, New Brunswick and Quebec, forming a region known as Acadia; to the west lay the vast untapped resources of the interior. Along the St Lawrence valley, the French grew wheat and trapped beaver for fur. These were the colonists' main products, although they had grown timber, hemp, and flax for ship-building and were manufacturing ironware. The St Lawrence valley was also home to whalers and seal hunters, who produced oil and skins.

South-west of the St Lawrence, the French ran trading routes down to the Gulf of Mexico. To the south and east stretched the rolling woods of New England and the thirteen English colonies which had gradually been established since the first settlements in Virginia in the early seventeenth century (see Chapter 8). These were threatened by the proximity of the French and by their alliances with Indian tribes from New Orleans on the Gulf of Mexico north to the Great Lakes, alliances which helped to pin down the British along the Atlantic coast. North and east along both shores of the St Lawrence was a wilderness protected by the greatest battlement in North America: Louisbourg. So powerful was it that the French King Louis XV (1710–74) imagined he could see its fortifications on the

Paris horizon. On average, 150 ships passed through Louisbourg each year: only Boston, New York and Philadelphia saw more naval traffic. As long as Louisbourg and the related fort of Fort Beausejour in Nova Scotia held, French North America was safe.

The French colonies were, by and large, more concerned with refinement than the English. One traveller who had toured both in 1749 found the Canadians (as the French colonists were already known) more agreeable:

> the difference between the favour and politeness which is my lot [in Canada] and that of the English provinces is like that between heaven and earth . . . the people [in Canada], even the common man, are much more polite than the people in the English provinces, and especially compared to the Dutch. (Eccles)

The French had imported their own social structures, and the upper classes of Quebec and Montreal were urbane and sophisticated, even if they were already tinged with the decadence which was to bring about the destruction of the French aristocracy in the revolution of 1789. The first road south and west from Quebec to Montreal had been built in 1734; French fashions and styles followed. By 1760, Montreal was a place to rival any in Europe. A British observer wrote:

> From the number of silk robes, laced coats and powdered heads of both sexes, and almost all ages that are perambulating the streets from morning to night, a stranger would be induced to believe Montreal is entirely inhabited by people of independent and plentiful fortunes. (Eccles)

A view of the St Lawrence river.

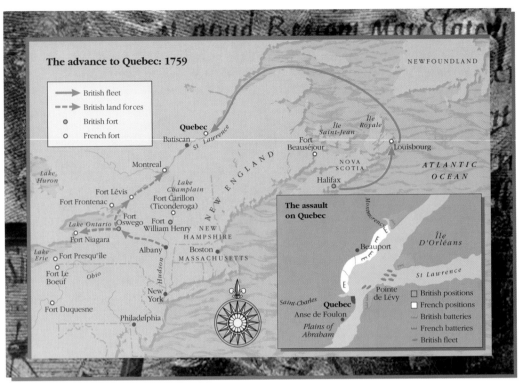

The advance to Quebec: 1759

British fleet
British land forces
British fort
French fort

NEWFOUNDLAND

Quebec
Batiscan
Île Royale
Île Saint-Jean
Louisbourg

Montreal
Fort Beauséjour
NOVA SCOTIA
Halifax
ATLANTIC OCEAN

Lake Huron

NEW ENGLAND

Fort Lévis
Lake Champlain
Fort Frontenac
Fort Carillon (Ticonderoga)
Fort Oswego
Lake Ontario
Fort William Henry
NEW HAMPSHIRE
Fort Niagara
Albany
Boston
MASSACHUSETTS
Lake Erie Fort Presqu'île
Ohio
Fort Le Boeuf
New York
Fort Duquesne
Philadelphia
Hudson

The assault on Quebec
Montmorency
Île D'Orléans
Beauport
St Lawrence
Pointe de Lévy
Saint-Charles
Quebec
Anse de Foulon
Plains of Abraham

British positions
French positions
British batteries
French batteries
British fleet

But Quebec was the jewel in the French crown. A city of around 8,000 inhabitants, it was the administrative, religious and commercial centre of the northern colonies. In the upper town, high above the St Lawrence, were the imposing Cathédrale and the Château St-Louis, residence of the Governor-General; near by was the convent of the Ursulines and the Hôtel Dieu, palace of the Bishop. In the lower town were the docks, warehouses and market-places. The forty-four streets which threaded through them were unpaved and liable to turn to mud when it rained.

Quebec was also the military stronghold of New France. The city's fortified walls stood on a 200-foot rocky cliff which dominates the St Lawrence River, 750 miles inland from the sea at the point where it narrows into the Great Lakes basin at the confluence of the St Charles, the Montmorency and the Chaudière rivers. Opposite Quebec, the Ile d'Orléans (4.8 miles wide and 27 miles long) splits the St Lawrence into two narrower channels, each constricted to north and south by treacherous tidal flats. The French thought it impossible for any warships to navigate the St Lawrence east or west beyond the island.

North America was a colonial war waiting to happen. The population of New France was probably between 55,000 and 60,000 (although some estimates put the figure as high as 82,000), overwhelmingly outnumbered by the one and a half million English colonists. The French colonies failed to attract enough immigrants, and this in turn made it hard for them to expand. The opposite was true of the English colonies, which enjoyed easier access along the eastern seaboard of North America and whose population tended to form communities whereas the French were more likely to work as trappers and to settle in smaller groups. These men and women, representatives of their respective countries of origin, were to act out European rivalries on North American soil. Resources were plentiful but access to them was difficult because routes were inadequate and river travel often hazardous.

Since 1670, when the Hudson's Bay Company had been formed under royal charter by Charles II, furs had become a staple export of the new colonies, but the animals themselves were becoming increasingly scarce. In 1747 the English colonists formed the Ohio

Land Company to open the fertile Ohio valley far to the south, and well to the west of their seaboard colonies; two years later it sent out the first scouts to explore both banks of the Ohio. Knowing that the British wanted land, the local Indians, with savage irony, stuffed soil into the mouth of any English colonist they killed.

But the British could not expand west without encountering the French; and the French could have no eastern access to their territories without crossing the British. In 1753, the Governor-General of New France responded to the English scouting activities on the Ohio by ordering 2,000 troops and engineers to build a line of forts down from the Great Lakes along the Ohio as far as Louisiana. This was the land of James Fenimore Cooper (author of the 1826 novel, *The Last of the Mohicans*), of frontier myth and pioneer adventure.

The first was Fort Presqu'île on the south shores of Lake Erie; it was followed by Fort Le Bouef. As the French moved inexorably into the Ohio valley, English settlers from the coastal colony of Virginia – who had already marked out the land for their own – became increasingly worried. They protested, and sent a delegation to Fort Le Boeuf, which was brusquely dismissed by the French commander. Roused to anger, the Virginians returned with a fighting force and attempted to establish their own fort on the Ohio River, only to be ejected by a French force of 500 men. When the French built Fort Duquesne further south on the upper reaches of the river, it proved too great a threat to the Virginian settlers, who sent soldiers under George Washington. He successfully ambushed a French detachment, but was forced to surrender to the numerically superior French at Great Meadows on 28 May 1754. Washington limped back to Virginia, bloodied and defeated. The English colonies then called on London to protect them and to drive the French out of the Ohio valley and the Great Lakes region.

The Road to War

Philippe de Rigaud Marquis de Vaudreuil, Govenor of Canada. (Painting by Henri Beau.)

Throughout 1754 and 1755 the French and British manoeuvred carefully for a winning position in North America. In October 1754 the British Major-General Edward Braddock was ordered to leave for North America with 800 men to take Fort Duquesne, sailing from London six months later. Braddock's land forces were to be the southern arm of a two-fronted offensive intended to sweep the French out of North America. At the same time, the British colonial forces were to launch a naval attack in the north to take the French forts at Niagara, at Lake Champlain and on the Nova Scotia border. But French intelligence gained a copy of Braddock's orders, and France immediately dispatched a convoy to Louisbourg and Quebec. A British fleet under Admiral Edward Boscawen pursued and caught the French convoy off Newfoundland, but captured only two ships; the rest, with eight companies of troops, reached their destinations safely. With them was the man the French had just appointed Governor-General of New France. His name was Pierre de Rigaud, Marquis de Vaudreuil (1703–1779), and he was destined to play a pivotal role in the defence of Quebec.

Command of the sea was vital for the European powers, both of which were two months' passage from the theatre of war. In addition, the St Lawrence became impassable in the winter months, in effect dictating a campaign season from May to September. In 1757, the French navy was ravaged by an epidemic of typhus; seamen and dockers fled the ports of metropolitan France, and French ships sometimes had to put to sea with skeleton crews of Frenchmen press-ganged into service. The British took advantage of their enemy's predicament and kept the French blockaded in their home ports. More than 300 French ships and 8,000 sailors were captured in the naval engagement. By 1758, the Atlantic and the route to the St Lawrence were dominated by the Royal Navy, the most powerful in the world.

The French fared better on land. Their forces consisted of an alliance of regular French army, Canadian militia made up of colonial volunteers, and Indian bands – Iowas, Ottawas and Hurons. On the British side were the army regulars and the settlers from the thirteen colonies. The guerrilla tactics of France's Indian allies were ideal for the densely wooded terrain: the fighters lived off the land, travelled light and fast, without baggage and unencumbered by a military structure. The British fighting style had evolved not in the humid summers and sharp winters of New England forests, but on the open plains of Europe. It was therefore better suited to open spaces, cavalry charges and collective discipline. But the tactics which had brought success for the British under the Duke of Marlborough at Blenheim in 1704 or most recently in the bloody encounter with the Scots at Culloden in 1746 were of no use in America.

Defeat for the British was thus all but inevitable. On 9 July 1755 Braddock was routed at Fort Duquesne by Canadian militia and their Indian allies. But there was another reason for this overwhelming victory: the Canadians, spotting that the organized British reloaded their muskets on the signal of a drumbeat, killed the officers and drummers, including Braddock himself. As a result, panic and confusion reigned in the British ranks. Two-thirds of Braddock's 2,200 force were slaughtered or captured, his artillery was lost, and, worse, the papers he was carrying, detailing the British plans of attack in the northeast, fell into enemy hands. A direct result of this new intelligence was the failure of the English settlers to take the fort at Lake Champlain after it had been strengthened by French reinforcements. An indecisive but crucial battle ensued, and thereafter the southern route through modern-day New York into Canada was effectively cut off. Despite this military triumph, the Canadians who had been victorious over Braddock thought that the French at Lake Champlain should have performed more creditably against the English settlers. These complaints struck a familiar note in Franco–Canadian rivalry.

The British forces had better fortune in Nova Scotia, where they took Fort Beausejour in late 1755 and diminished the French threat from the north. However, they then embarked on a policy which in the twentieth century has become known as 'ethnic cleansing', brutally expelling Indians and settlers from the area known as Acadia; even those who had pledged allegiance to King George II (1683–1760). Most of the Acadians fled to what later became Louisiana where their descendents still represent a French influence; the rest were dispersed to France, England, the eastern seaboard and the West Indies. No single British act of war could have done more to inspire the French and bind them to the Canadian settlers in the fight for their country. Throughout 1755 and 1756, the new Governor-General of New France, Vaudreuil, launched incursions into British protected territory, forcing the English settlers to dedicate large numbers of men in defensive positions along the lengthy western border with New France. These incursions also kept the French alliance with the Indians intact. Moreover, French forces controlled the rivers flowing into the Great Lakes region: this meant they could move more troops further and more quickly than the English settlers.

The land war, at that point, looked unwinnable for the British. One Anglo-American observer compared their position with that of the French:

> Our colonies are all open and exposed, without any manner of security or defense. Theirs are protected and secured by numbers of forts and fortresses. Our men in America are scattered up and down the woods, upon their plantations, in remote and distant provinces. Theirs are collected together in forts and garrisons. Our people are nothing but a set of farmers and planters, used only to the axe or hoe. Theirs are not only well trained and disciplined but they are used to arms from their infancy among the Indians; and are reckoned equal, if not superior in that part of the world to veteran troops. Our people are not to be drawn together from so many different governments, views, and interests; are unable, unwilling, or remiss to march against an enemy, or dare not stir, for fear of being attacked at home. They are all under one government, subject to command like a military people . . . and they have almost all the Indians of that continent to join them. (Eccles)

A series of defeats was turning 1755 into a catastrophic year for the British. The French and their Indian allies were marauding settlements and lonely farmhouses along the frontier, and the British could do little to defend such a long border. But what looked like a reversal of fortune occurred later in 1755 with the capture of the French commander, Jean-Armond Baron de Dieskau, at Lake George. In March 1756, however, the French sent a reputable soldier to take his place at the head of their forces in North America. His name was Louis-Joseph de St Véran, Marquis de Montcalm (1712–59).

The Men of War

The forty-four-year-old Montcalm had come out of retirement to fight in North America. Although a fine professional soldier, he was accustomed to the European style of warfare, having fought in the War of the Austrian Succession (1740–48), in which he was twice wounded. A short man, overweight, vivacious, vain, stubborn and opinionated, he was to act as second-in-command to the Governor-General of New France, Vaudreuil. The two men were very different, and when they first encountered one another in May 1756 it was at once clear that this crucial relationship would be fraught and uneasy. It was a meeting between the Old and the New Worlds.

Louis-Joseph Marquis de Montcalm. (Painting by Antoine Louis Francois Sergent.)

Vaudreuil, a large, good-natured and bluff man, was born and bred a Canadian, and he was convinced that the French had no real love of Canada. In contrast to Montcalm's preference for more formal European strategy, he believed in the successful guerrilla tactics which had foiled the British the previous year. He knew that the English colonies depended more on England for military aid than Canada relied on France. Above all, he knew how to handle the Indian allies.

Relations between the two men rapidly deteriorated. Montcalm said of Vaudreuil: 'However equal M. de Vaudreuil may be in talent, he will always have one basic fault: he is Canadian.' And he wrote to his wife on their estate in the South of France:

> I am subordinate general-in-chief, passing on messages, not involved in anything on some occasions, in everything on others: esteemed, respected, loved, jealous, hated, high, simple, sociable, difficult, polite, devoted, gallant and much desirous of peace. (Chapais)

A view of Quebec showing the entire story of the battle: the British troops landing, scaling the cliff face and establishing troop formation on the Plains of Abraham. (Published in London by Laurie & Whittle, Fleet Street, 1797.)

Two years later, in 1758, Montcalm would write of his 'secret hatred' of Vaudreuil: 'I have a greater reputation and more virtue than he' (Chapais). It is hardly surprising that two such determined egoists should clash, in culture, style and approach. Montcalm's classical outlook as a European-trained general led him to believe, in any case, that the French position was untenable, despite the successes achieved in the course of a concerted campaign throughout 1756 and 1757 – at Fort Oswego, Fort Carillon (also called Ticonderoga) on Lake Champlain and Fort William Henry in the Hudson valley towards Albany. South of Albany lay New York, and to the east, Boston. If the French thrust south from Albany, the English colonies could be split. In fact, British North America was now under threat and would have fallen to the French if Montcalm had indeed pressed on south to Fort Edward from Fort William Henry in August 1757. He chose not to. It was the worst decision of his career, and, it is arguable, one which ultimately cost France the continent. If he had pressed forward, the English colonies would have been divided, their supply lines cut and the colonies to the north-east isolated.

Montcalm's hesitation gave the British time to prepare a bold invasion of Canada. For them, the timing was perfect. Since his appointment in 1756 William Pitt, the bullish new Secretary of State for War, had been evolving a plan to crush the French and sweep them out of North America. An intelligent, aggressive, energetic and decisive politician, he saw the advantage of engaging the French overseas, attacking them where they were weakest. On 18 May that year war had been declared in Europe between the French and the British, the start of the Seven Years War. While the French concentrated on the war with England in Europe, the British developed a daring plan: to concentrate their forces in North America.

Assisted by the Royal Navy's command of the seas, Pitt sent regiment after regiment to the colonies until by 1758 the British troops in North America numbered 140,000 regulars and marines alongside one-quarter of the Royal Navy, and 22,000 colonial soldiers and militia. The French had only 12 of their 395 army battalions in North America, together with 2,000 marines and their Indian allies. Their contrasting global strategy was to occupy large amounts of enemy territory with relatively small forces. This policy inevitably caused Montcalm and Vaudreuil to feel neglected by Paris.

What Pitt planned were campaigns against Fort Duquesne in the south under Brigadier John Forbes; against the French forts on Lake Champlain under Major-General James Abercromby; and against Louisbourg in the north under Colonel Jeffrey Amherst and Admiral Edward Boscawen. Principal among Amherst's brigade commanders was James Wolfe, in charge of an elite force of 1,200 troops.

Wolfe (1727–59) was a weak, sickly, neurotic and mercurial thirty-one-year-old who suffered from tuberculosis and kidney disease. Yet he had extraordinary determination. He had performed with savage efficiency in the English action against the Scots at Culloden in 1746. In 1748, after fighting in Belgium, he had been stationed in Glasgow as a major in the 20th Foot Regiment. To each assignment he brought intelligence and dedication. He had a selflessness instilled by the professional and patriotic duty typical of the soldiers of his time. He wrote to his mother as he embarked on the Louisbourg campaign: 'All that I wish for myself is that I may at all times be ready and firm to meet the fate we cannot shun, and to die gracefully and properly when the hour comes' (DNB).

The hour had come for two nations and four men: on the French side, the clubbable Vaudreuil and the aristocratic Montcalm; and on the British the calculating Wolfe together with the naval commander Vice-Admiral Charles Saunders (1715–1775), a pirate by inclination who had risen to prominence in the Royal Navy by clever machination. He was to attempt to navigate the treacherous St Lawrence River.

The Battle for Quebec

Saunders and Wolfe knew the magnitude of the task that faced the British. Indeed, some of the English colonies were already pleading for peace on any terms. Pitt had realized that the French had become so strong that taking Quebec was the only way to end the war in North America. First, however, the British had to take Louisbourg, the great fortress dominating the St Lawrence and the key to control over New France. The defences withstood a sixty-day siege under Amherst's 8,000 troops, but the fortress at last fell on 27 July 1758 with the surrender of 5,000 men, who handed over 200 cannon and vast quantities of supplies. But the year was already too far advanced for an attack on Quebec: the St Lawrence would freeze over and become impassable by October. Wolfe commented acidly: 'If this force had been properly manag'd, there was an end of the French colony in North America in one Campaign' (Eccles). Wolfe had grown impatient with Amherst's tactics, more subtle and indirect than his own.

So the British would have to return the next year. But they did not leave without laying waste the villages and towns scattered along the upper reaches of the St Lawrence. Wolfe wrote of this scorched-earth policy: 'We have done a great deal of mischief – spread the terror of His Majesty's arms through the whole gulf: but have added nothing to the reputation of them' (DNB). He returned to England, and in November informed Pitt that he would be happy to serve in North America, and particularly in the river St Lawrence, if any operations are carried on there' (DNB). He then visited the fashionable spa city of Bath in the south-west of England, where he courted Katherine Lowther, an aristocratic girl whom he intended to marry. He was called back to London and, on 12 January 1759, given the commission to command the land forces for the expedition against Quebec.

The French ship Prudent, *captured by the British at Louisbourg.*

As the French advanced, the British troops fired with a volley which 'burst forth as if from a single monstrous weapon'.

Major-General James Wolfe sailed from Portsmouth on 14 February in Saunders' flagship *Neptune* with a fleet of forty-nine ships. When they arrived at Louisbourg, Wolfe selected men from the garrison and assembled an amphibian force of 8,600 troops, twenty-two great ships, five frigates, eighteen sloops and a flotilla of transport and supply vessels. Seven hundred and fifty miles up the St Lawrence, Montcalm and Vaudreuil waited, confident that the British ships could not navigate through the difficult tidal flats of the river and that, if they did manage to, Quebec's fortifications would hold off a siege – even though the supplies for the city were stored far up the St Lawrence at Batiscan. The French forces numbered 14,000, although only half were regular army. Time and the elements favoured the French, because Wolfe might be trapped in the St Lawrence when it began to freeze over once again in mid-autumn. He had only a short campaign season.

Throughout May and June, Saunders and his team of navigators, including the young James Cook, charted the waters of the St Lawrence. Cook was later to sail to the Sandwich Islands in the Pacific, and into history as the most famous European surveyor of Australia. On the St Lawrence, he gauged the currents, plumbed the shallows and, with Saunders' navigators, drew up detailed charts of the river. It was an extraordinary feat of seamanship. With precise measuring and piloting, Saunders guided his ships safely into the channel east of Quebec city itself on 25 June. The maps made from those soundings were so accurate that they were not bettered for many years to come. The Canadian commander, Vaudreuil, could not believe his eyes: 'The enemy have passed through sixty ships of war where we dared not risk a vessel of a hundred tons.' The British were knocking at the front door of Canada.

Wolfe camped on the Ile d'Orléans, opposite Quebec. The city was defended on three sides by water and on the fourth by fortifications. Wolfe remarked:

> My antagonist has wisely shut himself up in inaccessible entrenchments, so that I
> can't get at him without spilling a torrent of blood . . . the Marquis de Montcalm is
> at the head of a great number of bad soldiers, and I am at the head of a small
> number of good ones, that wish for nothing so much as to fight him.   (DNB)

Wolfe politely informed Vaudreuil of his intention to attack the city on behalf of King George II, and observing the conventions of the time the two commanders exchanged a series of notes, often accompanied with gifts of food or wine. Wolfe himself was in poor health, suffering from dysentery, and was subject to the jeering insubordination of his deputy, George Townshend.

Hostilities began in earnest when the French sent seven fireships into the midst of the British fleet on 28 June. Wolfe had decided to batter the city into submission and to lay waste the surrounding countryside. He had written to Amherst from the *Neptune*:

> If we find that Quebec is not likely to fall into our hands . . . I propose to set the
> Town on fire with Shells, to destroy the Harvest, Houses, and Cattle, both above
> and below, to send off as many Canadians as possible to Europe, and to leave famine
> and desolation behind me . . . (DNB)

On 12 July he began an incessant artillery barrage with 32-pound guns and 13-inch mortars set up at Pointe-Lévy on the south-east bank of the river. The cannon continued firing day and night throughout July, reducing parts of the city to rubble and forcing the Canadians into safe areas of the city beyond their range. The Cathédrale was hit and burnt down on the

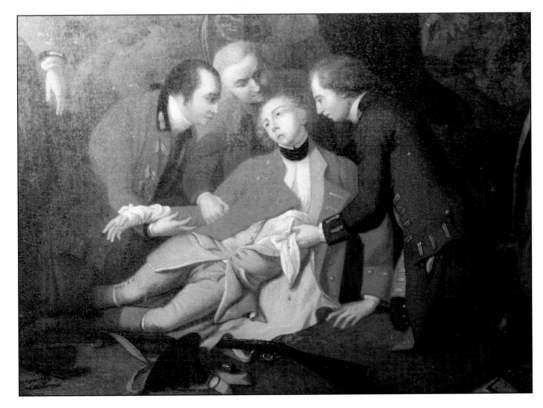

A detail from G. Roth's version of The Death of Wolfe.

22nd. Wolfe then turned to the firing of villages 100 miles down the St Lawrence and encouraged the scalping of corpses. Townshend thought it 'war of the worst shape' and Montcalm was incredulous: 'Would anyone believe that a civilized nation could become so rabid as to mutilate dead bodies in cold blood?' Wolfe's wish was to fight campaigns which were nasty, brutish and short. His relatively modern scorched-earth tactics were an affront to military protocol; this was the age, after all, when surgeons from one side were sent to tend the wounded of the other.

Montcalm had built entrenchments along the north-west bank of the St Lawrence at Beauport, on the other side of the St Charles River. As July wore on, the French dug in further, and Wolfe's costly attempts to land troops east of Beauport came to nothing. The only vulnerable side of Quebec was to the south, but Wolfe's access there was denied by two factors: the difficulty of navigating the river upstream from Quebec, and the height of the cliffs above any possible landing-place. On 18 July, however, six British ships slipped under the guns at Quebec and sailed into the narrow channel south towards Cap Rouge and Saint-Augustin. But there was still no place to land. Time was running out for Wolfe. His health was worsening, and the St Lawrence would become impassable inside two months. Unexpectedly, on a reconnaissance sortie upstream from Quebec on 8 or 9 September, he made a dramatic discovery: he realized that he could gain access to the southern side of the city and engage Montcalm's forces on the flat and open Plains of Abraham, if he were able to climb the towering cliffs with sufficient numbers of troops. He learnt that there was a tangled path up to the top of the cliff, and that the French had not thought it necessary to defend it. If he could exploit his discovery, he might just be able to overcome Quebec.

Wolfe and his command decided on a dangerous and risky plan which he executed on the dark moonless night of 13 September. He was in intense pain, and told his physician: 'Pray make me without pain for a few days and able to do my duty; that is all I want' (Connell). Wolfe knew this was his last chance to take the city. 'A vigorous blow at this juncture', he wrote, 'may determine the fate of Canada . . . The officers and men will remember what their country expects from them, and what a determined body of soldiers inured to war are capable of doing' (Reilly). He set off with 4,500 men packed into shallow longboats and followed the stern lights of the frigate *Sutherland*.

The British landed at Anse de Foulon. The French sentries patrolling the beach let them by on a password, which the British had discovered after capturing some French mariners further down the St Lawrence. Wolfe's men were now free to clear the cliff path of the tree-trunks and undergrowth which concealed it. Wolfe assessed the climb: 'I don't think we can with any possible means get up here, but however we must use our best endeavour.' Between 4.00am and 6.00am Wolfe landed not only the main body of 4,500 men but a further reserve force of 328. He had two days' supplies of food and ammunition, but this time he was at the unprotected back door of Quebec. From the time he landed, he had made no mistakes.

At 5.45am, Montcalm learnt of Wolfe's landing. Initially it seemed no more than a reconnaissance party, but, as the morning wore on, the full extent of Wolfe's force became clear. Montcalm panicked. Instead of waiting for reinforcements, he hurried his 5,000 men out on to the Plains of Abraham, south of Quebec. Wolfe was in the kind of territory he knew, and was able to fight in the style he favoured. Montcalm should have remained in Quebec and waited for 3,000 more troops to arrive from Cap Rouge under Colonel Bourgainville. The remainder of the French forces under Vaudreuil at Beauport were too distant to help immediately, but could have arrived to reinforce the garrison at

Quebec. Welcoming the opportunity of a European battle on American soil, Montcalm followed the one course of action which would ensure his defeat. Rather than delay or manoeuvre until Wolfe's supplies ran out and he was forced to withdraw an army down a steep cliff and load them on to small boats from a narrow shore, exposed to French attacks from the start to finish, Montcalm decided to fight. The battle of the Heights of Abraham was Montcalm's to lose, not Wolfe's to win.

At 8.00 am, a mile from Quebec, Wolfe halted in the light rain and deployed his troops into two ranks, giving orders that each musket was to be loaded with two balls, and that no man should fire on the enemy until they were forty yards away. Wolfe was now waiting for the French. Montcalm obliged. At 10.00am the French soldiers advanced, firing intermittently. At forty yards, a volley from the British cut them down. One soldier said: 'It was the most perfect volley ever fired on any battle field, which burst forth as if from a single monstrous weapon, from end to end of the British line.'

The second rank fired and the French were thrown into disarray. Within thirty minutes the battle for supremacy in North America was over. Montcalm had lost Quebec, and Bourgainville's reinforcements were to arrive too late. Montcalm himself was mortally wounded. He died the next day, and was buried in a British shell-hole by the Ursuline convent. His opponent also died in the battle. Wolfe had already been shot in the wrist and the groin when at 10.24 am he was fatally wounded in the chest. Informed as he lay dying that the French had been put to flight, he knew he had won the most important battle the British had fought in North America. Quebec surrendered on the afternoon of 17 September.

By the Treaty of Paris, signed in 1763 at the conclusion of the Seven Years War, France gave the whole of Canada to Britain. The great historian Chateaubriand wrote: 'France has disappeared from North America like those Indian tribes with which she sympathized.' But once France ceased to be a threat to the English colonies, there was little reason for them to continue in thrall to the British. In the year the French surrendered Canada, their Foreign Minister Charles Gravier, Comte de Vergennes, warned the British:

> Delivered from a neighbour whom they always feared, your other colonies will soon discover that they stand no longer in need of your protection. You will call on them to contribute towards supporting the burthen which they have helped to bring on you; they will answer you by shaking off all dependence.

An unstoppable movement had started. The events which led to the crucial battle for Quebec had in fact begun at Great Meadows on 28 May 1754. The ultimate beneficiary of the outcome at Quebec was a young Virginian who had fought at Great Meadows: his name was George Washington and he was to play a leading role in the great drama which culminated in the American Revolution of 1776. Without the British victory at Quebec, would the Anglo-American colonists havce felt that they no longer needed British protection in North America? And would the British crown have still risked the loss of colonial loyalty by insisting, as they did after 1759, that the settlers contribute to the colonies defence costs and by the imposition of unpopular taxes? Despite Wolfe's victory, Britain was still to lose its thirteen American colonies and the very lands the British had just won around the Great Lakes.

As for Canada, 200 years on from this turning point in history the relationship of the descendants of New France with their fellow citizens within Canada remains in question. For some, the memory of Wolfe and Montcalm dying together from wounds on the same battlefield represented a mutual sacrifice to a united future; for others, the battlefield at Quebec could never be the birthplace of a new nation.

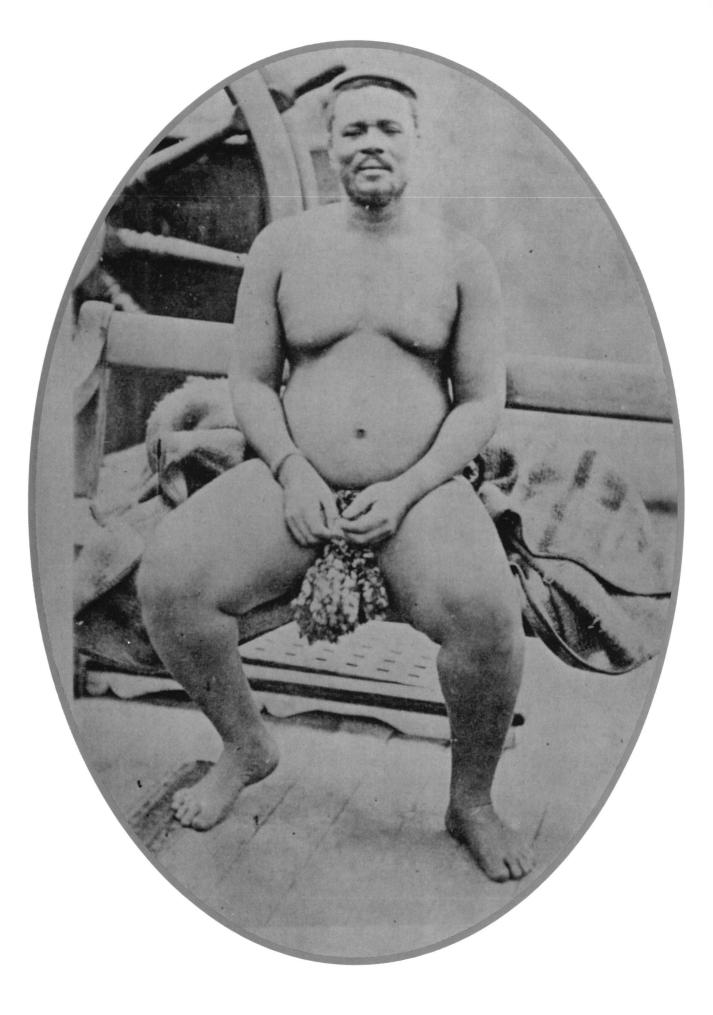

The Last African
KINGDOM

THE ZULUS SLAUGHTER THE BRITISH AT THE BATTLE OF
ISANDLWANA BUT LOSE THE WAR FOR SOUTH AFRICA.

. . . In answer to those statesmen – those mistaken statesmen who have
intimated the decay of the power of England and the decline of its
resources – I express here my confident conviction that there never was a
moment in our history when the power of England was so great and her
resources so vast and inexhaustible. (Benjamin Disraeli, *Works*)

THE BRITISH PRIME MINISTER Benjamin Disraeli (1804–81) disliked
dealing with Britain's colonies – 'millstones round our neck' as he called them
– but, when the Zulu wars began in 1879, troubles in Africa impinged on
English politics for the first time and rapidly swept the Disraeli Government
out of power. The wars opened with the Battle of Isandlwana, which marked
the start of a new British policy and the end of local autonomy for the Zulus.

The battle was fought on 22 January 1879 in the South African province of KwaZulu
Natal near the town of Nqutu, which was part of KwaZulu. Isandlwana (sometimes
rendered, Isandula, Isandhlwana, Isanlahana or Insanalwana) set off the process which was
to crush the Zulu nation within six months and push it into the margin of history for over a
hundred years. So Isandlwana was a turning point in the history of two nations and two
cultures. It was also the story of two men: the Zulu King Cetshwayo (or Cetewayo)
kaMapande and the man who had crowned him six years before in Zululand, Theophilus
Shepstone, the most famous administrator of nineteenth-century South Africa. Their
actions shaped a decade in the history of the British Empire's wars and conquests, stamping
their characters on British and South African history.

OPPOSITE: *Cetshwayo,
King of the Zulus in a
photograph taken in
1879.*

BELOW: *European
settlers move north in
search of new farmland.*

The British and Dutch in South Africa

By 1879, the British had been in South Africa for more than two generations. They had
arrived on the continent in 1795, defeating the Dutch navy off Simons Town and then colo-
nizing the Dutch-built port. Further settlement took place in 1806 when British forces

landed at the Cape of Good Hope, *en route* for the colonies in India. South Africa itself seemed ripe for take-over from the Dutch, who had been there for 200 years. The descendants of the first colonists had evolved into an independent and rugged people known as Boers or Afrikaners, whose principal concern was to find new grazing for their cattle. For twenty years, the land-hungry Boers had been fighting the African tribes for each acre of land.

The first Boer skirmish with an African tribe was with the most powerful and integrated of them all, the Xhosa, in July 1781. The engagement inaugurated a century of conflict between the settlers and the tribes and the first of nine frontier wars along the Xhosa's western border with what was to become the Cape Colony. The Xhosa remained until the beginning of the nineteenth century the most formidable of the Bantu-speaking tribes in South Africa. They grazed cattle and had no sense of private ownership. The Dutch settlers, with their own cattle to graze, drove them off their land. By the time the British arrived, with fresh European ideas of rationalism and capitalism, the fate of the African tribes was sealed. The Cape was the gateway to the uncharted riches and beauty of another New World. Unsurprisingly, the competing British and Dutch settlers were lured there by apparently unlimited possibility and by the promise of extensive territory.

From the first, the Boers resented the British. When the British declared the Cape a colony in 1806, it became part of the British Empire: this meant that the Cape Colony was to be self-supporting, that it had to buy from Britain, and that it had to supply the Empire with raw materials. Wool became a vital export, with new breeds of Merino sheep (from Spain) using up still more land. By 1820, when British settlement was gathering pace, the white population of the Cape was 47,000. Of these 43,000 were Boers – otherwise known as Voortrekkers.

Their dissatisfaction with the British in the Cape led the Voortrekkers to break free from the Colony in 1836–37 and to move north to the Orange river and beyond, and east along the coast to the territory now occupied by the Xhosa. This migration – the Great Trek – led to the establishment of the independent republics of Orange Free State (1842) and the Transvaal (1852).

The settlers – both British and Dutch – made their fortunes in farming. As a result, the pressure for land continued to increase in the 1830s and 1840s. Tribe after tribe of Africans – the Griqua, the Tswana, the Sotho, the Pedi, the Xhosa and finally the Zulu – clashed with the Boers and the British over land and water rights. But the European advance was inexorable.

The British expanded their interests east of the Cape, in 1843 annexing Natal, east of the Xhosa. Durban (formerly Port Natal, and renamed Durban in 1834) became a district of the Cape Colony in 1844 and a separate colony in 1856. British rule had arrived to stay. But between the British and the fertile expanse of the Transvaal to the north stood the Zulu nation. By the mid-nineteenth century, therefore, South Africa was poised on the brink of chaos: the British, the Boers and the African tribes were ready to go to war over the agricultural riches of the new land. But in 1867 it was suddenly more than mere land that was at stake: it was what lay beneath.

For in 1867 two young children, Erasmus and Louisa Jacobs, found what looked like a shiny pebble on the south bank of the Orange river near Hopetown in the Cape: it was in fact a 21,25–carat diamond. Richard Southey, Colonial Secretary of the Cape, saw a glittering prospect ahead. 'This diamond', he said, 'is the rock upon which the future success of South Africa will be built.' Four years later, gold was discovered in the Eastern

Transvaal and, in 1886, in the Witwatersrand to the west. Southern Africa was about to change forever.

It was against this background of unfolding opportunity for the British and Dutch settlers and diminishing resources for the African tribes that Theophilus Shepstone and Cetshwayo had grown up. The forces which shaped their lives were the forces which shaped South Africa's history.

King Cetshwayo ka Mapande

The Zulu kingdom had grown in power and strength during the early 1800s when the great chief Shaka (*c.*1787–1828) had developed the *amabutho* or 'age regiment' system to provide the tribe with soldiers. In essence, the Zulu had a regiment for each year, matching experience and fitness in war. At fourteen, Zulu boys joined the King's regiment for training in arms; when they were not fighting they tended the cattle. The result was the creation of a powerful army which, while not a standing force, could be called up at short notice.

When Shaka took over in 1816, the Zulu had an army of 500 men. Within a few months, he built up and trained a swift, deadly and disciplined fighting force of 2,000, each man committed to celibacy. The vicious stabbing spear, the assegai, became their standard weapon, and their battle plan was a brutal 'chest and two horns' formation perfected in action. Shaka's warriors scattered their rival clans across south-east Africa, conquering weaker neighbouring tribes and incorporating them into Shaka's chiefdom. At war, therefore, the Zulus were fierce and effective. When at peace, they tended livestock and organized themselves into homesteads.

By the early nineteenth century, the Zulu kingdom had a disciplined fighting force which formed the most mobile and feared army in Africa.

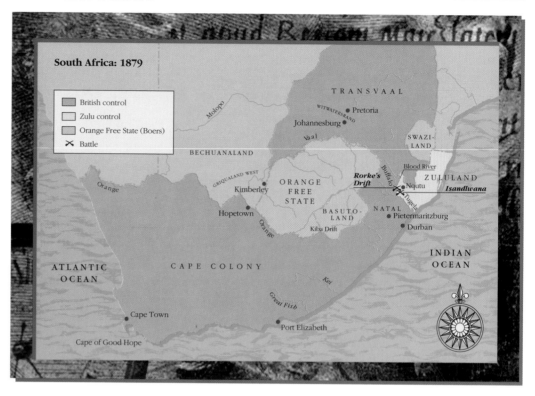

Throughout the nineteenth century, Zulu power grew. But this growth of power was part of a complex conflict – the *Mfecane* – with other tribes, provoked by the upheavals among the Nguni clans in the south-east following Shaka's imposition of militaristic rule. Shaka had risen from among the petty chieftains of the Nguni to establish the Zulus as the predominant force, at the hub of a network of alliances. But there was great tension among the chieftains and, on 22 September 1828, as he was speaking to a Sotho delegation which had brought a tribute of cranes' feathers, Shaka was murdered by his brother Mhangane and half-brother Dingane. Dingane then became king. In an attempt to expand his area of influence, he waged war against the Mfengu and the Ndebele north of the Vaal river, but suffered losses in the early 1830s. Most catastrophically of all, he attacked the Voortrekkers at Blood River, in Zululand, in 1838 and lost 3,000 men against the Voortrekkers' three. The chaplain to the Boer forces remarked triumphantly, 'The Kaffirs lay on the ground like pumpkins on a rich soil that has borne a large crop.'

After Blood River, Dingane fled north, and sought help from another of his half-brothers, Mapande, in a new action against the Swazi. Mapande sent a regiment, but Dingane was not satisfied with this contribution and determined to kill his untrustworthy brother, who duly fled south and enlisted the help of the Boers to invade Zululand and defeat Dingane. In 1840, Dingane was finally defeated and Mapande became king of the Zulus.

The Zulu system of loyalty and allegiance was vital to the tribe's survival. Each chief accepting Mapande's rule gave a reed from his hut; the collected reeds were woven into a grass wreath (*inkatha*) symbolizing the intertwined relationships at the heart of the Zulu Empire. It was into this warlike system that Mapande's son Cetshwayo (*c.* 1827–84) was born. After growing up in the royal village (*kraal*) at Ulundi, he graduated in 1852 to fight his first battle against the Swazi as a member of the uThulwana Regiment. He proved to be a bold and successful soldier, and was prominent in the 1856 Zulu war of succession, rallying the Zulu chiefs at the Battle of Ndondakusuka in December against his younger brother, Mbuyazi.

At twenty-nine, Cetshwayo had become the most powerful man in Zululand. He strengthened his position by a series of alliances among the Zulu chiefs and with the fractious British along the borders to the west, until he posed a serious threat to his father. Eventually, in a ceremony at Ulundi, their rivalry was contained: Cetshwayo was proclaimed Mapande's successor in return for pledging his loyalty to the Zulu King. The Zulu inheritance was secure.

Mapande lived until 1872, the first Zulu monarch to die naturally. Cetshwayo was duly crowned king, the first to accede in an orderly and systematic way. The spectacle was breathtaking: in August 1873 thousands of Zulu warriors and their chiefs gathered for the ceremony at Entonjaneni and proceeded to the sacred Zulu site of Makheni. There, they formed an enormous circle round the medicine man as he kindled new fire with the tribal firesticks and prepared to weave Cetshwayo's new *inkatha*. Cetshwayo was anointed with potions and charms mixed from the ashes of Mapande's *inkatha* and led to prayer at the graves of his forebears. There, the new King received the ancestral spear of the Zulus from his chief minister. The British sent representatives too, for they favoured Cetshwayo's kingship. Among them was Theophilus Shepstone (1817–93).

Theophilus Shepstone

Sir Theophilus Shepstone.

The Shepstone family had arrived on the Cape in 1820 when Theophilus Shepstone was three years old. His father, the Reverend William Shepstone, was a stone-mason and preacher, who helped build Wesleyville; the family settled there, beyond the Keiskamma river. In 1833, Shepstone's mother, Elizabeth, died giving birth to her sixth child. William Shepstone married again in 1835 and had another six children by his new wife, Anne.

During these formative years, Theophilus Shepstone lived a settler's life in various stations beyond the frontier, learning to speak Xhosa and Zulu. In 1834 he was appointed to his first Government post, as an interpreter in Xhosa and Zulu. By the 1840s, his skills as a translator and mediator were much in demand. On one occasion, after his mediation had proved unsuccessful, there was an attempt on his life. Shepstone survived unscathed, but a nearby German missionary was shot dead. In 1845 he was made diplomatic agent to the Bantu tribes of Natal, his intimate knowledge of Bantu affairs helping shape British policy. Believing passionately in humane treatment of the Bantu, because he thought it best not only for them but for British expansion in Africa, he became known as *somtseu* or 'white father'.

In 1846 he was appointed to a British Government commission charged with reporting on Bantu resettlement in Natal, a process which had begun in 1838. Shepstone understood the Bantu lifestyle, and disagreed with the Commission findings, which recommended a small settlement pattern and in his view ran counter to their culture. This was an example of a problem he faced every day: the need to balance his understanding of native culture against the British interests in the area. For Shepstone, humanism and imperialism were constantly at odds.

One solution was to settle the Bantu in large locations; this would preserve their agricultural lifestyle but would make them less tractable because they could not be easily governed. Settling them in small locations, on the other hand, would destroy their culture but guarantee their services as labourers on the growing numbers of sugar plantations. Although the Bantu were not settled according to Shepstone's recommendations, he did succeed in safeguarding their interests, and established the Natal Native Trust to protect their lands.

By the 1850s, Shepstone was faced with the problem of administering the Bantu lands. Having no staff, his solution was to adopt a form of indirect government, and his success as an administrator in balancing British and native African interests at this time was due wholly to his knowledge of and sensitivity to native African affairs. For the next thirty years, Shepstone was a force in the land. 'Governors of this colony', he said in 1873, 'have always been chiefly guided by my opinion.' He respected the Bantu laws, and thought that the most effective way of assimilating white settlers and native Africans was through education. He aimed for good government, for the protection of the Bantu through a system of individual land ownership, for their control by colonial law, and for equal political status and citizenship for the Bantu when they achieved the required standards of Westernization and development.

Shepstone the man – shrewd, patient and dutiful – was distinguished in appearance and possessed of an unshakeable religious faith. He thought that conversion to Christianity among the Africans would develop naturally. As his friend and assistant the writer Rider Haggard wrote: 'He believed that the Zulus should be taught to work and that their minds should be opened before attempts were made to Christianise them.' Shepstone was a model servant of British imperial government, achieving by his mastery of bureaucratic power and by the force of his personality a dominance in Natal affairs that lasted a generation.

In the 1860s, the British urged Shepstone to make use of his experience among the Bantu and to liaise with the Zulu King Mapande. Accordingly he undertook a series of difficult missions to Zululand, negotiating with Mapande and maintaining peace between the Zulu and the Swazi tribes. It was Shepstone who nominated Mapande's successor, Cetshwayo, in 1861, and the coronation in 1873 was a moment of triumph for the British administrator. That day he earned the respect of the Zulus when the new King honoured him with a royal salute; he further used the coronation to obtain the signing of a labour agreement under which a Zulu workforce would be provided for the industries developing in Natal.

Shepstone then devoted himself to border negotiations over the Transvaal–Zululand frontier, north-west of Natal. Although the tribal situation was complex and the talks protracted, he concluded them successfully, and was knighted by Queen Victoria in 1876. That same year he was appointed Special Commissioner in the Transvaal, to liaise between the native population and the British.

But in 1877 Shepstone's world began to change. He took a series of decisions which were to lead to the slaughter of British troops at Isandlwana and the biggest military disaster the Empire had seen in Africa.

Shepstone's Ultimatum to Cetshwayo

On 12 April 1877 Sir Theophilus Shepstone established himself in Pretoria and annexed the Transvaal as a British colony. Understandably, the Boers objected to this annexation of their republic, but they were not, for the moment, a threat. Shepstone had acquired a larger vision: a united federation of states in South Africa. Natal was already a British colony, and now the Transvaal had joined it. But between them lay the independent kingdom of Zululand.

Shepstone knew that, if the British were to expand, the Zulus had to be quelled or destroyed. Otherwise the Empire would suffer. After years of friendship with Cetshwayo, of understanding and supporting the Zulus, Shepstone turned against them, motivated by his desire for a federation. He chose the British Empire over native Africa.

The British sought a confederation of the Transvaal, Natal and Zululand under British rule. Shepstone therefore switched his allegiance to the Boers, championing their claim to Zululand. And he suddenly changed his attitude to Cetshwayo. He wrote in 1877:

> Had Cetshwayo's 30,000 warriors been in time changed to labourers working for wages, Zululand could have been a prosperous, peaceful country instead of what it now is, a source of perpetual danger to itself and its neighbours.

The logic of this opinion was inescapable. Shepstone and the new Governor of southern Africa, Sir Bartle Frere, knew that war with the Zulu would soon be unavoidable. A swift defeat of the Zulu would send a definite signal to the rest of tribal South Africa.

Frere and Shepstone started to muster troops and prepare for a campaign against the Zulu. Learning of this, Cetshwayo made it clear that he had 'no intention or wish to quarrel with the English'; he simply wanted to keep his independence by banning all missionaries, settlers and intruders from Zululand and by continuing to resist the Boers' claim to his territory.

In London, Disraeli's Government sent a letter to Frere in November 1878 urging consultation with the Zulus: 'by meeting the Zulus in a spirit of forbearance and reasonable compromise, it will be possible to avoid the very serious evil of a war with Cetewayo.' Frere also received a telegram at Pietermaritzburg, the provincial capital, on 30 November from the Colonial Office in London specifically forbidding war. He ignored it. The war that neither the British Government nor the Zulu chiefs wanted was about to begin.

The fuse was lit when British labourers, who had constructed a road from Kranz Kop in Natal down to the Tugela river at Middle Drift, attempted to complete the ford on the Zulu side of the river. Armed Zulus sent the workmen back to Natal and stripped and beat the road engineer. On 11 December Shepstone and Frere, in response to what they saw as Zulu misbehaviour at Middle Drift, provoked Cetshwayo by issuing an ultimatum he could not obey. Representatives of the British and the Zulus met under a canopy strung between two trees at what became known as the Ultimatum Tree on the bank of the Tugela. Shepstone and Frere demanded the impossible: within two weeks a British resident (administrator) should be allowed into Zululand, the Zulu forces and the 'age regiment' system should be disbanded, the ban on marriage in the Zulu army should be lifted, and missionaries should be readmitted to Zululand. The text of the ultimatum arrived in London on 2 January 1879, only nine days before it expired.

Cetshwayo, anxious to avoid conflict, requested more time. He knew that a war would be dangerous and disruptive, and that he had more to lose than the British. He wrote to

Shepstone: 'The king . . . declared and still declares that he will not commence war but will wait till he is actually attacked before he enters on a defensive campaign.' By that January the British had amassed 15,000 troops (army regulars and the Natal Native Contingent raised by Shepstone) divided into three columns under the command of Lieutenant-General Lord Chelmsford (1827–1905). Cetshwayo still had no inclination to be the aggressor:

> It is the Whites who have come to fight with me in my own country, and not I that go to fight with them. My intention is only to defend myself in my own country, where they made me King a few years ago.

Back in London, the Empire, extended but not exhausted, prepared to go to war. The *Illustrated London News* wrote on 1 February:

> The British Empire is but slowly emerging from the troubles in which it was involved by the Russo-Turkish War in the South-East of Europe, and by the Afghan War on the North-Western frontier of India, only to catch a glimpse of an approaching Zulu War in South Africa. Suffice it to say that an ugly war is now before us; and that, although there can be no solid ground for doubting its issue, the lasting outcome of it may prove extremely disastrous, not only for the colony of Natal, but even to the Cape Colony itself.

On 11 January the British forces had invaded Zululand. The London writer did not know that the disaster had already happened.

Lieutenant-General Lord Chelmsford.

The Zulu War of 1879

Lord Chelmsford was a pillar of the Victorian establishment: courteous, gentlemanly and hard-working, a career soldier who had served the Empire in India and Abyssinia and had lately resigned the governorship of the Cape Colony. His force, No. 3 Column of the 24th Regiment, consisted of 4,709 men, 302 wagons and 1,500 oxen. He supervised and deployed it meticulously, but he had no proper intelligence staff, and relied either on rumour or on reports of the black Border Police for information on the Zulus' intentions.

The terrain and conditions did not suit him. The air was hot and humid, and the ground underfoot rough, broken and stony. His troops crossed into Zululand at the settlement of Rorke's Drift on the Mzinyathi river, heading north into a thick mist. The river was not deep, the water reaching the horses' saddle flaps. But in order to transport the wagons across the water, engineers built a pontoon bridge of barrels and planking. One man, Henry Harford, described the crossing:

> In order to scare away any crocodiles that might be lurking in the vicinity, the leading Company formed a double chain right across the River, leaving a pathway between for the remainder to pass through. The men forming the chain clasped hands, and the moment they entered the water they started to hum a kind of war-chant, which was taken up by every company as they passed over. The sound that this produced was like a gigantic swarm of bees buzzing about us, and sufficient to scare the crocodiles or anything else. Altogether, it was both a curious and grand sight.

Part of Chelmsford's column headed north-east and pitched a temporary camp four miles away by the Batshe river in a sheltered valley between two mountains. On 12 January the British skirmished with warriors of Chief Sihayo – an ally of Cetshwayo – near his homestead. The Zulus were defeated and the British became more confident. Eight days later, the remainder of the column marched from Rorke's Drift, crossed the Batshe river by the temporary camp, and turned south-east towards the plain below the craggy hill of Isandlwana.

On the plain, the ground was flat and the terrain wild and open. There, on the 20th, No. 3 Column camped for the night. The troops made few preparations; they did not dig trenches or make fortifications because Chelmsford planned to move on soon; neither did they form a wagon ring or *laager* because the wagons were due to return to Rorke's Drift to collect more supplies. The camp was without formal defences. But, as one soldier said, 'Nobody from the

Their cumbersome ox-drawn wagons slowed the British advance as they crossed into Zululand at the settlement of Rorke's Drift.

General downwards had the least suspicion that there was a chance of the camp being attacked.' One unit of No. 3 Column was out on scouting duties under Major Dartnell. Chelmsford himself left the camp with a party at 2.00am on the 22nd to rendezvous with Dartnell to the east. Sixty-seven officers and 1,707 British troops remained, including 104 mounted infantry and 800 Natal Native Contingent. Colonel Pullein commanded. The *Regulations for Field Forces in South Africa*, written by Chelmsford in 1878, specified the following:

(17) By day the camp should be guarded against surprise by vedettes [mounted sentries] thrown out at some distance on all surrounding points of observation. Horses and oxen when out grazing should have mounted guards. The former will be knee-haltered.

(18) By night horses should be picketed and oxen placed in a wagon-laager.

(19) The camp should be partially entrenched on all sides.

None of these instructions had been followed. In the light of the early morning, scouts with Chelmsford's party of 1,200 men located Zulu activity. The Zulus waited for the British to spread their resources.

Later that morning, at 10.30am, reinforcements of five troops of the Natal Native Horse arrived from Rorke's Drift. They did not stay at the camp, but rode out on reconnaissance. The British forces were now divided into three.

At noon Cetshwayo attacked. George Hamilton-Browne, Commandant of the 1st Battalion of the 3rd Natal Native Contingent, looked on in horror:

I saw a puff of smoke rise from the hills on the left of the camp. It was followed by another. They seemed to come from a huge black shadow that lay on the hills. Presently another puff, and in a moment I knew they were bursting shells. Not a cloud was in the sky, and I knew that the shadow resting on the hills must be the Zulu army moving down to attack the camp.

The Zulu warriors swarmed down and overwhelmed the small British force left to defend the camp.

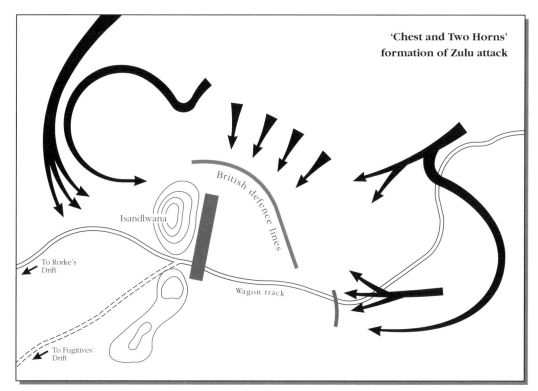

'Chest and Two Horns' formation of Zulu attack

British defence lines

Isandlwana

To Rorke's Drift

Wagon track

To Fugitives' Drift

The Zulu forces advanced in their classic 'chest and two horns' formation, almost completely encircling the British camp.

The British soldiers at Isandlwana heard the same swarming of bees which had helped them cross the river ten days before; but this time they heard it as the Zulu army advanced with a low humming noise. The Zulus had been sighted four miles away. This gave the British time to form a half-square defence a few hundred yards north of the camp itself, stretching one-and-a-half miles and facing the rising ground to the north-east. There they waited.

Cetshwayo had the most mobile and feared army – or *impi* – ever seen in Africa. He had mustered his men, five days before, at the kraal of Nodwengu. Estimates vary, but his force numbered at least 20,000. The Zulus were equipped with guns (some 10,000 in various states of repair had been bought by Cetshwayo from local white traders) and with the assegai so effective in close combat. Throughout the late morning they swept down from three sides and, moving at a fast walking pace and in the classic 'chest-and-two-horns' attack pattern, outflanked the defences to surround the British. At 1.30pm, they burst through the enemy line. At that moment, there was a solar eclipse and the battle-field was thrown into eerie darkness. A shadow had fallen across the Empire.

Some of the British retreated, only to be cut down by the Zulus as they attempted to cross the River Mzinyathi at a place now known as Fugitives' Drift. The Queen's colours, taken from the field by two lieutenants, were found in the water, both men having been caught and killed. Others made a stand, killed by the Zulu spears as the ammunition ran out or their guns overheated. One Zulu recalled:

> The sun turned black in the middle of the battle; we could still see it over us . . .
> Then we got into the camp and there was a great deal of smoke and firing.
>
> One party of soldiers came out from among the tents and formed up a little above the ammunition wagons. They held their ground there until their ammunition failed them when they were nearly all assegaied.
>
> Those that were not killed at this place formed up again in a solid square in the neck of Isandhlwana. They were completely surrounded on all sides and stood back to back and surrounding some men who were in the centre. Their ammunition was now

When the Zulus burst through their line, the British soldiers were forced to scatter.

finished, except that they had some revolvers which they fired at us at close quarters. We were unable to break their square until we had killed a good many of them, by throwing our assegais at short distances. We eventually overcame them all this way.

One lucky escapee, a cavalryman named James Brickhill, later wrote:

> Our flight I shall never forget: no path, no track, boulder everywhere – on we went, borne now into some dry torrent bed, now weaving our way amongst the tree of stunted growth, so that unless you made the best use of your eyes you were in constant danger of colliding against some tree or finding yourself unhorsed at the bottom of some ravine.
>
> Our way was already strewn with shields, assegais, blankets, hats, clothing of all descriptions, guns, ammunition belts.

A fellow soldier staggering among the rocks and stones called out to Brickhill. 'For God's sake, give me a lift!' Brickhill replied: 'My dear fellow, it's a case of life and death with me,' and closing his eyes he spurred on his horse. Brickhill survived, but years later he was still haunted by the desperate soldier's plea.

Another Zulu remembered:

> I myself only killed one man. Dum! dum! went his revolver as he was firing from right to left and I came beside him and stuck my assegai under his right arm, pushing it through his body until it came out between his ribs on the left side. As soon as he fell I pulled the assegai out and slit his stomach so I knew he should not shoot any more of my people.

The Zulus had annihilated the army of the world's greatest power.

The British had been ill-prepared and ill-organized, and had made the mistake of dispersing their forces. In addition it is possible that their rifles had let them down. The standard issue .45 Martini Henry rifle had an effective range of 500 yards and was designed to fire twelve rounds in three minutes; but it may have overheated. The British faced the further problem that they could not distribute the extra 200 cartridges per man (standard reserve supply) quickly enough because the front line was hundreds of yards from the supply wagons. Many of the British died fighting hand to hand. A British sergeant arrived on the battlefield later:

> I could not help crying to see so many of our poor comrades lying dead on the ground, when only a few hours before that we left them all well and hearty. You could not move a foot either way without treading on dead bodies. Oh, Father, such a sight I never witnessed in my life before. I could not help crying to see how the poor fellows were massacred.

The last soldier held out until 5.00pm from a small and sheltered cave under Isandlwana Hill. He was the last of the British casualties. All the supplies of No. 3 Column, including 800 Martini Henry rifles and ammunition, fell into Zulu hands.

The Zulu had an overwhelming superiority in numbers; their tactics were decisive, and they were able to sustain heavy losses (around 1,000 died at Isandlwana). Shepstone was dismayed by Cetshwayo's extraordinary victory. The Zulu King had taken first blood, repelling the invading power. But he lamented his losses and blamed his commanders for taking no officers as prisoners.

The Mounted Infantry Company of the 1st Welsh Regiment visit the memorial to the colonial dead at Isandlwana in 1884, exactly five years after the battle.

But the Zulu plan seemed to be working. Cetshwayo hoped to crush the British columns, defend his border and sue for peace as quickly as possible. He knew that the British in Natal had a relatively small force, but white traders had told him of their great army beyond the sea. If the war continued, he knew he would lose.

Only when the smoke of Isandlwana cleared was it possible to see how important the battle was to both nations. It was a turning point in British colonial policy, and it sealed the fate of the Zulus. The London papers, hearing the news a month later, thought the war premature, even if ultimately inevitable; the *Illustrated London News* (8 March 1879) added that no such disaster as that at Isandlwana should have been possible in a well-disciplined force. Disraeli fell into a depression, brought on by the bad news of Isandlwana and the prospect of a long South African campaign; Chelmsford and Shepstone retreated into over-caution; and the campaign which followed was mired in sloth and indecision. Later that summer, the British Government was further embarrassed when Louis Napoleon's son, the Prince Imperial, who had volunteered for the campaign, was found hacked to death by Zulu spears after an ambush. Queen Victoria was distressed. Government prestige fell.

Isandlwana had a personal impact on Cetshwayo and Shepstone. Respect and friendship had long disappeared, but both men suffered losses in the battle. To Shepstone himself the battle seemed haphazard and risky, with a small force scattered all over the country. His son George had died at Isandlwana, on a rocky knoll at the south-western foot of the hill, where some of the British attempted a last stand. Cetshwayo had won the victory which was to lose him the war.

After Isandlwana

In London, life could never be the same again. At 6.40pm on 10 February 1879 the British War Office received this telegram from Lord Chelmsford, Commander of British forces in Natal:

> I regret to have to report a very disastrous engagement, which took place on Jan 22, between the Zulus and a portion of No 3 Column, left to guard the camp about ten miles in front of Rorke's Drift. The Zulus came down in overwhelming numbers; and, in spite of the gallant resistance made by five companies, two guns, two rocket-tubes, 104 mounted men and 800 natives, they overwhelmed them.

It was a defeat from which Disraeli would never recover. The agricultural and industrial depression of the 1870s had made his Government deeply unpopular, and a massacre of Britons at Kabul in September 1879 made matters worse. His administration would topple the following year. But now, at the Battle of Isandlwana, the Empire had been defeated for the first time in Africa. *The Times* (6 March 1879) called it 'the greatest disaster which has ever happened to British arms in South Africa'.

In the evening of the same day of Isandlwana, the garrison of 139 British troops had repelled the Zulu at Rorke's Drift, one of the most famous defences in military history. But the British Empire would never forget Isandlwana. Initially stung by the loss, in the spring and summer of 1879 the British launched a concerted campaign under Frere and Chelmsford which cost the Zulu 10,000 casualties, and laid waste to the Zulu capital of Ulundi on 4 July. Disraeli wrote to Queen Victoria on 26 May that Chelmsford had invaded Zululand without knowledge or provision: 'A dreadful disaster occurred in consequence, and then Lord Chelmsford became panic-struck . . . and found himself at the head of 20,000 of yr. majesty's troops in order to reduce a country not larger than Yorkshire' (Moneypenny & Buckle). Chelmsford, Frere and Shepstone needed Ulundi to obliterate Isandlwana. Cetshwayo was captured on 28 August and sent to Cape Town, where he complained to the Governor of the Cape Colony:

> I have done you no wrong, therefore you must have some other object in invading my land. I wish the English nation to tell me when they see this my letter if they find anything in it for which I deserved to be treated as I have been treated, taken captive from my country. Does the English nation think that I would have been so stupid as to plan an invasion of any of their territory?

The answer was that after Isandlwana the British had suffered such trauma that the Zulu could never again be trusted. After dismantling the economic and political basis of the Zulu nation, deposing its king, destroying its centres of royal authority and killing its warriors, the British turned their back on the consequences. By October 1879, the last of the British troops had left Zululand. A nation had withered in ten months. After the Zulus had been defeated, and after Disraeli's Government fell in April 1880, British attitudes softened under the Liberal administration of William Gladstone. In 1882 Cetshwayo was invited to meet Queen Victoria in London; he stayed in Kensington and caused a ripple of excitement among Victorian women. The British allowed him to return to Zululand to reign over part of his former kingdom. This he did in 1883, but he died a broken man the following year.

Sir Theophilus Shepstone, too, was a spent force. He retired in 1880, like Frere discredited and distrusted after the 1879 Zulu campaign. Then followed an undignified squabble with the British Government over his pension, which brought disillusion to his last years. He died in June 1893. He was victim not so much of his own duplicity to the Zulu as of the failure of British colonial administration to avoid war with them.

Cetshwayo visits Queen Victoria in London in 1882.

The after-history of Isandlwana saw South Africa not in British but in local settlers' control, following the Act of Union in 1910 – the result of the bitter Boer-British war of 1899–1902. Had that battle not taken place, the Zulu nation would have survived and the British may not have had to leave South Africa as they did. Isandlwana tipped the balance between European and African, and pointed the way towards a South Africa that remained divided for over a hundred years.

The British buried their dead at Isandlwana, erecting memorials to those killed; today the battlefield has an eerie and mournful air. It was the place where two nations faced each other for the first time in their history and where the greater was found wanting. History was turning as the Zulus swept down on the British redcoats that clear, hot day in January 1879. Only two months later, at Hamilton's Amphitheatre in Holborn, London, a new theatrical show was born: 'The battle of Isandula, illustrating the thrilling episode of the heroic stand against 20,000 Zulus by the gallant 24th, from authentic sources' (*Illustrated London News*, 8 March 1879). The battle had already become a legend.

L'EROE DEL GIORNO, L'AMMIR°

· 11 ·

The Battle
OF TSUSHIMA

JAPAN'S NAVY DESTROYS THE RUSSIAN FLEET AND
A NEW MILITARY AND ECONOMIC SUPERPOWER EMERGES.

> Whether by land or sea, battles derive their importance from the nature of
> the issues at stake rather than from the magnitude of the forces engaged.
> If greater fleets than those of the present war have been put forth, seldom
> has the prize of victory been greater than was that for which the fleets of
> Russia and Japan have twice contended in ordered battle.
>
> (Captain W. C. Pakenham, RN, *Reports From Naval Attachés*)

THE BATTLE OF TSUSHIMA, on 27 May 1905, was the decisive encounter between the two imperial powers of Japan and Russia, one emerging and one declining. At the end of that fateful day at sea in the Straits of Tsushima between Korea and Japan, the balance of power in Asia altered forever.

OPPOSITE: *The devastating defeat of the Russian war fleet in the Straits of Tsushima in 1905.*

The battle was a turning point in Japan's advance to world-power status, an advance which had started just four decades earlier. The Japanese achieved this crushing defeat of Russia as a result partly of their speedy technological development and partly of the ineffectiveness of a dying Russian Empire. In 1905 Japan was still new to the industrial world, but it was learning and catching up rapidly. Tsushima was the test and proving place for its naval skills and strategy, recently acquired from more advanced countries such as Holland, France, and especially Britain; and the battle brought it face to face with the might of the Western powers.

One man, the remarkable Admiral Heihachiro Togo, 'Japan's Nelson', carried his country's hopes: his sense of honour and duty knew no limit. The Russian fleet was commanded by the experienced and imposing Vice-Admiral Zinovi Petrovich Rozhestvenski. The Tsarist Empire had been at war with Japan since 1904. The Battle at Tsushima would bring a year of costly conflict to an end.

In the nineteenth and early twentieth centuries, a nation's strength was increasingly gauged by its sea power. A powerful navy was vital for the maintenance of overseas territories and the protection of sea lanes, the life-blood of any nation aspiring to the status of a great industrial (and military) power.

Nineteenth-Century Japan

Togo and the Japanese had come a long way to earn that dawn encounter at the Straits of Tsushima. The battle represented so much more than a trial of strength and nerve with the Russians. It would shake the politicians of the West and alert them to a new force in the East that threatened the comfortable balance of power in the world. The old feudal Japan, long eyed by eager foreign traders and colonists, was now their technological equal.

Over 350 years earlier, in 1542, the Portuguese had discovered Japan – by accident. A junk, carrying three Portuguese, was on a voyage to Macao from Siam when she was blown off course and landed on the small island of Tanegashima, south of the province of Satsuma. The foreigners were made welcome, and the curiosity of the Japanese about their arquebuses (early portable guns, often supported on tripods), started a trading relationship with Europe that would last for less than a hundred years, before Japan closed its ports to all foreigners.

Feudal Japan was ruled on behalf of the Emperor (who at that time was little more than the nation's figurehead), by a military government called the *Bakufu* (camp government) under a military dictator known as the Shogun. The Shogun in turn, by various means, controlled the feudal lords (the Diaimyo), and these and their vassals followed the severe and implacable code of discipline of the samurai warrior class. This moral creed was based on the uncompromising and unsentimental application of duty and focus: the duty of the samurai was not to seek victory but simply to fight to the death; it was also their duty to remain focused – for, according to one samurai saying, 'To chase two rabbits means catching neither.' Above all, the members of this warrior class were brought up so that, faced with a life-and-death situation, they were unafraid to choose death.

In the early days of trading, some of the feudal lords welcomed the Portuguese Jesuit missionaries as part of the new, potentially lucrative relationship. Buddhism, having superceded the beliefs of the Shinto cult as the dominant religion of Japan, was tolerant enough to accept this influx. By 1551 the Jesuits had baptized 150,000 Japanese into the Christian faith. But six years later, with the number of converts growing ever larger, the tide turned against these Christian proselytizers and the new military overlord, Hideyoshi, sought to expel them from Japan. But he had only mixed success, and in 1616 the new Shogun, Hidetada, felt driven to declare war on Christians. In 1635 alone, 280,000 Japanese Christians were put to death. By the end of that decade the only foreign presence in Japan was a Dutch trading post on the island of Deshima, just off Nagasaki.

An imperial edict of 1648 declared: 'In the future and as long as the sun shall light the world, let no man attempt to land in Japan even as an ambassador and let this order never be infringed on pain of death.' The Japanese avoided contact with foreigners for the next 200 years.

RIGHT: Feudal Japan was ruled by the Shogun, according to the disciplined code of the samurai warrior class.

Then, in 1853, four black ships appeared off Edo. The American Commodore Matthew Perry had arrived with a force sufficient to protect him from the hostile inhabitants. He carried with him a letter from the American President Franklin Pierce (1804–69) to the Emperor of Japan requesting him to open his country to foreign trade. Perry did not stay long, but he returned the next year, this time with ten ships and gifts of whisky, watches, guns and miniature steam engines – a marvel of Western technology.

The Japanese were thrown into confusion. This display of Western military might (it seemed to the Japanese that the US ships 'belched fire') and technological wizardry was enough to break any further resistance to the foreign intruders. Actual force was not needed, nor was it sanctioned by the American President. The Japanese signed a treaty by which they undertook to give assistance to shipwrecked sailors, to supply stores and provisions to all foreigners and to allow American ships to anchor in Japan's ports. It was a humiliation the Japanese would never forget.

Thus it was that from this time on, Japanese ports were gradually opened up to all the great powers trading throughout Asia. Japan, already aware of the impact of Western imperial power on China, were now themselves subject to treaties which exempted foreigners from Japanese law and adherence to Japanese customs within the so-called Treaty Ports. But this impunity could not be ignored forever.

Commodore Matthew C. Perry.

In 1862, a British merchant called Charles Lenox Richardson was killed in Satsuma province for failing to show enough respect to Samurai horsemen on the road. The British Government demanded reparation and the seizure and punishment of the murderers, but the Diaimyo of Satsuma province refused to oblige. The British accordingly dispatched a squadron of warships to Kagoshima, the Satsuma capital. They reached the harbour in August 1863. There the squadron, under the command of Admiral Kuper, sank Kagoshima's three defending ships and, after the provincial capital had refused to capitulate, opened fire on the city itself. Kuper reported:

> considering the heavy fire which was kept up from the ships, point-blank range, the effect must have been considerable. Many guns were observed to have been dismounted . . . one half of the town was in flames and entirely destroyed.

The defenders, including the samurai Kichizaemon Togo and his three sons, Shirobei, Sokuro and Heihachiro, were helpless. Their old-fashioned cannon, loaded with gunpowder and then with earth to prevent the powder igniting against the heated cannon balls, were no match for the modern British guns. Kuper's squadron delivered broadside after broadside as it cruised the harbour at will. There was nothing for the proud samurai to do but rage impotently on the beach, calling on the British to come ashore and fight like men. The British ignored the challenge; they suffered only thirteen killed and sixty-three wounded. The Japanese dead and wounded were never counted.

The first sighting of Commodore Perry and his black ships off Edo. (A nineteenth-century Japanese woodblock print by Yoshi Toshi.)

After more than 200 years of isolation, the Japanese began to send envoys abroad to learn about the Western powers.

It was a national humiliation. And it was a personal humiliation for the sixteen-year-old Heihachiro Togo. Like many Japanese of his age, he felt that his country was being abused and exploited by the imperial powers of the West. He realized, even then, that Japan had to modernize, and he wanted to be part of that process.

In the ensuing years, the Japanese launched a campaign to learn as much as possible about the Western powers and their civilization. Over the next four years, sixty-eight envoys were dispatched on fact-finding missions to the West, and by 1868 over 150 Japanese had had direct experience of Western society and technology. The original language of communication with the outside world had been Portuguese and then Dutch. The Japanese soon recognized that in order to deal with the two greatest world powers, Britain and America, they would need to learn English.

But it was not only a new language which the Japanese were learning but a new approach to the military arts. Already, new military leaders were emerging, men such as Aritomo Yamagata and Tsuugumichi Saigo, who had learnt military tactics in Europe.

Many in Japan feared that this would alienate the samurai and leave control in the hands of people unversed in the traditional customs of war and lacking the martial spirit. The samurai ethic, however, had proved to be fundamentally conservative and resistant to change. If Japan were to alter itself, the samurai would have to find a new role. Nationalism was to provide the overriding incentive for co-operation.

That year, 1868, the real power of the monarchy was restored in Japan and the Emperor was replaced at the centre of the political stage, after 250 years of military dictatorship created by the dynasty of Tokugawa Ieyasu. The young Emperor Meiji was to become the symbol for a group of younger samurai who seized power and disempowered the Shogunate. They began to build a modern government structure and, at the same time, to dismantle the class system of feudal lords and samurai. The new capital of the imperial Government was transferred from Kyoto to Edo, renamed Tokyo.

By an extraordinary political decision, supported by the samurai, the Japanese set in motion the changes that were to make them one of the world's foremost economic and industrial powers. The old order would soon perish. The overwhelming influence of the old samurai class was gone and the samurai themselves were either brought into the imperial administration as civil servants or encouraged to join the armed forces. Many of them voluntarily, and with some aid from the Government, began to earn their own living for the first time, something which their tradition had previously forbidden. They also gave up what were literally their most valued possessions, their swords. One young samurai, Heihachiro Togo, decided to join the navy.

Heihachiro Togo

Admiral Togo, 'the Japanese Nelson'.

Togo was born in 1848 in the port of Kagoshima near Kyushu, Satsuma province, into a samurai family. The feudal Japan of his youth was economically backward and industrially weak. It was vulnerable to the powerful interests of Britain, America and France. This much Togo had seen from the action at Kagoshima in 1863.

Three years later, in 1866, his father encouraged his sons to join the newly instituted Satsuma naval force. Like many of his contemporaries, Togo began to learn English, and in 1871 he was selected to train under the guidance of Britain's Royal Navy at Greenwich in London. He spent that summer at Southampton and Plymouth, learning English and looking at ships in the docks. He studied everything and committed all that he saw to memory. In the autumn he returned to London to board the marine training ship, the *Worcester*. He was to remain in England for the next seven years.

His commanding officer on the *Worcester*, Captain Smith, described Cadet Togo as 'not what you would call brilliant, but a great plodder; slow to learn, but very sure of what he had learnt'. He overcame his classmates' racist jibes about 'Johnny Chinaman' and passed out second in his class in 1873. Over the next two years, his training programme continued, including a five-month voyage on *HMS Hampshire* in February 1875, during which he rounded the Cape of Good Hope and visited Melbourne. He returned to England for training in mathematics at Cambridge, where he contracted a disease of the eye that threatened his sight; the Japanese Embassy intervened, and he was rushed to Harley Street in central London for surgery. His sight was saved.

Togo's stay in England taught him that a small island could control a vast empire by using an efficient, modern and disciplined navy. The 1870s were a period of expansion in the Japanese military: in 1873 the Government introduced conscription for the army, and in 1876 took Japan into a war with Korea, imposing on it the same harsh trade treaties which had been forced on Japan by the Western empires. The Japanese navy commissioned ships to be built in England for its new fleet. Togo himself stayed on in England to supervise the building of the first of these ships, the *Fuso*; he came to know every plate and rivet of it.

But there were troubles in Japan which were to affect Togo while he was still in England. In the new Japan, the samurai resented the Government's change of tactics from persuasion to compulsion. The final blow was the formal decree that forbade them to carry swords. A last-ditch stand by the 'flower of the samurai' against the Meiji authorities was led by Takamori Saigo in 1877 from the Satsuma province. It was unsuccessful. Among these 15,000 rebellious subjects were Togo's family, and his elder brother Sokuro was killed in the final defeat of Saigo's forces at Shiroyama. Togo grieved for his brother, but he did not feel responsible for his family's attitudes. It was the end of old Japan, and Togo was part of the new.

A Japanese woodblock of a horse-drawn tramway from the end of the nineteenth century. Traditional Japan was in the process of transforming itself into a modern industrial nation.

At home, the Japanese had grasped the importance of modernizing not only the armed forces but the industrial base of the country. Until as late as the turn of the twentieth century, Japan was still a predominantly rural and agricultural country. But when Togo returned to Japan in 1878 the Japanese fleet was well on the way to becoming the model of a modern fighting navy, strongly influenced by the British, especially by the tactics of Admiral Nelson.

Japan had itself changed during Togo's absence: railways, telegraph, factories and sky-scrapers, funded by massive foreign investment, were altering the face of the country. All over Japan, a new and confident outlook was rapidly forming, inspired by the cry, 'Enrich the country, strengthen the military.' Japan was booming, and nationalism was flourishing under the similar slogan of the army commander Marshal Aritomo Yamagata, 'Wealth and Strength'.

Togo joined the newly established Naval College at Tsukiji, where thirty British offi-cers taught the young Japanese, and rose through the ranks to the royal yacht *Jingei*, on which he became first lieutenant. He was then posted to the *Amagi*, an old wooden ship, where he was appointed lieutenant commander and then commander. His first captaincy, in 1883–4, was of the *Daini Tihu*, a small 125-ton and 135-foot inshore coaster. His experience in the building of the *Fuso* proved vital to the Japanese navy, whose senior officers understood that to compete with the Western powers it would have to manufacture its own ships. They had copied British construction methods, but were determined to build their ships to a higher standard than the British: to this end, they learnt the designs and methods, and then improved them. It was through such skill and perseverance that the Japanese navy came to be the first to install torpedo tubes on its ships.

In June 1885, Togo was duly sent to oversee the construction of the ship *Yamato* and became its captain in 1886. He was still under forty years old. But he was then laid low by rheumatic arthritis, and spent the next year bedridden. In 1890 he was ready to serve again, and rejoined the navy as chief of staff to the commander of the naval base at Kure, the protected harbour in the Inland Sea.

Japan, China and Russia

Throughout the 1880s and 1890s, Japan presented an aggressive and expanding front in Asia, most dramatically in the conflicts with Korea and China. As early as 1880 the British decided that closer links with Japan would be prudent and would help protect their own interests in Asia: a £1 million British loan followed, which was used by the Japanese to build telegraph cables and railway track.

As Japan grew imperially, its strategic needs changed. Across the Straits of Tsushima lay Korea, with the Sea of Japan to the north-east and the Yellow Sea to the south-west; Korea itself was wedged between Japan's most powerful regional competitors, China and Russia. The speed of Japan's emergence as a new force threatened the established balance of power in Asia, and to the cautious Japanese Korea was 'the dagger pointing at the heart of the nation' from which a hostile power was most likely to launch an attack.

By 1894, the Japanese felt that Chinese influence in Korea had reached a level which threatened the Japanese trade treaties established in the 1870s. A brief but decisive war followed between China and Japan. The first shot, on 1 August that year, was fired by

Captain Heihachiro Togo, commanding the *Naniwa*, which engaged with the Chinese cruiser *Chi Yuen* and then with a troop carrier, the *Kowshing*. His initial encounters with the Chinese were swift and brutal, his men sinking the *Kowshing* and machine-gunning the Chinese survivors. An important strand of samurai ethic was still alive in Japan: implacable contempt for defeated forces.

By the end of 1895, the Japanese had secured high-profile land and naval victories, at Seoul, Pyongyang and the capital of the Chinese Liaotong peninsula, Port Arthur (which later, as a result of the great powers' intervention, Japan was forced to give up). These successes exposed the weakness in China's control over Korea and alarmed the major colonial powers, Germany, France and Britain. When the Chinese eventually sued for peace, the Japanese had demonstrated that they had created a first-rate military machine in little over twenty years.

Togo himself had performed with his customary cool and detachment throughout the campaign. One of the wiliest and most aggressive of Japan's commanders, he was appointed President of the Naval War College in 1896. During his four-year appointment, he was able to make a detailed study of the Straits of Tsushima, which he believed would one day be vital to the defence of his country. He would eventually be proved right.

Togo could see that the next great struggle would be against Tsarist Russia, which was beginning to overreach itself, enlarging its empire through Manchuria towards Korea. To establish a hedge against Russian expansion in Korea, the Japanese sought alliance with Britain. For the British, this would also provide a useful military ally in their own check of Russian expansion in Asia. An Anglo-Japanese agreement was duly signed in 1902, satisfying the Japanese that they need not fear opposition from the most powerful naval force in the world. Now they felt sufficient confidence to enter a round of hard bargaining with Russia.

On 6 February 1904, after a long period of tense negotiations, Japan broke off diplomatic relations with Russia. It was the inevitable outcome of their conflicting interests in mainland Asia. War was declared on the 10th. The night before, in a lightning move, Togo's fleet had attacked and trapped the Russian ships at the strategically important Port Arthur. The pre-emptive strike was typically Japanese. It was a tactic which the samurai would recognize as one of their own: 'Win first, fight later.' Japan was now at war with the mighty Tsarist Empire. The next months would make or break the new Asian power. That same year, Togo was promoted from Commander-in-Chief of the Combined Fleet to full Admiral.

Tsushima, 1905

Admiral Togo took a dispassionate view of the enemy now facing him. The Russian navy had once been great, but, in parallel with the rest of the decadent Russian ruling class, had fallen into slack and undisciplined ways, operating through favouritism and bribery, with rich men buying commissions in order to show off their smart uniforms in the cities. Togo remarked from his observation of Russian ships in the 1890s and 1900s:

> The Russians are too ready to use their warships as freighters for military supplies. Any ship used frequently as a cargo carrier loses her fighting quality.

By 10 March 1904, Togo had exploited the vulnerability of the Russian fleet under the great Admiral Makarov by establishing a stringent blockade of the entrance to Port Arthur by means of sunken ships and carefully placed submarine mines. For the time being, after a brief engagement with the Russians, he had only rendered Makarov's fleet ineffective; it would not come into the open sea to fight, as its ships were trapped in the harbour. Togo had learnt from Makarov's book of naval tactics, which he had ordered to be translated into Japanese. He had therefore added not just British but Russian naval expertise to his own.

Makarov tried to break out of Port Arthur in the spring of 1905, but found himself caught between Togo's cruisers and the sea mines laid by the Japanese. Worse was to come. His flagship, the *Petropavlosk*, was destroyed by a mine, and Makarov himself went down with it. For the world's press, enraptured by the contest between the two contrasting empires, the 'yellow Admiral' had defeated the 'white Admiral'.

Without control of the sea around Korea and Japan, the Russians would have little chance of winning the war. Tsar Nicholas II (1868–1918) had decided to dispatch the Baltic fleet a gruelling 18,000 miles to Japan to relieve them. The Vice-Admiral in charge was the physically impressive Zinovi Petrovich Rozhestvenski (1848–1909), an impatient man ready to quarrel with anyone. He was also vain; to make his fleet stand out from the rest of the Russian navy he ordered that every funnel of the ships under his command be painted a gaudy yellow and every hull a shiny black. But he faced a daunting task. He was to sail 18,000 miles into unfamiliar waters to confront an enemy of great skill, power and bravery. He could expect no quarter from Togo's fleet. The ships of the Russian Baltic Fleet, the lees of the Empire, were in any case a sorry contrast to Togo's superior force. Moreover, their sailors were demoralized through shortage of funds and unprepared through lack of training. As if all this were not enough, Rozhestvenski himself had never commanded a fleet in battle.

The forty-five warships of the Baltic fleet left the Gulf of Finland in October 1904: they would sail around Africa, cross the Indian Ocean, and head through the Malacca Straits in Indonesia to Vladivostok. Rozhestvenski tried, but failed, to lose his oldest and weakest ships, which he feared would impede him, by sending them through the Suez Canal. Togo was delighted. His enemy would be tired, sea-weary from the seven-month voyage, and unable to refuel with coal at any of the ports controlled by the British, who were bound to Japan by the 1902 treaty.

Communications in the Russian fleet were poor. In the Atlantic, the Russians had mistakenly attacked a fleet of English fishing trawlers from Hull, believing them to be the enemy torpedo boats. Several fishermen were killed. The Russian guns fired for twelve minutes before the ceasefire order was transmitted and understood – their ships had not been fitted with the latest Marconi communications equipment. This was one of the most significant differences between the resources available to Rozhestvenski and Togo: the Japanese had immediately installed the most modern and efficient communications system they could find.

Off the coast of Africa, Rozhestvenski ordered his fleet to spend a day engaged in target practice. An old fishing boat was towed behind a destroyer, and the Russian gunners

Vice-Admiral Rozhestvenski, leader of the Russian Baltic fleet.

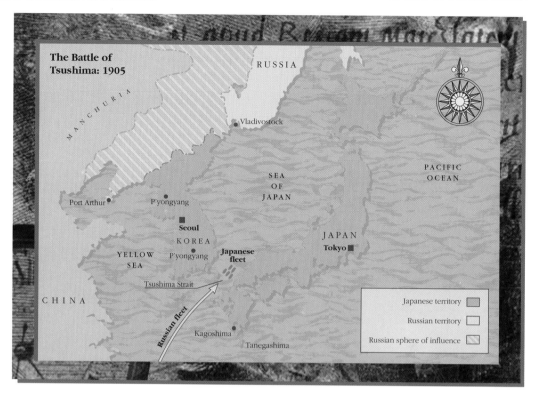

loosed thousands of shells at it. They managed only one hit, and that was on the destroyer itself, which promptly sank. When the news of the blockade of Port Arthur reached Rozhestvenski on 5 January 1905, it came as a severe blow. Depressed, he sent this telegram to his Admiralty:

> I have not the slightest prospect of recovering command of the sea with the force under my orders. The dispatch of reinforcements composed of untested and in some cases badly built vessels would only render the fleet more vulnerable.

Togo too knew that the Russian fleet was vulnerable: it kept station sloppily, the ships were so heavy with supplies that their decks were awash, and their livery of shiny black hulls and bright yellow funnels made them easy targets. Besides, Togo knew where he was going to fight, on the waters he knew well. He waited with sixteen ships in the Straits of Tsushima, certain that Rozhestvenski would choose that route north-east to Port Arthur. The Russian Vice-Admiral was indeed heading for Vladivostok, hoping to avoid encountering Togo altogether. As the Russians entered the China Sea in April 1905, Togo braced himself for the fight. Seven months' waiting was now at an end.

The Russians reached the Straits of Tsushima during the foggy night of 16 May 1905. Visibility was less than 4,000 yards. One of Rozhestvenski's commanders commented:

> How can they find us in this? It's 20,000 to one against anyone running into us accidentally. We have been going for 24 hours without being seen. If it's the same tomorrow, we'll give them the slip! They haven't come on us! ... what a stew they must be in! What fun.

But, at 2.45am, the Japanese cruiser *Shinano Maru* sighted the Russian battle line: an auxiliary ship was carelessly burning lights. As dawn broke on the morning of 27 May, Admiral Togo sent a signal to the Minister of the Navy in Tokyo: 'The Russian fleet has been sighted. I am going to attack it and annihilate it.'

Togo set course to intercept the Russian fleet by 2pm at a point where it would be strung out and exposed as it headed for the island of Okinoshima. He had originally planned an attack strategy using torpedo boats throughout a four-day battle, but the weather was too rough for the smaller vessels to operate, and he was forced to plan instead for an exchange between battleships. The fleets met at 1.55pm. Togo issued this general order to his fleet:

> The combined squadrons are at last to meet the enemy. We have developed a high fighting efficiency, and now that we are to defeat the enemy, there is little more that I can say to you . . . In battle the most important thing is caution. We must not fear a formidable enemy, or make light of a weak one, and we must not be taken by surprise.

In contrast, Vice-Admiral Rozhestvenski's Orders of the Day for 27 May were more cautious:

> Our squadron is not only equal in strength to the enemy's, but we are superior in the number of battleships. The Japanese, however, have had more experience of war than us, and are more skilled in gunnery and warfare. You must not forget this. Though they may fire with greater rapidity than us, we must not imitate them and waste ammunition. The Japanese are of unparalleled loyalty to their Imperial family and state. They are a nation who hate dishonour and think nothing of sacrificing their lives in the cause of heroism . . .

Though Togo's battleships were faster and better armed than Rozhestvenski's, he had fewer ships at his command. His fleet consisted of four battleships, eight heavy and sixteen light cruisers and twenty-one destroyers, as well as the fifty-seven torpedo boats rendered useless in the heavy seas. Rozhestvenski's forty-five warships were by themselves a match for Togo's entire fleet. But Togo had the distinct advantage of Marconi radio links between his ships. The Russians were communicating by flags, a method that was sometimes as hazardous as it was slow: Rozhestvenski's signalled order 'Steer North 20 Degrees East' was kept flying by mistake throughout the battle and caused much confusion among his fleet.

By 2pm, thirty-six Russian ships had entered the Straits of Tsushima, and the two fleets were on collision course. Togo immediately ordered the manoeuvre which put his battleships across the path of the Russian fleet: at 2.08pm, each Japanese ship turned at right angles to the oncoming Russians. It was a dangerous and daring plan, borrowed from Nelson at Trafalgar. In executing it, Togo exposed himself to the forward guns of the Russians. At 3pm, his fleet moved to cross the Russian line. He had thereby managed to cut off their path to Vladivostok. More than this, he had crossed the 'T': this meant that he could now fire broadsides at the Russians, who could only use their forward armaments with great care, for fear of hitting their sister ships in front.

Togo's flagship, the *Mikasa*, sustained the first of forty-eight direct hits. Although it smashed the compass at the Admiral's side as he stood on the bridge, he ignored the incoming shells and waited until the Russian ships were at point-blank range. He then let loose a murderous volley of controlled fire on the enemy. His fleet was launching new armour-piercing shells at three times the Russian rate of fire. Within thirty minutes, the Baltic fleet was crippled, its rangefinders and navigation instruments destroyed, and the decks of the ships covered with blood, bodies and severed limbs. The flagship officer, Commander Vladimir Semenoff, later wrote:

It seemed impossible even to count the number of projectiles striking us. Shells seemed to be pouring upon us incessantly one after another. The steel plates and superstructures on the upper deck were torn to pieces, and the splinters caused many casualties. Iron ladders were crumpled up into rings, and guns were literally hurled from their mountings. In addition to this there was the unusually high temperature and liquid flame of the explosion, which seemed to spread over everything. I actually watched a steel plate catch fire from a burst.

On the bridge of Togo's flagship, a Royal Navy observer watched the 13,500-ton battleship *Imperator Alexander III* under attack from Togo's rain of fire:

To the left, at about 5,000 yards, the *Alexander* has just sunk with all hands. The forward gunners put three shells into her magazine at which point she blew up, sending her fully ten feet into the air, landing bottom up and sinking. It all took place within a minute.

One Russian survivor, from the 13,000-ton *Ossylaba*, described the panic and fear on board as his ship went down:

The battleship was heeling at such an angle that it was evident that she would be on her side in a few seconds. Water was streaming in. Not waiting for orders, everyone rushed aloft, shouting frantically. My God, how the wounded groaned now! The fitter sailors trampled them underfoot, mercilessly stamping on them as they struggled to get out. There were so many people crowding the hatches that they could go neither forward nor back. Many crawled over other people's heads.

Rozhestvenski's fleet was smashed, the ships crippled and the sailors decimated. With the seas now less heavy, Togo sent in his torpedo boats throughout the night to finish off those Russian ships which had patched the leaks and were pressing on to Vladivostok. All through the night, the torpedo boats launched their deadly cargo along the spotlight beams from the Russian ships.

By 10.30am on 28 May, the Russian flagship *Nicholas I* signalled surrender. But Togo ignored the signal and continued to pour shells into the stricken Russian ships, perhaps remembering how the British had raked his home town with a hail of shells over forty years before. One of his deputies called to him that the spirit of Bushido, the ethical code of the samurai warrior, required that the Japanese show generosity to a defeated foe – in this instance to cease fire. The Japanese did so. But only three Russian ships reached Vladivostok.

At sea on 27–28 May, the Russians lost thirty-four ships and 4,830 sailors, and 5,917 prisoners of war were taken, the wounded Rozhestvenski among them. Togo visited him in hospital with this dispassionate advice: 'Defeat is a common fate of a soldier. There is nothing to be ashamed of in it. The great point is whether we have performed our duty.' The Japanese dead numbered 117; and their losses in ships amounted to only three torpedo boats.

The *Japan Chronicle*, published weekly in Kobe, reported on 30 May 1905:

The Baltic Fleet, of which we have heard so much during the last nine months, is now no more. Some of the finest ships are in Japanese hands, others are at the bottom of the sea; while the men neither drowned nor killed are now prisoners. Little else, it may be said, was expected, but the comparatively easy victory which Admiral Togo appears to have gained will set people wondering why the Baltic Fleet persisted on its voyage when, once Port Arthur had fallen, everything was against the

Russians. The vessels were of a composite character and the best of them had not any opportunity of docking for the last seven months; they were fighting an enemy close to his base while twelve thousand miles from their own.

The consequences of the war were far-reaching. The Russian Baltic fleet was destroyed, and the Japanese would win the war for Korea. Russia itself would go through spasms of social upheaval later in 1905, and the ruling Romanov family would in 1917 cease to govern (see Chapter 12). All these events were a direct result of Togo's victory at Tsushima.

The Russian Tsar accepted the mediation of the President of the United States, Theodore Roosevelt (1858–1919), who arranged for peace negotiations to take place at Portsmouth, New Hampshire. The resulting treaty was signed on 23 August 1905. Russia was forced to evacuate Manchuria and to recognize Japan's sphere of influence in Korea. Japan was now a significant imperial power in East Asia.

The Battle of Tsushima was thereafter marked in Japan by Navy Day, 27 May, and was celebrated by the Japanese until 1945. In the wake of the victories of the 1905 war, Japan had arrived. It was now a major maritime and therefore established imperial power. At the victory celebrations which coincided with his appointment as Chief of the Imperial General Staff on 20 December 1905, Admiral Togo said:

> The gods award the crown to those who, by their training in peacetime, are victorious even before they go into battle. But the gods soon take the crown away from those who relax in the pleasures of peace. After a victory, tighten your helmet.

The statue of Admiral Togo that stands in Kagoshima in Satsuma province.

Togo died in 1934, and was given the first state funeral accorded to a man who was not at least a prince of the imperial family. His samurai message, 'Win first, fight later', was never to be forgotten. Certainly, Admiral Yamamoto, as he planned the raid on the US fleet at Pearl Harbor in 1941, must have been influenced by this philosophy.

Although Togo's reputation slumped in the anti-military era which followed the Japanese defeat in the Second World War, a statue to him was erected in the 1980s in Kagoshima, in his native province of Satsuma. A bloodstained map from the bridge of the Japanese flagship, the *Mikasa*, together with a lock of Nelson's hair, was kept in a wooden case made from the timbers of Nelson's ship, the *Victory*, at the Japanese Naval Academy as a treasured momento of Japan's triumph over the Russians at Tsushima.

Togo had taught Japan in 1905 that complete victory was everything. His country was to fight two more wars within a generation with the same implacable dedication. The samurai ethic had passed into modern Japanese consciousness. By the Battle of Tsushima, the balance of power in the East had irrevocably changed. The extraordinary transformation, in less than one hundred years, of a small island, for so long feudal in structure and hostile to outsiders, to a modern, sophisticated world power would have ramifications throughout the twentieth century.

· 12 ·
The Russian
REVOLUTION

LENIN'S BOLSHEVIKS LEAD THE RUSSIAN REVOLUTION
WHICH GIVES THE WORLD A NEW IDEOLOGY – COMMUNISM.

The capitalists have always called 'freedom' the freedom to make money
for the rich, and the freedom to die of hunger for workmen. The capitalists call 'freedom' the freedom of the rich, freedom to buy up the press, to
use wealth, to manufacture and support so-called public opinion . . .
Actual freedom and equality will exist only in the order established by the
Communists, in which it will be impossible to become rich at the expense
of another . . .   (Vladimir Ilyich Ulyanov – 'Lenin', 1919 Congress
of the Communist International)

HISTORY TEACHES THAT no oppressed class has ever come to power, and
cannot come to power, without passing through a period of dictatorship.
That was what Lenin told the 1919 Congress of the Communist
International in his Chairman's address. Two years before he had staged
the most daring coup of his time: the Russian Revolution of October
1917 had overthrown one of the greatest political orders in Europe; it had ended one
empire and begun another. 'The Revolution', declared Lenin, 'does not need historians.'

The Russian Empire at the turn of the century was greater than the USA, China and
India combined, with a population in 1906 of 150 million. Russia looked east to Asia and
west to Europe, poised between two worlds. The 1917 Revolution changed all that.
From Lenin's achievement Russia evolved a harsh Communist regime which for seventy
years held the country in the grip of an implacable new ideology. Under Lenin and his
successors Josef Stalin and Nikita Khrushchev, Russia was to survive the hostility of the
capitalist West and, for a while, to stand as a model for others to emulate.

Lenin is rare in history because he achieved something that would not have come
about through the action of politics, of an interest group, or of any other individual. The
Russian Revolution of 1917 was neither predictable nor inevitable; but it was clear that
Lenin had the charisma and expertise to transform his ideas into political realities. His
character suited the times. Communist Russia from the start bore the stamp of one man.

OPPOSITE: *Lenin
addresses the crowds in
Petrograd, in 1917.*

Lenin and Russia up to 1905

Lenin was born Vladimir Ilyich Ulyanov in April 1870 in Simbirsk, a small town on the River Volga. His father was an inspector of schools, and helped to establish hundreds of them in the Simbirsk region. At Simbirsk itself, the high school was run by Fyodor Kerensky, father of the man who, though eleven years younger, was to become Ulyanov's greatest political rival.

Kerensky's father wrote the reference which helped his pupil, the young Vladimir Ulyanov, gain a place at Kazan University as a law student in 1887: 'There is not a single instance on record, either in school or out of it, of Ulyanov's evoking by word or deed any adverse opinion from the authorities and teachers of his school.' He was 'talented, invariably diligent, prompt and reliable', but, Kerensky added, 'I could not but observe in him an excessive introversion and lack of sociability . . . in short, an aversion to companionship.' To act as a referee for a Ulyanov from Simbirsk in 1887 took courage, for in March of that year Ulyanov's brother Alexander had been arrested in St Petersburg for carrying a bomb with which he intended to kill Tsar Alexander III (1845–94), whose father had been assassinated six years before. He was tried and executed.

Alexander Kerensky (1881–1970), was later to write:

The Ulyanov family in 1879 in Simbirsk. From left to right: Olga, Alexander, Anna; (seated) Maria Alexandrovna Ulyanov with her daughter Maria on her lap, Dmitri, Ilia Nikolayevich Ulyanov, Vladimir.

Although Alexander Ulianov entered my life only fleetingly, he left an indelible impression, not as a person but as an ominous threat that played upon my childish imagination. The mere mention of his name evoked a picture of a mysterious carriage with drawn green blinds driving through the town at night to take people into the unknown. (Abraham)

It was a time of civil unrest. For almost 300 years the Romanov family had ruled Russia under a system which gave autocratic and unlimited power to the tsar or emperor. The royal family kept itself aloof from the people, but discontent with the Romanovs in town and country was spreading. Serfdom in Russia had recently been abolished, but society was still predominantly rural, with four-fifths of the people living in villages, most of them in grinding poverty. There were frequent university protests by student revolutionaries.

It was as the brother of one such martyred student revolutionary that Ulyanov attended Kazan University. The assassination attempt by his brother and his brother's subsequent execution left him with an entrenched hatred of the Tsarist regime. Despite his introverted nature, he was soon drawn into student politics and was arrested and expelled with thirty-nine other students after a demonstration in protest against restrictive university regulations. He applied to be allowed back into the university, and the authorities finally relented in 1890; Ulyanov became an external student, passing the Bar exam in November 1891. Yet it was not to law but to Marxism and economics that he then turned his attention. Alexander Kerensky, too, was to become a lawyer and a socialist.

Little in Ulyanov's early life foretold the future revolutionary. But it was clear that his uncompromising outlook and sheer force of will would bring him into conflict with other absolutes. One of his closest associates during the 1890s, Peter Struve, noticed that he had grown to hate authority in all its forms. As Struve later wrote:

LEFT: *The Jordan staircase of the Winter Palace.*

He hated not only the existing autocracy (the Tsar) and the bureaucracy, not only the lawlessness and arbitrary rule of the police, but also their antipodes – the 'liberals' and the 'bourgeoisie'. That hatred had something repulsive and terrible in it; for being rooted in the concrete, I should say even animal, emotions and repulsions, it was at the same time abstract and cold like Lenin's whole being. (Pipes)

BELOW: *Tsar Nicholas II and Alexandra in the Winter Palace at St Petersburg, January 1903.*

In 1893, Vladimir Ulyanov arrived in St Petersburg, the location of the country's premier law faculty and the city that one day would bear his name as Leningrad. Prematurely bald, short and stocky, he was described by a British diplomat as having the appearance of a provincial grocer. But he had a hypnotic power over others, which in part arose from his extraordinary faith in his ideas and in himself.

In the winter of 1895–6 he was arrested for inciting strikes, and like many other revolutionaries he spent three years in Siberian exile. One of his comrades, Nadezhda Krupskaya, wanted to be exiled to the same place, but this was allowed only if they were married. So Lenin, to whom all obstacles existed only to be knocked down, married her. Their exile was less stark than might be supposed and, as intellectuals with some money of their own, they lived in relative comfort, Vladimir sometimes hunting game in the Siberian forests. The exile would have been longer had he not, before his arrest, passed off one of his manuscripts as the work of an associate, who was consequently sentenced to an extra two years of imprisonment and exile. This deception gives some indication of Ulyanov's fear of physical privation. During his imprisonment, he read, translated and studied, absorbing ideas and feeding his mind; he also wrote prolifically and first adopted at this time the pseudonym 'Lenin'.

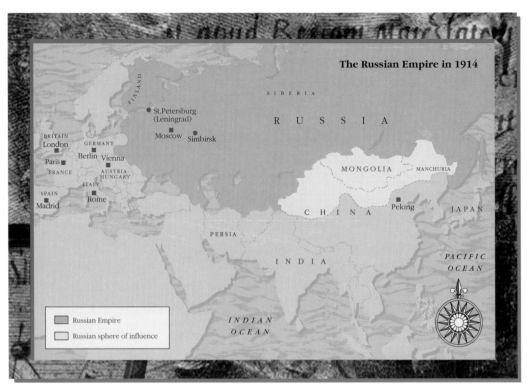

On his release, Lenin travelled to Geneva to join the Russian Social Democratic Party before moving to Munich, where he founded and co-edited the party newspaper *Iskra* ('The Spark'). From its first issue in December 1890 it became influential in Communist circles both internationally and within Russia:

> Revolution is a tough business. You can't make it wearing white gloves and with clean hands . . .
>
> Give us an organization of revolutionaries, and we will overthrow Russia.

During this time, Lenin became convinced of the need for professional, dispassionate revolutionaries. It was this conviction which in March 1902 inspired him to write the pamphlet *What Is to Be Done?* in which he urged that an 'organization of revolutionaries must chiefly and above all include people whose profession is revolutionary activity'. This important essay was part of his attempt to take over the Social Democratic Party. As a result of Lenin's ruthless tactics, the Party split at its Second Congress in 1903, into a majority and a minority, or 'Bolsheviks' and 'Mensheviks', the former led by Lenin. Bolsheviks and Mensheviks alike were driven by Marxist ideology, but Lenin's faction believed in making the revolution happen, unlike the Mensheviks, who expected the effect of economic and political circumstances combined to produce a social crisis and general upheaval. Both wings believed in collective ownership of property and of the means of production.

Lenin could tolerate no dissent, neither opposition nor criticism. The world was divided into friends and enemies. He knew no compromise. In 1904, Leon Trotsky (born Lev Bronstein; 1879–1940) compared him to the French revolutionary Maximilien Robespierre, 'who knew only two parties – that of good citizens and that of bad citizens. This political aphorism is engraved in the heart of Maximilien Lenin.' He could be cruel in the cause, and was referred to as a 'thinking guillotine'. Lenin knew no intellectual or moral fear. His strengths were unblinking commitment to the Bolshevik cause, a capacity for prolonged thought and hard work, and the will to attend to detailed organization. His weakness was his cowardice in the face of physical danger.

In 1905 an uprising rocked Tsarist Russia for the first time, but, despite their commitment to ideology and their determination to translate this into political action, Lenin and the Bolsheviks had little to do with the events of that year. The history of Russia was shaped on this occasion by external circumstances. For a year the great Tsarist Empire had been locked in a war for control over Manchuria with the rising power of Japan which had inflicted a series of humiliating defeats on the Russians. The war was the harebrained idea of Nicholas II (1868–1918), who had been Tsar since his father's death in 1894. Fired by his belief in Russia's imperial destiny he provoked the conflict against the advice of his ministers, who feared that both international and domestic instability would result. The Manchurian setbacks were therefore a severe rebuff to his expansionist plans and a blow to his prestige. Russia had been forced to sustain devastating losses on land (at Mukden in Manchuria the Russians lost 89,000 men) and at sea (off Port Arthur and in the Straits of Tsushima). It was the fall of Port Arthur (only recently leased from China) in December 1904 and the capture of 25,000 Russians which started a chain of events that would lead directly to the toppling of the Tsar.

Leon Trotsky, in a photograph taken in 1920 by Moisei Nappelbaum, the great Russian photographic portraitist of the period.

The war had exposed him as a muddled and ineffectual leader who was over-ambitious and out of contact with his people. A wave of unrest and discontent swept across the country. The cry for political reform was to prove irresistible. In early January 1905, 120,000 workers in St Petersburg staged a strike for better conditions. At 6am on Sunday the 9th, at the Narva Gate in the south-west of the city, a group of demonstrators led by a priest named Georgy Gapon was fired upon by Tsarist troops. Two hundred died and 800 were wounded. It became known as 'Bloody Sunday' and triggered a year of revolt which shook but did not overturn the Romanov throne. Nicholas, however, was fatally discredited. In London, the future Labour Prime Minister Ramsay Macdonald condemned him as 'a blood-stained creature'.

Workers' unions were now formed. Strikes spread like wildfire, and Russia stood on the edge of an abyss, almost in a state of civil war. The Tsar's uncle, Grand Duke Sergei, was blown up, riots and massacres occurred across the country, the sailors of the battleship *Potemkin* mutinied in June, and the strikes continued into the autumn. In St Petersburg, strike committees merged into a Workers' Council, or 'Soviet', led by Leon Trotsky. Aspiring to the status of an alternative political and economic administration, it represented an important aspect of the 1905 revolution, as the 'dress rehearsal' for 1917.

On 17 October, Tsar Nicholas signed under duress the 'October Manifesto', which granted to his subjects civil liberties, electoral rights and a say in legislation. Principal among the reforms was an advisory body, the newly formed State Duma, a representative assembly or council for the people of Russia. One of the Duma's few independent voices was the thirty-four-year-old Alexander Kerensky.

Throughout his life, Kerensky remained a constitutionalist, a democrat with revolutionary leanings. Lenin, however, was a revolutionary with democratic leanings. While Kerensky believed in the rule of law, Lenin trusted only in revolution; while Kerensky wanted the poor to become rich by working, Lenin wanted them to become richer by the redistribution of wealth from the rich; while Kerensky was flexible and charismatic, Lenin was obsessive. Despite being an elected member of the Duma and a committed democrat, Kerensky toured the country meeting revolutionaries and planning the Tsar's overthrow:

Dear friends and comrades. We can rid ourselves of the Tsarist crooks. These cowards and clowns must be swept out of our country.

All men must be able to decide Russia's future. I will lead a fight so that all Russians will be free. (Abraham)

The Tsar's court continued aloof. The Tsar abhorred politics and was happiest in the bosom of his family, and the Empress – of German birth and English upbringing – felt Russian high society as strange. The 1905 uprising failed to solve Russia's fundamental problem – there was still a gulf between the rulers and the ruled. Lenin waited.

Russia 1905–1917

Russia had tasted the chaos of revolution in 1905. The Tsar's regime had been rocked but not displaced. Peter Stolypin, according to the British ambassador in St Petersburg 'the most notable figure in Europe', was appointed Prime Minister, charged with implementing a programme of cautious reform. He challenged the unthinking impatience of the revolutionaries – 'You want upheavals, but we want a great Russia' – and pursued them with such gusto that the hangman's noose became known as the 'Stolypin necktie'. But he was the one man able to steer Russia through this uneasy period towards a stable society.

The years after 1905 were relatively calm. Stolypin gradually promoted social and agricultural reforms, and the third Duma, elected in 1907 (Nicholas had dissolved the first two for promoting revolution), lasted until November 1912. Scientific and cultural life in Russia experienced a period of enormous creativity. The country produced innovative leaders in science and engineering such as Dmitri Mendeleyev, Alexander Popov, Ivan Pavlov and Igor Sikorsky. Russian literature had rolled down the nineteenth century into the 1890s and 1900s with writers such as Leo Tolstoy, Anton Chekhov, Maxim Gorky and, later, Boris Pasternak, whose *Dr Zhivago* is set against the unfolding events of the Russian Revolution. The great Moscow Art Theatre and the Alexandrovsky Theatre in St Petersburg featured work by Konstantin Stanislavsky and Vsevolod Meyerhold. The ballet, too, prospered, and Russia was home to the choreographer Serge Diaghilev and the dancers Vaslav Nijinski and Anna Pavlova. Its musical life was particularly rich, with composers such as Sergei Rachmaninov, Alexander Scriabin, Sergei Prokofiev, Nikolai Rimsky-Korsakov and Igor Stravinsky.

But in 1911 an event took place which would change Russia forever. Paradoxically, it happened at a performance of Rimsky-Korsakov's opera *Tsar Sultan* in Kiev, with Tsar Nicholas looking on from his imperial box. Peter Stolypin was shot by a revolutionary impatient for more and quicker change. He died four days later. Tsar Nicholas was no longer safe; he had lost a conservative reformer who might have guided Russia through the social changes that had become so vital. Count Kokovstev became Prime Minister.

The beginning of the end came in August 1914. It was at this point that the threat of German expansion in the West became a reality. The Kaiser's Government declared war. Russia began a war effort that sent 15 million troops into the field, the largest force of men under arms in the world. But they were no match for the German war machine. The German commander General Paul von Hindenburg wrote shortly after the war:

> In the Great War ledger, the page on which the Russian losses were written has been torn out. No one knows the figure. Five millions or eight millions? We too have no idea. All we know is that sometimes in our battles with the Russians we had to remove the mounds of enemy corpses in order to get a clear field of fire against fresh assaulting waves.

It was a wide road to war and a narrow path home. The army was ill-equipped, ill-trained and, after early losses of skilled officers, ill-led. Within a year, the Russian army had suffered four million casualties. So great were the numbers of wounded that some were even taken to the Winter Palace in Petrograd, as St Petersburg was renamed in 1914, which was soon filled to overflowing; they were also billeted in domestic houses around the city.

In 1915, the Tsar took personal command of the army. Keen to impress his authority and bolster morale, he toured the units on active duty and thereby unwittingly associated himself with the worst suffering, losses and defeats in living memory. At home, the royal family failed to provide leadership. The Tsarina Alexandra fell under the spell of the maniac mystic Gregory Rasputin, welcomed by the royal family as the man to control her son Alexis' haemophilia. With Rasputin's advice, the ruling dynasty might have survived; he was shrewd and cunning, and had the ear of the family. But by causing the dismissal of several ministers, including the Prime Minister Kokovstev, he made powerful enemies, and on 16 December 1916 he was poisoned and shot several times and killed by Prince

The July 1917 demonstrations, when dissent amongst the striking workers was at its height.

Yusupov, heir to the greatest fortune in Russia (it earned him the equivalent of a ton of gold each year). The Romanovs lost a trusted adviser.

The winter of 1916–1917 was cold, even by Russian standards, the air raw and the ice heavy on the streets. The cold led to hunger, and hunger to frustration directed against the Tsar and the Government. The angry peasants were uncertain about the decline of old communal structures following Stolypin's agrarian reforms. There was open disaffection in the upper ranks of Russian society provoked by the clumsy and botched management of the war.

The Cossacks, who had remained loyal to the Tsar in 1905, and represented the toughest and most dedicated defenders of the Empire, were by 1917 actually promoting the revolution, albeit covertly. The capital, Petrograd, was in disarray: food supplies were disrupted by the war and there were consequent shortages. Queues started at 4am each day for bread, sugar and tobacco; and Petrograd soon filled with untrained military recruits, earmarked for replacement regiments, who had no wish to fight at the front.

In February 1917, the Duma was reconvened. The strain on all sections of society from fighting Germany, the world's mightiest military power, had subdued the Russian will. It had become clear to people all over the country that the Tsar had to go; he now resembled the luckless Charles I of England and Louis XVI of France. Kerensky realized that Nicholas' abdication was essential to prevent a catastrophe. He told the Duma: 'If you will not listen to the voice of warning, you will find yourself face to face with facts, not warnings.'

Strikes in the capital that very month brought the seething discontent to the surface. Troops, angry about the war, refused to obey orders to disperse the demonstrators, thus turning industrial and political unrest into the Revolution of 27 February. On 2 March, in response to the crisis, a provisional government was formed under Prince Georgy Lvov, a liberal with much experience of local government and rural problems. His administration comprised other nobles like himself, intellectuals and reformers, with little representation for the workers or peasants. Kerensky, a lone socialist but with his power growing, was Minister of Justice:

> My memories of the first weeks of the Provisional Government are among the
> happiest of my political career. There were eleven of us in this government, of whom
> ten belonged to the liberal and moderate conservative parties. (Abraham)

The Provisional Government attempted to establish rights and recognize freedoms. Kerensky wrote that it 'tried to draw as many people as possible into the business of constructing the new order, thus instilling into the population a feeling of responsibility for the fate of the country as a whole'. Capitalists welcomed the February Revolution and the new administration: Russian bonds rose, and London brokers urged clients to buy oil and gold shares.

On the day of its formation the Provisional Government suggested to Tsar Nicholas that he should abdicate. He did so on 4 March, and left Petrograd four days later. On 21 March, Kerensky visited him at Tsarskoe Selo, where he was being held under house arrest:

> The whole family was standing huddled in confusion around a small table near a
> window in the adjoining room. A small man in uniform detached himself from the
> group and moved forward to meet me, hesitating and smiling weakly. It was the
> Emperor. On the threshold of the room in which I awaited him he stopped, as if
> uncertain what to do next. He did not know what my attitude would be. Was he to
> receive me as a host or should he wait until I spoke to him? Should he hold out his

hand, or should he wait for my salutation? I sensed his embarrassment at once as well as the confusion of the whole family left alone with a terrible revolutionary. I quickly went up to Nicholas II, held out my hand with a smile, and said abruptly 'Kerensky,' as I usually introduce myself. (Pipes)

After 303 years of ruling Russia, the Romanovs were deposed. After the defeat of the 1905 revolution, like many other revolutionaries, Lenin returned to his European exile. Lenin heard the news in Zurich. Between 1905 and 1914 he had been honing and perfecting his ideas by writing for revolutionary publications and by reading Marx and Engels; he had also evolved tactics based on those of eighteenth-century French revolutionaries. Cold and single-minded, he had been relieved by Stolypin's death, since his agrarian reforms would have removed support for the Bolsheviks had they been implemented fully.

Lenin had spent 1912–14 in the Austrian Polish city of Cracow to be close to the Russian frontier. From there in 1913 he had written to the great writer and revolutionary Maxim Gorky, expressing his wish for war:

A war between Austria and Russia would be a most useful thing for the revolution (in all of Eastern Europe) but is not very likely that Franz Joseph [Emperor of Austria, 1848–1916] and Nicky will give us this pleasure.

But, happily for Lenin, hostilities duly broke out. He was arrested as a Russian spy by Austrian police in Cracow at the outbreak of the war (Austria was allied to Germany), but was released as an 'enemy to Tsarism' and crossed into Switzerland. The war had answered his deepest desires. He publicly expressed his hopes that Russia would lose to Germany: what he wanted was *civil* war, the consequences of which, he believed, would be revolution. He had waited long enough. Now he was ready to move.

The ID card issued in the name of K.P. Ivanov, a worker, which was used by Lenin while in hiding in 1917.

Lenin arrives at the Finland Station, Petrograd, 1917.

He made many unsuccessful attempts to return to Russia, one of them involving disguise as a deaf-mute Swede. In the event the Germans, knowing he would cause disruption, organized his return. As Winston Churchill wrote in his *The World Crisis*: 'They turned upon Russia a most grisly of all weapons. They transported Lenin in a sealed truck like a plague bacillus into Russia.'

He arrived at the Finland Station, Petrograd, on the night of 3 April. On the station platform, he gave the now famous speech attacking Kerensky and the Provisional Government. It showed his political instinct and timing. It would ring throughout the world:

> The people need peace. The people need bread and land. And they give you war, hunger, no food, and the land remains with the landowners.

October 1917

The revolution of October 1917 came about because of two turning points in Russian history: the outbreak of the First World War in the summer of 1914 and the arrival of Lenin in Russia in April 1917. Had Lenin not reached Russia, the revolution of 25 October (7 November, New Style) would not have happened.

The Bolshevik Party in March 1917 was in no shape to bid for power; but by declining to support the Provisional Government and by refusing to compromise, Lenin and the Bolsheviks were perfectly placed to profit when the situation deteriorated and loyalties became polarized. They began to infiltrate the local workers' soviets.

Against this implacability, Lenin's rival Kerensky, though now Minister of Justice, would find nothing in his legal training or in his belief in law and reason to help him. He had known that the Tsar had to abdicate, but when that was achieved he put his faith in the democratic process.

Kerensky, thirty-six years old in 1917, became War Minister in early May. On 16 June he launched a summer offensive against Austria. It was disastrous. Trains returning from the battle fronts could hardly bear the weight of the deserters crammed into them and their axles caught fire. Deserting troops shot their officers. The disaffection in the army swelled the ranks of Lenin's Bolsheviks, based at the Smolny Institute in Petrograd. Lenin demanded that power be transferred from the Provisional Government to the soviets. Since his return to Russia, Lenin had campaigned recklessly and tirelessly to bring down the Government, inciting the army to ignore orders, the workers to seize factories and the peasants to take land.

He also had a brilliant and valuable ally, the propagandist Leon Trotsky, exiled after the 1905 revolution and newly returned to Russia in May. Trotsky had fled to Paris, then to Spain and the USA. He was the most assured orator and manipulator of images, and was central to Bolshevik propaganda in the crucial days before the takeover. Together he and Lenin waged psychological warfare, wearing down their opponents with argument and using information to attract support. Because of them, a few thousand Bolsheviks would

Trotsky addressing the Red Army during the civil war.

Alexander Kerensky, Prime Minister of the Provisional Government.

hold sway over a nation of 150 million. Another advantage the Bolsheviks enjoyed was a commitment to the idea of a Marxist world revolution, and therefore the belief that the Russian revolution was only the first phase, perhaps not even the most important. As Lenin said in 1918, 'There is no room for morality in politics.'

Suddenly, the popularity which Kerensky – known as the 'Persuader-in-Chief' – had steadily won through moderate domestic policy (as Justice Minister) and bullish nationalism (as War Minister) evaporated. Not long before, crowds had gathered for hours to shake his hand. His path, according to one witness, 'was strewn with flowers. Soldiers ran for miles after his motor car, trying to shake his hand.' He returned to Petrograd from a visit to the front, realizing that the Bolsheviks, who were holding out the prospect of an end to the war, were gaining ground rapidly in the soviets. A mass demonstration, led by the Bolsheviks, prompted Kerensky to order Lenin's arrest. On 29 June, Lenin, disguised as a railway worker, fled to Finland. He remained there until July, when the Bolsheviks attempted another coup, but this too failed, and their leader, now charged as a German agent, was forced once more into hiding. This period, later known as the July Days, embraced three Bolshevik bids for power.

On 11 July, Kerensky was made Prime Minister. In late August he secured dictatorial powers from the Cabinet. He took control of the Provisional Government, banished the Romanovs to Siberia and moved into the Winter Palace. He sympathized with the aims but not with the violent, unconstitutional methods of Lenin's Bolsheviks. Even so, he felt that the only danger would come from a royalist coup and not from the Bolsheviks.

Kerensky sensed he was vulnerable after the July Days, and appointed General Lavr Kornilov as Commander-in-Chief to revive the army and monitor national security. Kornilov demanded sweeping powers. Kerensky demurred; worse, he then realized that Kornilov might pose a threat and set about undermining him. The new Commander-in-Chief wanted to preserve Russia's war effort (which was now seriously undermined by Bolshevik pacifist agitation at the front and almost total demoralization of the troops in the rear). He advocated military rule as the best way to restore discipline and order. The Prime Minister pressed him into a position where he appeared to have attempted a coup. Kerensky prevailed and Kornilov was dismissed. But the episode weakened Kerensky's authority. It was Lenin and the Bolsheviks, not Kerensky, who gained from the 'Kornilov Affair'.

Kerensky further weakened his position when, on 8 September, as part of the Government's revolutionary programme, he abolished the old Department of Political Counterintelligence, thereby extinguishing his prime source of information on the Bolsheviks. Meanwhile, throughout the autumn of 1917, the Bolsheviks increased the pressure on the Provisional Government by packing and manipulating the soviets, which had now begun to meet together in congress. The First All-Russian Congress of Soviets had opened on 3 June; the Second, due to open on 20 October, was postponed, while the Bolsheviks attempted to increase their following.

Maxim Gorky described the coup plotters, led by Lenin and Trotsky, as 'crazed fanatics'; the US ambassador thought them 'altogether too crazy'. But by October the

Bolsheviks had come to dominate the workers' and soldiers' soviets. As October advanced, Lenin and Trotsky realized that action, while their power within the Societs held, was imperative. 'We prepared to assault the government,' wrote Trotsky, 'but our agitation rested on the claim that the enemy was getting ready to disperse the Congress of Soviets and it was necessary mercilessly to repulse him' (Pipes).

On 24 October Kerensky, suspecting an imminent coup, ordered troops to close down the Bolshevik newspapers. That night, Lenin scribbled this note:

> I am writing these lines in the evening of the 24th, the situation is most extremely critical. It is clearer than clear that now, truly, to delay the uprising is death.
>
> With all my strength I want to convince my comrades that now everything hangs by a hair, that we are confronting questions that are not resolved by consultations, not by congresses . . . but exclusively by the people, by the masses, by the struggle of the armed masses.
>
> Power seizure is the task of the uprising: its political goal will become clear after power has been taken.

Lenin was driven by the need to smash what Karl Marx had called the 'bureaucratic-military machine' of the state, its organizational apparatus. He applied himself to this moment with all the uncompromising zeal he could muster; it was clear to him that the revolution should happen now or never. Disguising himself with a wig and glasses and covering his face, he made his way to the Smolny, the Bolshevik headquarters.

That night, 24–25 October, the Bolsheviks took control of Petrograd. It was the model of a modern revolution: silent, swift, virtually bloodless, and carried out with surgical precision. The Bolsheviks systematically took the railway stations, post offices, telephone exchanges, banks and bridges. No shots were fired. They cut the phone lines from the Winter Palace, but missed two private lines which enabled the Government ministers gathered in the Malachite Room to communicate with the outside world. Kerensky telephoned the front-line commanders to ask for help; none was forthcoming.

Between 9am and 10am, 25 October, Kerensky slipped away from the Winter Palace disguised as a Serbian officer. He managed to borrow a car from the American Embassy, complete with American flags and driver, and set off to GHQ at Pskov for help. At 10am, Lenin issued this manifesto:

> The Provisional Government has been deposed. State power has passed into the hands of the organ of the Petrograd Soviet of Workers' and Soldiers' Deputies, the Revolutionary Committee, which heads the Petrograd proletariat and the garrison.
>
> The cause for which people have fought – namely, the immediate offer of a democratic peace, the abolition of landed proprietorship, workers' control over production, and the establishment of soviet power – this cause has been secured.
>
> Long live the revolution of workers, soldiers and peasants!

Only the Winter Palace remained in Government hands. It was under siege from the Bolsheviks, although throughout the day the so-called 'siege' was so slack that the American journalists John Reed (who later wrote of the events in his famous book, *Ten Days That Shook the World*, in 1919) and Louise Bryant were able to stroll in to the Palace. Servants in Tsarist uniform took their coats and showed them round.

The ministers there awaited Kerensky's return with reinforcements. He did not come back, but went immediately into hiding. Meanwhile, the delayed Second Congress of Soviets at the Smolny was postponed hour after hour; it could not open until the fate of the

Government ministers was sealed. As night fell, the Cossacks defending the Winter Palace withdrew. Finally, when the Palace was defended only by military cadets and a women's battalion, it was taken not by assault, but by the steady infiltration of the mob. Defenders and attackers rarely caught sight of each other in the Palace's 1,500 rooms, and the total casualties were only five killed though several were wounded, mostly by stray bullets.

Trotsky knew the way forward: 'Now we only have to expand our victory.' Once Petrograd was secure, the Bolsheviks turned their attention to Moscow. Opposition there from the Committee of Public Safety loyal to Kerensky's Government was stronger than anything encountered in the capital. After a struggle, the Kremlin was taken on 2 November. Bolshevik power had taken hold in Russia.

After 1917

Alexander Kerensky never returned to Petrograd. He had been unable to find sufficient help and had gone into hiding before escaping to Finland. From there, he left for the United States and lived out his life in exile.

The Tsar's family was executed by the Cheka, the Bolsheviks' secret police, in Ekaterinburg (later Sverdlovsk during the Soviet era) in the foothills of the Ural mountains on 17 July 1918. They were staying under house arrest when a detachment of troops arrived. The man who commanded them, Jacob Mikhailovich Yurovsky, head of the Ekaterinburg Cheka, wrote:

> I told the Romanovs that in view of the fact that their relatives continued their offensive against Soviet Russia, the Executive Committee of the Urals Soviet had decided to shoot them. Nicholas turned his back to the detachment and faced his family. Then, as if collecting himself, he turned around, asking 'What? What?' I rapidly repeated what I had said and ordered the detachment to prepare. Its members had been previously told whom to shoot and to aim directly at the heart to avoid too much blood and to end more quickly. Nicholas said no more. He turned again towards his family. The others shouted some incoherent exclamations. All this lasted a few seconds. Then commenced the shooting which went on for two or three minutes. I killed Nicholas on the spot.

From the moment of their seizure of power, the Bolsheviks began to eliminate rival parties, and on 28 January 1918 Lenin established the Red Army to defend the gains of the revolution. He nonetheless brought to an end Russia's disastrous participation in the war, with Trotsky as Commissar for Foreign Affairs conducting the negotiations with the Germans that culminated in the Treaty of Brest-Litovsk in March 1918. The Third Congress of Soviets, overseen by the Bolsheviks, passed the Declaration of the Rights of the Toiling and Exploited Masses and on 8 January 1919 proclaimed the Soviet Russian Republic. In early March, the Bolshevik Government left Petrograd and established itself in Moscow, the new capital of the Republic. Meanwhile, civil war was raging in Russia, between the Bolshevik Red Army and the anti-Communist opposition known as White Russians and backed by troops supplied by the United States, Britain, France and Japan. In 1920, after two years of conflict which had directly followed the heavy losses of the 1914–1918 war, the Bolsheviks consolidated their hold on the country by at last crushing the foreign-backed opposition.

OPPOSITE: The Storming of the Winter Palace. *(Painted by R.R. Frents in the late 1920s.)*

The deciding factor in their successful revolution was the quality of their leaders, Lenin and Trotsky. They had brought about the October Revolution and carried the Bolsheviks to victory in the civil war by force of will.

Although Lenin had so effectively begun the revolutionary task, he did not live to finish his work. He died in January 1924, broken by illness and railing at his successor, Josef Vissarionovich Dzhugashvili – known as Stalin. It was to be Stalin's task to secure the political gains of the revolution and shape it to the demands of economics and power politics from his appointment as first General Secretary of the Communist Party in 1922 to his death in 1953. Stalin's own successors faced the double problem of resolving, in the face of a rapidly changing world, the internal tensions of both Lenin's revolution and Stalin's administration, the one implacable and the other unwieldly.

Lenin did not ride to victory on the crest of a revolutionary wave of Bolshevism. Russia in the autumn of 1917 was a state of chaos, breaking apart. It was a combination of government weakness and Bolshevik strength among the workers and troops in Petrograd which gave Lenin the opportunity he needed. The revolution changed Russia into the first modernist state: brutish, totalitarian, ideologically driven. It proved to be one of the most momentous events in modern history. For seventy years a huge area of the world was controlled by a powerful new ideology, an ideology which menaced the rest of the world. Hitler failed to destroy it in the Second World War, and it survived for another forty-five years at the heart of the Cold War, a period of lethal stalemate at once achieved and threatened by the new weapons of mass destruction. Not until 1989–91 was Lenin's legacy finally dismantled.

The October Revolution was carried through by the sheer force of Lenin's character. He succeeded, as Mirabeau said of the great revolutionary Robespierre, because 'he believes all he says'. Lenin's own view was less portentous. He simply said that starting the world revolution in Russia was like 'picking up a feather'.

OPPOSITE: Be On Guard!: *This cartoon, produced towards the end of the civil war, was a warning against foreign intervention. It shows a Red Army soldier stamping on Poland in reaction to their invasion of the Ukraine under Marshall Pilsudsky.*

The Mushroom CLOUD

THE DECISION TO DROP THE ATOMIC BOMB
ON HIROSHIMA HERALDS THE NUCLEAR AGE

To avert a vast, indefinite butchery, to bring the war to an end, to give
peace to the world, to lay healing hands upon its tortured peoples by a
manifestation of overwhelming power at the cost of a few explosions,
seemed, after all our toils and perils, a miracle of deliverance.

(Winston Churchill, *Triumph and Tragedy*, 1953)

O N 6 AUGUST 1945 the United States dropped the world's first atomic bomb
on the Japanese city of Hiroshima. The blast killed over 130,000 people. Three
days later, the United States dropped a second atomic bomb on the city of
Nagasaki killing 73,884 and wounding 76,796. On 10 August, Japan surrendered. Since then, no atomic bomb has been used by one nation against another.

The development of the atomic bomb brought scientists, military leaders and politicians
together throughout America and set in motion a series of decisions which culminated in
President Harry S. Truman's order of 25 July 1945 to attack Japan with a new and terrifying
weapon of unconceivable destructive power.

OPPOSITE: *The
Trinity Test: Fireball
and 'mushroom cloud'
formation following the
detonation of the
world's first atomic
bomb in the desert near
Alamagordo, New
Mexico, July 16 1945.*

The Scientists: A Means to the End

In the summer of 1939, two Hungarian refugee scientists working in the United States,
Eugene Wigner and Leo Szilard, persuaded Albert Einstein, the prominent émigré scientist to write to the American President, Franklin D. Roosevelt (1882–1945), urging him
to devote resources to the development of a new form of weapon which would unleash
the power within the nucleus of an atom.

The atom had been discovered by the British scientist Ernest Rutherford in 1919. The
science which grew out of that discovery, nuclear physics, advanced in 1934 when the
Italian scientist Enrico Fermi produced new elements by the process of nuclear fission –
that is, splitting the atom's nucleus by allowing it to be struck by a neutron (a sub-atomic
particle). His findings were confirmed in 1938 by two scientists in Berlin, Otto Hahn and
Fritz Strassman. In 1939 Fermi moved to the United States and continued his research as a
professor at Columbia University. During the late 1930s, the scientific community became

ABOVE LEFT:
Albert Einstein.

ABOVE RIGHT:
Professor Enrico Fermi.

aware of the immense destructive power of a nuclear chain reaction. This is what happens when the splitting of the nucleus releases two or three other neutrons which in turn strike other nuclei, and so on. This takes place in an instant, producing massive energy. Scientists thought the element most conducive to this process was the naturally unstable uranium–238 and its related isotope (that is, one of two or more forms of an element which contain a different number of neutrons) uranium–235. Einstein alerted Roosevelt in his letter of 2 August 1939 from Nassau Point, Long Island:

> In the course of the last four months it has been made probable – through the work of [Jean] Joliot in France as well as Fermi and Szilard in America – that it may become possible to set up a nuclear chain reaction in a large mass of uranium, by which vast amounts of power and large quantities of new radium-like elements would be generated. Now it appears almost certain that this could be achieved in the immediate future. This new phenomenon would also lead to the construction of bombs, and it is conceivable – though much less certain – that extremely powerful bombs of a new type may thus be constructed.

Wigner and Szilard feared that Germany had already made headway in this area, with experiments on nuclear fission reported from Berlin in 1938. Einstein told Roosevelt that scientists at the Kaiser-Wilhelm-Institut in Berlin were conducting advanced work on uranium. He encouraged the President not only to be aware of new research that was taking place in uranium production and in chain reactions but also to provide further funds for American research. On 11 October 1939 the message was underlined by Roosevelt's friend, a Wall Street banker called Alexander Sachs, who met the President to discuss Einstein's letter. The American Government immediately established a preliminary project, the Advisory Committee on Uranium, which met for the first time on 21 October 1939, seven weeks after the opening of the Second World War. It was the start of an extraordinary scientific, military and political journey.

Eight months later, in June 1940, at the time of the fall of France, the Uranium Committee was subsumed into the National Defense Research Committee (NDRC) under Vannevar Bush, President of the Carnegie Institution. The NDRC in turn became an advisory body to the Office of Scientific Research and Development (OSRD), established on 28 June 1941, six days after German forces invaded the Soviet Union. Bush was also to run the new office, a body which strengthened the scientific voice in the Government and ensured that efforts were increasingly focused on the scientific possibility of an atomic bomb. The former Uranium Committee became codenamed S–1, Section One of the OSRD. The structure for research was in place. But the political and military implications, should the bomb prove to be feasible, were not yet part of Roosevelt's concerns.

In October 1941, Bush briefed Roosevelt on the state of atomic research, citing a 2 July report of British scientific research (codenamed MAUD) confirming that an atomic bomb was indeed a feasible weapon. The refugee German physicists Rudolf Peirels and Otto Frisch had calculated that a critical mass (the amount needed to maintain the chain reaction) of ten kilograms of uranium or similar matter was sufficient to produce an enormous explosion. Not only could existing aircraft carry a bomb of these dimensions, but they believed it could be ready in two years. Roosevelt swiftly ordered Bush to investigate the practicality of producing such a bomb and to determine its cost and design. Bush was to discuss this problem for the first time with the military.

Now, in late 1941, the scientific research towards producing an atomic bomb had therefore received a measure of military, political and consequently economic support. The momentum had come from the scientific community. Throughout the following year, Bush would co-ordinate research from industry and universities across America.

7 December 1941

On 8 December 1941, the United States went to war. The previous day, the Japanese had attacked the American Pacific base of Pearl Harbor on Oahu in the Hawaiian Islands. The pre-emptive attack took place while Japanese envoys were holding talks in Washington designed to resolve Japan's objections that the US sanctions were strangling its oil supplies. Over 3,300 American personnel were killed, four battleships destroyed, and a large part of the US Pacific fleet destroyed or damaged; 188 American aircraft were destroyed on the ground at Pearl Harbor's airfields. Roosevelt declared:

> Yesterday, 7 December 1941 – a day which will live in infamy – the United States of America was suddenly and deliberately attacked by naval and air forces of the Empire of Japan . . . No matter how long it may take us to overcome this premeditated invasion, the American people, in their righteous might, will win through to absolute victory.
>
> . . . I ask that the Congress declare that since the unprovoked and dastardly attack by Japan on Sunday, December 7, 1941, a state of war has existed between the United States and the Japanese Empire.

When the United States, and Britain and its allies (but not the Soviet Union) declared war on Japan in 1941 they faced a formidable enemy: powerful, well-armed and determined. Two days later, on 10 December, Japan's Axis allies Germany and Italy declared war on

America. Nonetheless, Winston Churchill knew the moment he heard of Pearl Harbor that the war was won:

> To have the United States at our side was to me the greatest joy . . . now at this very moment I knew the United States was in the war, up to the neck and in to the death . . . Hitler's fate was sealed. Mussolini's fate was sealed. As for the Japanese, they would be ground to powder . . .

The conflict which had erupted in Europe in 1939 had become a global war that would be fought in Western and Eastern Europe, in the Soviet Union, in the Mediterranean, in Asia and in the Pacific and the Atlantic. But the war with Japan started badly for the United States and its allies. Within six months the Japanese had taken Guam, Wake, Hong Kong and Manila. And after the Battles of Coral Sea and Midway in May and June of 1942, and the American landings on the Solomon Islands in August, it became clear just how costly to America the fanatical defence of the Japanese would be. It was the prospect of heavy losses of life against an implacable enemy which became a public and military concern over the war in the Pacific.

The Politicians: Henry L. Stimson and Franklin D. Roosevelt

Responsibility for the United States war effort fell on the President, Franklin D. Roosevelt, and the Secretary of War, Henry L. Stimson (1876–1950). Between them, they provided the political will and the Government resources to develop the atomic bomb.

Franklin D. Roosevelt, President of the United States, with Henry L. Stimpson, Secretary of War, Representative May, George C. Marshall and Senator Sheppard. Washington, September 16 1940.

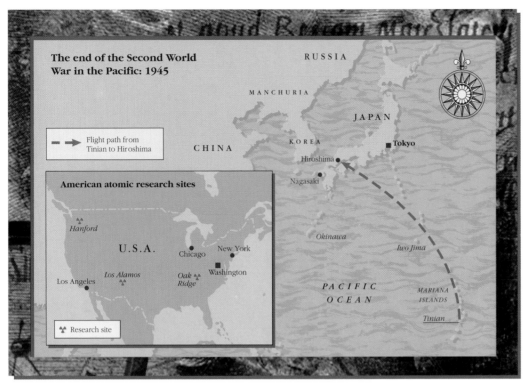

Before the Second World War, Stimson had pursued a long and distinguished career in public service under Presidents Taft, Coolidge and Hoover as a United States Attorney-General, Secretary of War, Governor-General of the Philippines and Secretary of State. Seventy-four years old when the United States entered the war, he first learnt about the atomic issue – from Roosevelt – in the autumn of 1941. It was Stimson who, as chief presidential adviser on the military employment of atomic energy, was responsible for making the scientific research not only available to the military but also palatable to the politicians:

> At no time, from 1941 to 1945, did I ever hear it suggested by the President, or by any other responsible member of the government, that atomic energy should not be used in war. All of us of course understood the terrible responsibility involved in our attempt to unlock the doors to such a devastating weapon; President Roosevelt particularly spoke to me many times of his own awareness of the catastrophic potentialities of our work. But we were at war, and the work must be done.

The work continued. Roosevelt appointed a Top Policy Group comprising Stimson, Bush, Vice-President Henry Wallace, James B. Conant (Bush's assistant and the President of Harvard University) and the Army Chief of Staff, George C. Marshall. This group was to handle the policy decisions relating to uranium and the atomic bomb.

The original atomic research had been done in Berlin in 1938, and the feasibility of an atomic bomb had been confirmed by the British report in 1941. These facts, now that America was at war, aroused the fear that the Germans were ahead in atomic research and would be the first to bring atomic weapons to the battlefield. Through the Top Policy Group, the Americans began to co-ordinate their atomic research and their war effort. By 1942 the atomic programme under Stimson had a clear goal and the resources to pursue it. On 19 January of that year Roosevelt approved production of an atomic bomb. Stimson hoped that they would have enough time to carry it out.

PO Box 1663, Santa Fe, New Mexico

Atomic research gathered pace rapidly throughout 1942 in all areas related to producing the atomic bomb: electromagnetics, reactor and gas technologies, metallurgy and ordnance. In charge of the research itself was a New York-born scientist called Robert Oppenheimer (1904–67), thirty-eight years old and a graduate of Harvard and Cambridge Universities. So completely was he devoted to his scientific studies as a professor at the California Institute of Technology and the University of California, that he read no newspapers or current magazines, and had no radio or telephone. His first connection with the atomic energy programme arose when he attended a meeting of the National Academy of Sciences in the autumn of 1941. As a result, he joined the Metallurgy Laboratory in Chicago and established a theoretical group in Berkeley, California.

Soon, Oppenheimer was co-ordinating his work with Wigner at Princeton and with Fermi at Columbia. The challenge was to find a means of producing uranium–235, which is very scarce. Four methods existed: gaseous diffusion, centrifuge, electromagnetic and pile or reactor. The S–1 committee pushed forward with all four throughout 1942. Most important, Colonel James Marshall established the Manhattan Engineer District for the development of substitute metals, including another unstable element, plutonium.

In the autumn the atomic bomb project, now known as the 'Manhattan Project', received a boost. General Leslie Groves, an impressive engineer who had overseen the construction of the Pentagon (US military headquarters), was appointed to lead it. A brusque, egocentric and wily man, he met Oppenheimer at Berkeley in early October 1942 and was persuaded of the need for a central laboratory. Oppenheimer later wrote:

Dr Robert Oppenheimer, Director of the Laboratory at Los Alamos.

I became convinced, as did others, that a major change was called for in the work of the bomb itself. We needed a central laboratory devoted wholly to this purpose, where people could talk freely with each other, where theoretical ideas and experimental findings could affect each other, where the waste and frustration and error of the many compartmentalized experimental studies could be eliminated . . .

Groves liked Oppenheimer, and wanted him to run such a laboratory: 'Why, Oppenheimer knows about everything. He can talk to you about anything you bring up. Well, not exactly. I guess there are a few things he doesn't know about. He doesn't know anything about sports.'

General Groves was a determined man, totally focused on his goal. His scientists would have to move from research to development and production in record time. To help them liaise with the military, Stimson and Bush established the Military Police Committee. Meanwhile, Groves pressed for a unified laboratory. He moved the Manhattan Project to Washington, and established there a new bomb laboratory under Oppenheimer. Material suitable for nuclear fission would be produced at installations in Hanford, Washington, and Oak Ridge, Tennessee. From there raw nuclear material would be supplied for Oppenheimer's bomb laboratory. Los Alamos in New Mexico, 7,000 feet up in the mountains, was chosen as its new location. Its address was PO Box 1663, Santa Fe, New Mexico. Its existence was the highest military secret. But time was running out. Oppenheimer recalled:

> The last months of 1942 and early 1943 had hardly hours enough to get Los Alamos established . . . The program of recruitment was massive. Even though we then underestimated the size of the laboratory, which was to have almost 4,000 members by the spring of 1945, and even though we did not at that time see clearly some of the difficulties which were to bedevil and threaten the enterprise, we knew that it was a big, complex and diverse job.

On 2 December 1942, Enrico Fermi at Stagg Field, Chicago, successfully used 400 tons of graphite, 6 tons of uranium and 50 tons of uranium oxide to produce the first self-sustaining nuclear chain reaction at the power level of 0.5 watts. This chain reaction would create the atomic bomb's destructive power. This prompted Roosevelt on 28 December to approve a budget of $500 million for the Manhattan Project. This move was the logical result of his earlier decision to act in response to Einstein's advice in 1939.

Major General Lesley R. Groves who had overall reponsibility for the Manhattan Project.

By the end of the war the Manhattan Project under Roosevelt, Stimson and Groves would spend $2.2 billion on the facilities in New Mexico, Washington and Tennessee as well as on research projects at universities from Berkeley to Columbia. It would involve over 200,000 scientists, technicians and engineers. The Project was in essence a large production company building, hiring and contracting facilities and expertise to create a product which would be researched, developed and delivered to the military in only two and a half years from the start of 1943. S–1, of which the Manhattan Project was a part, was the largest scientific and industrial enterprise in history.

Life at Los Alamos, a military posting for civilian scientists, was hard, situated as they were in the harsh desert of New Mexico, far from the urban and university comforts many were used to. But it was an ideal location for such a top-secret project. As Oppenheimer wrote: 'The notion of disappearing into the New Mexico desert for an indeterminate period and under quasi-military auspices disturbed a good many scientists.' But there was another side to Los Alamos.

Almost everyone realized that this was a great undertaking. Almost everyone knew that if it were completed successfully and rapidly enough, it might determine the outcome of the war. Almost everyone knew that it was an unparalleled opportunity to bring to bear the basic knowledge and art of science for the benefit of his country. Almost everyone knew that this job, if it were achieved, would be part of history.

Work continued steadily, and secrecy was maintained throughout 1943 and 1944. Few people, even at the highest levels of government, knew about it. Moreover, everything concerning the Manhattan Project had to be conducted with the utmost speed.

One man who knew nothing of the Manhattan Project between 1942 and 1945 was the Chairman of the Special Committee to Investigate the National Defense Program, which had been formed in 1941. He was the future Vice-President and President, Harry S. Truman. The job of the Truman Commission (as it was also known) was to root out inefficiency and waste in the military. In the summer of 1943, in a telephone conversation with Stimson, Truman learned of a secret project, costing millions, at a plant at Pasco, Washington, one of the facilities on the Manhattan Project:

A reconstruction of the scene when the prototype reactor built by Enrico Fermi's team in Chicago went critical for the first time on 2 December 1942.

Stimson: Now, that's a matter which I know all about personally, and I am one of the group of two or three men in the whole world who know about it.
Truman: I see.
Stimson: It's part of a very important secret development.
Truman: Well, all right then—
Stimson: And I—
Truman: I herewith see the situation, Mr Secretary, and you won't have to say another word to me. Whenever you say that to me, that's all I want to hear.

Even the Truman Commission was to know nothing of Oppenheimer and the Manhattan Project and was prepared to leave it at that. It was a tribute to Stimson's status and probity. Even when Truman became Roosevelt's Vice-President in 1944, he remained in ignorance. But in April 1945 he was to be quickly apprised of the secret.

Franklin D. Roosevelt and Harry S. Truman

The news of President Roosevelt's death broke at 5.47pm Eastern War Time, Thursday, 12 April 1945. He had been signing papers just two hours earlier, when he suddenly complained of a severe headache. He died of a cerebral haemorrhage at 3.45pm local time, Warm Springs, Georgia. He was sixty-three years old.

The news flashed around the world, to Churchill in London, and to Stalin in Moscow, where the American Ambassador was hosting an Embassy party. In Berlin, the news of Roosevelt's death caused the ecstatic Minister of Propaganda, Joseph Goebbels, to

President Harry S. Truman.

telephone Hitler with the claim that this was a turning point in the war ordained by fate. Roosevelt had been close to achieving victory: the forces under his direction as Commander-in-Chief stood at the gates of Berlin and were closing in on the shores of Japan's home islands. Surely, Goebbels felt, his death would encourage those Americans anxious to make peace with Germany in order to unite against the Soviet Union.

At 7pm that day, the United States congressional leadership assembled in the Cabinet Room in the West Wing of the White House, Washington, to witness the Vice-President take the Oath of Office. When Truman began the ceremony, he glanced at the clock on the mantel:

> It said nine past seven when I started to swear the oath – I remember. I looked at it. And I remember the faces all around me.

He was succeeding a renowned world statesman with over twelve years' experience in the White House, and his country was at war. In his diary, Secretary of War Harry Stimson wrote that Truman had borne himself well, considering the shock he had been subjected to, and how little he knew.

On Wednesday, 25 April, Stimson told Truman about the Manhattan Project. The first words of his memorandum read: 'Within four months we shall in all probability have completed the most terrible weapon ever known in human history, one bomb of which could destroy a whole city.' Stimson recalled the meeting:

> He was very nice about it. He remembered the time that I refused to let him go into this project when he was chairman of the Truman Committee and was investigating it, and he said that he understood now perfectly why it was inadvisable for me to have taken any other course than I had taken.

The war, meanwhile, continued. The Japanese within their home islands remained determined. On 9 March the Americans had mounted a firebomb raid on Tokyo. Over 300 B–29 bombers (developed to fly long-range bombing missions from the Pacific islands to Japan) under the command of General Curtis LeMay left the Mariana and Pacific Islands and launched an incendiary attack on the enemy capital, killing nearly 100,000 and wounding over a million Japanese. The attack caused a firestorm which destroyed nearly all the wooden houses and left the city flattened. But still the Japanese fought on.

The same month, 60,000 US Marines had landed on the volcanic island of Iwo Jima. It was a fortress of bunkers, tunnels and fortified caves garrisoned by 20,000 Japanese. In the worst casualty ratio in Marine Corps history, the American dead reached 6,800 and their wounded over 20,000. The Japanese dead were 20,000, only 1,000 defenders allowing themselves to be taken alive. No less daunting than the Japanese determination was the appearance of their suicide bombers, piloted by airmen who were prepared to die with their bombs. These *kamikaze* attacks were deadly at the later battle for the island of Okinawa: thirty American ships were sunk by them and 300 more damaged.

Iwo Jima confirmed what the American military had long feared: beating back the Japanese island by island could be costly beyond belief, and probably beyond what public opinion in America would tolerate. Nonetheless, Roosevelt had agreed to an invasion of Japan, scheduled for 1 November 1945.

The Military: 6 August 1945

Germany surrendered to the Allies on 7 May 1945. The war in Europe was over, but the war in the Pacific continued. The Japanese Government showed little sign of weakening, although on 7 April the Japanese Prime Minister, Kautaro Suzuki, had formed a new Cabinet to bring the war to an end. There were several ways in which the war with Japan might be concluded. The US Navy under Admiral William D. Leahy had effectively blockaded Japan, cutting its supplies of food and fuel. Meanwhile, LeMay's B–29 bombers scoured Japanese targets at will, with little opposition from the depleted Japanese air force. Waiting to starve Japan into surrender was one option.

Another was the prospect of Soviet military help. At the Yalta Conference between Churchill, Roosevelt and Stalin during February 1945, at which they planned the shape of post-war Europe, Stalin had promised Soviet action against Japan two or three months after the defeat of Germany, once their ground forces in Europe could be redeployed. Yet another option was to accept that Japan was moving towards surrender in the summer of 1945. On 22 June the Japanese Supreme War Council approved efforts to negotiate peace with the United States through Soviet mediation. And on 12 July the Japanese Foreign Minister, Togo, instructed his Ambassador in Moscow to ask the Soviet Union to mediate an end to the war with the United States, but only on conditions. Unconditional surrender was not to be contemplated. The Allies were indeed to pursue this option as far as they could.

In the face of Japan's refusal to agree to unconditional surrender, two other options remained. First was the original invasion plan timetabled for November and ratified by Truman on 18 June in hopes of Soviet help in due course. General Douglas MacArthur and Admiral Chester Nimitz began to prepare battle plans for the invasion. But the Army Chief of Staff General George Marshall estimated that an invasion of Japan would cost at least a quarter of a million American casualties. Stimson thought the figure would be even higher:

The Manhattan Project was conducted in hurriedly contructed buildings which constituted the atomic research centre at Los Alamos.

Given the increasingly fanatic resistance of Japanese forces, such as on Iwo Jima and Okinawa, casualties during the invasion might total one-half million . . . [and be a] far more bitter finish fight than in Germany.

The last option was to use the atomic bomb. In essence, Truman never seriously considered an alternative to the bomb: the Manhattan Project had a logic and momentum all its own. Japan would certainly be defeated. But each day's delay in securing Japan's surrender cost more American lives. After the Allied victory in Europe, Truman's best efforts were directed to ending the war in the Pacific.

Scientific opinion was divided. With the ending of the war in Europe, there grew increasing concern among scientists about whether they had the moral right to drop their new ultimate weapon on Japan without warning. Oppenheimer was their spokesman by virtue of his position as leader of the Manhattan Project, and he repeatedly sought answers to the crucial question of whether the Americans should alert the Japanese to the horrifying potential of the bomb. Would the Japanese then believe them? Would they move Allied prisoners into their cities? How widespread was the damage likely to be inflicted by the bomb anyway? What were the long-term implications?

Truman and Stimson had established an Interim Committee in April 1945 to decide the great question. Stimson, its chairman, felt that 'the first and greatest problem was the decision on the use of the bomb: should it be used against the Japanese, and if so, in what manner?' His committee reported on 1 June 1945, after discussion with Oppenheimer and all members of its advisory Scientific Panel. Having acknowledged at the time that the scientists were not unanimous on the initial use of these weapons, Stimson later recalled that the Interim Committee had finally adopted the following recommendations:

(1) The bomb should be used against Japan as soon as possible.
(2) It should be used on a dual target – that is, a military installation or war plant surrounded by or adjacent to houses and other buildings most susceptible to damage and
(3) It should be used without prior warning [of the weapon's nature].

On 2 July, Stimson outlined the proposed terms of Japanese surrender to Truman. They entailed demilitarization and the prosecution of war criminals in exchange for economic and electoral freedoms designed to guard against future Japanese aggression. On the 15th, Truman arrived in Berlin for the Potsdam Conference (17 July–2 August) with Churchill and Stalin to discuss post-war settlements. During the conference, Truman received important news from the Manhattan Project at Los Alamos.

At 5.30am on Monday, 16 July the plutonium test bomb 'Trinity' had been detonated in the New Mexico desert, producing a nuclear chain reaction which created extraordinary heat and pressures in millionths of a second. As the reaction cooled to 500,000 degrees Fahrenheit in about one ten-thousandth of a second, a shock-wave developed, hot at first, then cooling to become visible. The double flash of light – too closely spaced to be detected by the eye – created by the detonation and reaction was so bright that many observers were temporarily blinded, even though they were looking through smoked glass. Seconds after the explosion the blast reached the observers, a huge wave of searing heat which knocked some of them to the ground over 10,000 yards away. As the shock-wave cooled, the air behind it heated. A great fireball of orange and yellow rose up, and from within it a second column rose and spread, rapidly flattening into a mushroom-shaped cloud above the desert. The nuclear age had found its distinctive image.

Truman and Joseph Stalin at the Potsdam Conference in July 1945.

Oppenheimer told an audience after the war:

When it went off in the New Mexico dawn, that first atomic bomb, we thought of Alfred Nobel, and his hope, in vain, that dynamite would put an end to wars.

News of the 'Trinity' test reached Truman in Potsdam with more details following in a coded cable to Stimson:

Doctor has just returned most enthusiastic and confident that the little boy is as husky as his big brother. The light in his eyes in discernible from here [Washington] to Highhold [Stimson's farm 250 miles away] and I could have heard his screams from here to my farm [fifty miles].

Truman therefore had a new option in his dealings with the Allies over the fate of Japan. In the second week of the conference, on 24 July, he told Stalin that he had a new weapon of great power; Stalin, who knew from his intelligence service of the 'Trinity' test, casually replied that he hoped the weapon would be used to good effect against Japan. Two days later, the Potsdam Conference, stiffened by Truman's resolve, issued a proclamation calling on Japan to surrender unconditionally or face 'prompt and utter destruction. The terms were too humiliating for the Japanese, and they rejected them on 29 July.

But four days before, President Truman had authorized the use of the atomic bomb against one of four Japanese cities. He had consulted his Secretary of State James F. Byrnes, Secretary of War Stimson, Army Chief of Staff Marshall and General Henry 'Hap' Arnold of the US Army Air Force. Arnold thought Japan would be defeated by conventional strategic bombing. But Marshall likened the situation in Japan with that in Europe, where Germany had not been beaten by air power alone. A land invasion of Japan would prove costly, as Marshall pointed out: 12,500 Americans had been killed in eighty-two days of fighting at Okinawa; undaunted, the Japanese had lost 100,000 men:

We had just gone through a bitter experience at Okinawa. This had been preceded
by a number of similar experiences in other Pacific islands, north of Australia . . . We
had had the one hundred thousand people killed in Tokyo in one night of bombs,
and it had had seemingly no effect whatsoever. It destroyed the Japanese cities, yes,
but their morale was not affected as far as we could tell, not at all. So it seemed
necessary, if we could, to shock them into action . . . We had to end the war, we had
to save American lives.

General MacArthur, who would be responsible either for a land invasion or for the army
of occupation when Japan fell, was neither informed nor consulted about the atomic
bomb. The Supreme Allied Commander in Europe, Dwight D. Eisenhower, was dining
with Stimson at his headquarters in Germany when the cabled news of the 'Trinity' test
arrived. It was the first he knew of the weapon. He reported:

So then [Stimson] told me they were going to drop it on the Japanese. Well, I
listened, and I didn't volunteer anything because, after all, my war was over in Europe
and it wasn't up to me. But I was getting more and more depressed just thinking
about it. Then he asked my opinion, so I told him I was against it on two counts.
First, the Japanese were ready to surrender and it wasn't necessary to hit them with
that awful thing. Second, I hated to see our country be the first to use such a weapon.

Truman was adamant. Russian help would not be needed. No invasion was necessary.
The atomic bomb would be used on Japan. On 24 July 1945 Truman sent this order to
General Carl Spaatz of the US Strategic Air Force:

1. The 509 Composite Group, 20th Air Force will deliver its first special bomb as
soon as weather will permit visual bombing after about 3 August 1945 on one of the
targets: Hiroshima, Kokura, Niigata and Nagasaki . . .
2. Additional bombs will be delivered on the above targets as soon as made ready by
the project staff . . .
4. The foregoing directive is issued to you by direction and with the approval of the
Secretary of War and the Chief of Staff, U.S.A. It is desired that you personally
deliver one copy of this directive to General MacArthur and one copy to Admiral
Nimitz for their information.

Spaatz followed Truman's directive. At 2.45am on 6 August, the *Enola Gay*, a B–29 bomber
from 509 Composite Group, took off from Tinian Island carrying 'Little Boy', its gun-
model uranium bomb, bound for Hiroshima. Flying the B–29 was Colonel Paul Tibbetts,
heading north-west by north at 4,700 feet. At 5.52am the *Enola Gay* climbed to 9,300
feet over Iwo Jima to rendezvous with two observation planes. By 7.30am 'Little Boy' had
been fully armed by the bomb crew, ready to be dropped. Tibbetts climbed to 31,000
feet, flying at 285 knots (328 mph). Over Hiroshima, Thomas Ferebee, the *Enola Gay*'s
bombardier, loosed the bomb. Tibbetts banked away steeply. Forty-three seconds later
'Little Boy' exploded at 8.16:02 Hiroshima time at 1,900 feet above the courtyard of
Shima Hospital with a force equivalent to 12,500 tons of TNT. Fifty-three seconds after
the explosion the first shock-wave hit the B–29. Tibbetts recalled:

A bright light filled the plane. The first shock-wave hit us. We were eleven and a half
miles slant range from the atomic explosion, but the whole airplane cracked and
crinkled from the blast . . . We turned back to look at Hiroshima. The city was
hidden by that awful cloud . . . boiling up, mushrooming, terrible and incredibly tall.

The city was devastated over an area of five square miles. The temperature at the site of the explosion had reached 5,400 degrees Fahrenheit, and the blast wave had emanated from the hypocentre at two miles per second, destroying everything in its path. Eighty thousand people were killed instantly (50,000 to 60,000 died in the next several months); five years later, by 1950, the death toll had risen to 200,000 as a result of the continuing effect of radiation. Seventy thousand of Hiroshima's 76,000 buildings were destroyed or damaged: the city, in other words, had been ruined in an instant. Those who were not at once eviscerated or burnt shrieked in pain; others looked on in disbelief:

> The streets were deserted except for the dead. Some looked as if they had been frozen by death while still in the full action of flight; others lay sprawled as though some giant hand had flung them to their death from a great height . . . Nothing remained except a few buildings of reinforced concrete . . . For acres and acres the city was like a desert except for scattered piles of brick and roof tile. I had to revise my meaning of the word destruction or choose some other word to describe what I saw. Devastation may be a better word, but really, I know of no word or words to describe the view.

Two days later, Russia declared war on Japan. One day after that, on 9 August 1945, the United States dropped an implosion-model (the alternative detonation mechanism to the gun-model uranuim bomb) plutonium bomb on the city of Nagasaki. 'Fat Man' exploded at 11.01am 1,650 feet above the city, killing 73,884 people instantly and causing an overall death count of 140,000. Five days later, on 14 August, Japan agreed to unconditional surrender. The Second World War had ended.

The scientists at Los Alamos had created a nuclear future. The events set in motion by Albert Einstein's letter to Roosevelt six years before had produced a weapon of terrifying destructive power. Szilard was horrified. But Oppenheimer took a measured and dispassionate view, secure in his belief that scientific discoveries are made not because they are useful but because they are possible. In November 1945 he addressed the Association of Los Alamos Scientists in Washington:

> When you come right down to it, the reason we did this job was because it was an organic necessity. If you are a scientist you cannot stop such a thing. If you are a scientist you believe that it is good to find out how the world works; that it is good to find out what the realities are; that it is good to turn over to mankind at large the greatest possible power to control the world and to deal with it according to its lights and values . . .
>
> It is not possible to be a scientist unless you believe that the knowledge of the world, and the power which this gives, is a thing which is of intrinsic value to humanity, and that you are using it to help in the spread of knowledge, and are willing to take the consequences.

By September 1949, four years after Hiroshima, and partly thanks to intelligence obtained in the US, the Soviet Union also had the bomb. Just three years later, both superpowers had a weapon which eclipsed the power even of the atomic bomb - the hydrogen bomb. A thousand times more powerful, a single bomb could destroy a small country. This was one of the legacies of the Manhattan Project.

BIBLIOGRAPHY

CHAPTER 1
Aeschylus, tr. Benardete, S.G., *Persae*, Chicago, 1942.
Byron, G., *Poems*, London, 1985
Herodotus, tr. Rawlinson, G., *The Histories*, London, 1992

CHAPTER 2
Cotterell, A., *The First Emperor of China*, London, 1981.
Cottrell, L., *The Tiger of Ch'in*, London, 1962
Greil, W.E., *The Great Wall of China*, London, 1909
Tzu, Sun, tr. Griffith, S.B., *The Art of War*, London, 1971

CHAPTER 3
Augustus, *Res Gestae Divi Augusti*, Oxford, 1967
Cassius Dio, *Roman History: The Reign of Augustus*, tr. Scott-Kilvert, I., London, 1987
Chisholm, K., and Ferguson, J., (eds.), *Rome: The Augustan Age. A Source Book*, Oxford, 1981
Cicero, *see* Chisholm, K., and Ferguson, J., (eds.)
Horace, tr. Shepherd, W.G., *Epodes*, Cambridge, 1961–1967
Plutarch, *Lives of Noble Grecians and Romans*, New York, 1994.
Propertius, tr. Musker, R., *Elegies*, Cambridge, Bk I 1961, Bk II 1967, Bk III 1966
Suetonius, *Twelve Caesars*, London, 1970
Virgil, tr. Mackail, J.W., *Aeneid*, London, 1908
Zanker, P., tr. Shapiro, A., *The Power of Images in the Age of Augustus*, Michigan, 1988

CHAPTER 4
Collins, R., *The Arab Conquest of Spain*, Oxford, 1989
Collins, R., *Early Medieval Spain: Unity in Diversity 400–1000*, London, 1983
Gibbon, E. *The History of the Decline and Fall of the Roman Empire*, London, 1982
Lewis, B. *The Muslim Discovery of Europe*, London, 1982

CHAPTER 5
Boccaccio, G., *Decameron*, Oxford, 1993
Horrox, R., *The Black Death*, Manchester, 1994

CHAPTER 6
Barbaro, N., (ed.) Cornet, E., *Giornale dell' assedio di Constantinopoli*, Vienna, 1856
Garraty, J.A., and Gay, P., *The Columbia History of the World*, New York, 1972
Nicol, J.M., *The Immortal Emperor*, Cambridge, 1992
Runciman, S., *The Fall of Constantinople, 1453*, Cambridge, 1965

CHAPTER 7
Chamberlain, R. S., *Conquista y Colonización de Yucatan*, Mexico, 1982
Cieza de León, P. de, *La cronica de Peru* (Parts I–IV), Madrid, 1553
Hemming, J., *The Conquest of the Incas*, London, 1993
Pizarro, H., *Confesion de Hernando Pizarro*, Madrid, 1540
Porras, B.R., *Pizarro*, Lima, 1978
Ruiz de Arce, J., *Relación de servicios; Advertencias que hizo el fundador del vínculo mayorazao a los sucesores en él*, Madrid, *c.* 1545

Wright, R., *Stolen Continents: The Indian Story*, London, 1993
Xerez, F. de, *Verdadera relación de la conquista del Perú y provincia del Cuzco*, Seville, 1534

CHAPTER 8
McLuhan, T.C. (ed.), *Touching the Earth*, New York, 1971
Mossiker, F., *Pocahontas, The Life and the Legend*, London, 1977
Rountree, H.C., *Pocahontas's People: The Powhatan Indians of Virginia Through the Centuries*, London, 1990
Rountree, H.C., *The Powhatan Indians of Virginia: Their Traditional Culture*, Oklahoma, 1989
Smith, J., *The Generall Historie of Virginia, New England and the Summer Isles*, London, 1624

CHAPTER 9
Chapais, T., *Le Marquis de Montcalm: 1721–1759*, Quebec, 1911
Connell, B., *The Plains of Abraham*, London, 1959
Dictionary of National Biography: From the Earliest Times to 1900 (22 vols), Oxford, 1908
Eccles, W. J., *France in America*, Ontario, 1990
Reilly, R., *Wolfe of Quebec*, London, 1973

CHAPTER 10
Blake, R., *Disraeli*, Oxford, 1969
Knight, I., *Zulu: Isandlwana and Rorke's Drift, 22–23 January 1879*, London, 1992
Morris, D.R., *The Working of the Spears*, London, 1965
Mostert, N., *Frontiers*, London, 1992

CHAPTER 11
Hoyt, E.P., *Three Military Leaders: Yamamoto, Yamashita, Togo*, London, 1993
Pakenham, W. C., *Reports From Naval Attachés*, London, 1905

CHAPTER 12
Abraham, R., *Alexander Kerensky. The First Love of the Revolution*, London, 1987
Buchan, F., *A History of the Great War*, Boston, 1922
Fischer, L., *The Life of Lenin*, London, 1965
Pipes, R., *The Russian Revolution, 1899–1919*, London, 1990

CHAPTER 13
Churchill, W., *Triumph and Tragedy*, Boston, 1953
Churchill, W., *The Grand Alliance*, Boston, 1950
Einstein, A., in the Roosevelt Papers, Franklin D. Roosevelt Library, Hyde Park, New York
Fanton, J.F., Stoff, M.B., and Williams, R.H., (eds.), *The Manhattan Project*, Philadelphia, 1991
McCullough, D., *Truman*, New York, 1992
Oppenheimer, R.J., *Autobiographical Sketch*, New York, 1954
Rhodes, R., *The Making of the Atomic Bomb*, London, 1988
Safire, W. *Lend Me Your Ears: Great Speeches in History*, New York, 1992
Truman, H.S., *Memoirs of Harry S. Truman: 1945 Year of Decisions*, Vol. I, New York, 1955

INDEX

PICTURE ACKNOWLEDGEMENTS: AKG London: 105; The Ancient Art & Architecture Collection: 13, 18, 25, 26, 32 top left, 43, 60, 71, 72-73; **Bibliotheque Royale, Brussels:** 82 bottom; **British Library:** 76, 86, 90, 91, 101; **David King Collection:** 184, 189, 196, 197, 201, 202; **E.T. Archive:** 168, 172-3, 174, 176; **Harry Truman Library, USA:** 214; **Hulton Deutsch:** 46, 47, 50, 51; **The Illustrated London News:** 161, 175, 179; **Killie Campbell Afrikana Library:** 62, 165; **Los Alamos Historical Society:** 206 right, 212-213; **Los Alamos National Laboratory/ Science Photo Library:** 204; **Mary Evans Picture Library:** 87, 111, 120, 121, 134; **The Metropolitan Museum of Art** (Jan Mitchell and Sons Collection, Gift of Jan Mitchell, photograph by Justin Kerr): 112 top; **ML Design:** 16, 24, 32 bottom, 56, 65, 80, 96, 112 bottom, 128, 140, 156, 163, 180, 209; **The Museum of Art at Brigham Young University:** 129; **Natal Archives Depot:** 152, 157, 160, 167; **National Archives, USA:** 206 left, 211, 217; **National Archives of Canada:** title page, 141, 143, 144-5, 147; **National Atomic Museum:** 210, 215; **National Trust at Quebec House, Westerham:** 136, 149; **New York State Office of General Services:** 132; **Peter Newark's Pictures:** 53, 55, 78, 83, 110, 113, 114, 117 top, 124, 126, 138, 171; **Prado Museum, Madrid:** 88-9; **Sonia Halliday Photographs:** 92, 97, 99, 106; **Roosevelt Library, USA:** 208; **S.C.R. Photo Library:** 192, 195; **Transatlantic Films:** half-title page, 4, 12, 14, 15, 17, 21, 28, 31, 34, 37, 38, 40-41, 49, 57, 62 top and bottom, 64, 69, 82 top, 85, 94, 95, 108, 116, 117 bottom, 122, 128 top, 139, 148, 153, 153, 155, 164, 170, 183, 187 top; **The Trustees of the British Museum:** 44; **The Virginia Historical Society:** 8, 127, 135; *Nicholas & Alexandra - The Family Albums* (by Prince Michael of Greece, Tauris Parke Books, London, 1992): 187; *The Russian Century* (by Brian Moynahan, Chatto & Windus Ltd, London, 1994): 198; *Vladimir Ilich Lenin* (Editorial "Planeta", Moscow, 1983):186; *The Three Worlds of Captain John Smith* (by Phillip Barbour, Macmillan, London, 1964): p.128